**PICCOLO ENCYCLOPEDIA
OF USEFUL FACTS**

# PICCOLO ENCYCLOPEDIA
# OF USEFUL FACTS

JEAN STROUD

Cover Illustration by Brian Webb
Text Illustrations by Robin Lawrie

# A Piccolo Original

PAN BOOKS LTD : LONDON

First published 1973 by Pan Books Ltd,
33 Tothill Street, London, SW1.

ISBN 0 330 23413 7

*2nd Printing 1973*

© Jean Stroud 1973

*Made and Printed in Great Britain by*
*Cox & Wyman Ltd, London, Reading and Fakenham*

# CONTENTS

# 1 THE SOLAR SYSTEM

## The Solar System

The centre of the Solar System is the Sun. The Sun is one of the millions of stars that make up the Universe. The Earth is one of nine major planets which revolve round the Sun, bound to it by the force of gravity. The Sun, the planets, their satellites and a large number of other lesser bodies including comets and asteroids as well as interplanetary dust and gas form the Solar System. The origin of the Solar System is not known; it is thought that its age must be at least 5,000 million years.

## The Galaxy

The Galaxy, more popularly known as The Milky Way, is a mass of stars. It is a glowing band of light seen on dark nights stretching around the sky along the line of the galactic equator. Galileo discovered that The Milky Way consists of an enormous number of faint stars. They are whirling about in space. The Milky Way is, in fact, the visible sign of the Galaxy.

The Milky Way system (the Galaxy or Galactic system) is a huge star system of which the Sun is a member. The diameter of the Galaxy is about 100,000 light-years. The maximum thickness is about 20,000 light-years. The Sun lies about 25,000 light-years from the centre. The Galaxy rotates round its centre – the Sun takes about 225,000,000 years to complete one revolution known, unofficially, as a 'cosmic year'.

There are about 1,000 million galaxies similar to the Milky Way, each made up of thousands of millions of stars, dust and gas, and only three are visible to the naked eye. These are the Andromeda Spiral (which closely resembles ours in shape, size and number of stars) in the northern hemisphere, and the two Nebulae of Magellanic clouds in the far south.

Galaxies are units of the Universe in the same way as atoms are units of matter. They are of various shapes. The nearest galaxy is about two million light-years away from Earth.

# The Sun

| | |
|---|---|
| Age | At least 6,000 million years old |
| Diameter | 865,000 miles |
| Surface Area | 12,000 times that of Earth |
| Temperature | Surface: About 6,000°C<br>Internal: About 35,000,000°C |
| Distance from the Earth | 92,868,000 miles |
| Volume | 1,300,000 (Earth=1) |
| Mass | 330,000 (Earth=1) |
| Density | 0·25 (Earth=1) |
| Force of Gravity on the Surface | 27·7 (Earth=1) |
| Period of Rotation on its Axis | 25·38 days |
| Speed of Rotation at its Equator | 4,407 mph |

# The Moon

| | |
|---|---|
| Diameter | 2,158 miles |
| Surface Area | 14,660,000 sq. miles |
| Temperature (on lunar equator) | Day:   estimated +220°F<br>Night:  estimated −250°F |
| Distance from the Earth | Maximum: 252,700 miles<br>Minimum: 221,460 miles |
| Volume | 0·0203 that of the Earth |
| Mass | 1/81·3 of that of the Earth (=0·0123) |
| Density | 3·3 (water = 1); 0·06 (Earth = 1) |
| Speed in Orbit | 2·287 mph (0·63 miles per second) |
| Time of Revolution | 27 days, 7 hours, 43 minutes |
| Synodic Period (Interval between<br>one new Moon and the next) | approx 29·5 days |

Note: To convert Fahrenheit to Centigrade see p. 63.

# The Planets

| Planet | Distance from the Earth Maximum (in miles) | Minimum (in miles) | Distance from the Sun (in miles) | Period of Revolution Round the Sun | Equatorial Diameter (in miles) | Maximum Surface Temperature (F) | Number of Satellites | Surface Gravity (Earth = 1) |
|---|---|---|---|---|---|---|---|---|
| Mercury | 136,900,000 | 49,100,000 | 36,000,000 | 88 days | 2,900 | +770? | 0 | 0·37 |
| Venus | 160,900,000 | 25,700,000 | 67,200,000 | 224·7 days | 7,700 | +800? | 0 | 0·89 |
| Earth | — | — | 92,868,000 | 365·3 days | 7,927 | +140 | 1 | 1·00 |
| Mars | 247,000,000 | 34,000,000 | 141,500,000 | 687 days | 4,219 | +80 | 2 | 0·39 |
| Jupiter | 597,000,000 | 362,000,000 | 483,300,000 | 11·9 years | 88,700 | −200 | 12 | 2·54 |
| Saturn | 1,023,000,000 | 773,000,000 | 886,100,000 | 29·5 years | 75,100 | −240 | 9 | 1·13 |
| Uranus | 1,946,000,000 | 1,594,000,000 | 1,783,000,000 | 84·0 years | 29,300 | −310 | 5 | 1·09 |
| Neptune | 2,891,000,000 | 2,654,000,000 | 2,793,000,000 | 164·8 years | 27,700 | −360 | 2 | 1·41 |
| Pluto | 4,506,000,000 | 2,605,000,000 | 3,666,000,000 | 248·4 years | ± 9,000? | ? | 0 | ? |

# The Constellations

A Constellation is a group of stars within a definite region of the sky. The word means 'star groups'. For as long as man has existed on this planet, the positions of the stars have remained virtually unchanged and by knowing the positions of the constellations it is possible to locate stars, planets, comets and meteors. For thousands of years man has used his knowledge of the constellations to guide himself from place to place during journeys over the surface of the earth. On a cloudless night between 2,000 and 3,000 stars are visible to the naked eye. With the aid of a great astronomical telescope, like the one on Mount Wilson in California, something like 50,000,000 stars can be seen.

The largest constellation is *Hydra* (the Sea Serpent) which contains at least 68 stars visible to the naked eye. The smallest is *Equuleus* (Little Horse) which has only five stars.

The following constellations are the most important ones in the northern hemisphere:

| Scientific Name | English Name |
|---|---|
| Andromeda | The Chained Lady |
| Auriga | The Charioteer |
| Bootes | The Herdsman |
| Canis major | The Greater Dog |
| Canis minor | The Smaller Dog |
| Cassiopeia | The wife of Cephus |
| Cygnus | The Swan |
| Gemini | The Twins |
| Leo | The Lion |
| Lyra | The Lyre or Harp |
| Pegasus | The Winged Horse |
| Perseus | The Legendary Hero |
| Sagittarius | The Archer |
| Scorpius | The Scorpion |
| Taurus | The Bull |
| Ursa major | The Great Bear |
| Ursa minor | The Little Bear |

# The Stars

Any celestial body, whether fixed or planetary, is called a star. A star is a heavenly body that shines with its own light, produced by substances raised to a high temperature.

The stars are classed according to their brightness as seen from the Earth. The unit of brightness is called the *magnitude*. Magnitude 0 is the brightest. Stars as faint as the sixth magnitude can be seen by the unaided eye. The nearest star (Bungula in Centaurus) is 25,000,000,000,000 miles away.

# The Twenty Brightest Stars

| Star | Magnitude | Star | Magnitude |
|---|---|---|---|
| Sirius | −1·43 | Agena | 0·66 |
| Canopus | −0·73 | Altair | 0·80 |
| Rigil Kentaurus | −0·27 | Aldebaran | 0·85 |
| Arcturus | −0·06 | Acrux | 0·87 |
| Vega | 0·04 | Antares | 0·98 |
| Capella | 0·09 | Spica | 1·00 |
| Rigel | 0·15 | Fomalhaut | 1·16 |
| Procyon | 0·37 | Pollux | 1·16 |
| Achernar | 0·53 | Deneb | 1·26 |
| Betelgeuse | 0·90 | Beta Crucis | 1·31 |

# Glossary of Astronomical Terms

**Atmosphere** – The gaseous mantle surrounding a planet or other body.

**Black Body Radiation** – A theoretical body which completely absorbs all radiation reaching its surface and reflects none – thus appearing quite black.

**Celestial Sphere** – The imaginary sphere, concentric with the observer, on which the stars appear to be fixed.

**Circumpolar Stars** – Those which can never set, because their distance from the celestial pole is less than the distance of the pole from the horizon at the place of observation.

**Conjunction** – Apparent closeness of two heavenly bodies.

**Corona** – The outermost region of the Sun's atmosphere.

**Cosmic Rays** – High-energy particles reaching the Earth from outer space.

**Cosmogony** – Study of the origin and development of the universe or of any particular part of it.

**Cosmology** – Study of the universe as a whole, its general nature and structure.

**Craters (Lunar)** – Circular formations of all sizes that are a prominent feature of the Moon.

**Ecliptic** – The path that the centre of the Sun's disc traces out on the celestial sphere. Also the projection of the Earth's orbital plane on the celestial sphere.

**Light, Speed of** – 186,000 miles per second.

**Light-Year** – The distance travelled by light in one year – just under 6,000,000,000,000 miles.

**Magnitude (visual)** – The unit of brightness of a star. A star of the first magnitude is said to be 100 times brighter than one of the sixth magnitude.

**Meteor** – A small particle of rock or metal ore hurtling through space. When they enter the Earth's gravitational field they look like 'shooting stars'.

**Milky Way** – The luminous band seen in the night sky, made up of large numbers of faint stars.

**Novae** – Individual faint stars that suddenly brighten to a brilliant maximum, then fade again.

**Occultation** – The covering up of one celestial body by another. An eclipse is, strictly speaking, an occultation of the Sun by the Moon.

**Parsec** – A measure of distance. A parsec is 3·26 light years (approx. 19,000,000,000,000 miles).

**Poles, Celestial** – The two points where the Earth's axis intersects the celestial sphere.

**Pulsar** – One theory is that it is a rotating neutron star of immense density. The discovery of the first pulsar (or pulsating radio source) was in 1968.

**Pulsating (or expanding) Universe** – A model universe of galaxies in which expansion takes place so that the distance between galaxies constantly increases.

**Quasars** – Popular name for quasi-stellar objects. Mysterious objects which appear as sources of strong radio frequency radiations. They are seen as small star-like objects on photographs, and their existence was established in 1962.

**Scintillation** – The official term for 'twinkling'.

**Specific Gravity** – The density of any substance, compared with that of an equal volume of water.

**Red Shift** – The phenomenon in which the spectral lines of galaxies are shifted towards the red end of the spectrum. The red shift indicates that the galaxies are receding.

**Spectroscope** – An instrument for the analysis of light.

**Sun-Spot** – One of the numerous dark patches which may be seen on the Sun's surface.

**Supernovae** – Extremely luminous novae. Only three supernovae have been identified in our own Galaxy, the brightest on record being in the constellation Cassiopeia, which reached an apparent magnitude of $-3 \cdot 5$.

**Zenith** – Point of heavens directly above the observer.

# 2 HOW LIFE BEGAN

## How Life Began

More than a million different kinds of animal inhabit the earth. But no one really knows how life began. It probably began about 1,000 million years ago in some ancient sea. Some scientists believe that chemicals in the sea and air combined to form organic compounds, that these joined together and developed the characteristics of life.

The first speck of life must have been very simple – it may have been somewhat similar to the viruses we know today – but, most important, it was able to reproduce. Life evolved over millions of years – and changes are still taking place today.

| Era | Period | Important Geological Past | Millions of years ago |
|---|---|---|---|
| PALAEOZOIC (Age of Ancient Life) | Cambrian | Mild climates. Invertebrates only – jellyfish, starfish, worms and sponges. No land animals. | 550 |
| | Ordovician | Flooding of continents. Very powerful earth movements. First vertebrates appear, known as *Ostracoderms*. | 445 |

**Silurian**

Warm climate. Coral reefs develop. Spiders and scorpions become first air-breathers. Invertebrates widespread. First land plants appear but are still leafless.

375

**Devonian**

'The Age of Fish' – ancestors of all modern fish evolve. Amphibians appear. Plants with roots, stems and leaves evolve. Ferns, seed-ferns and horsetails develop. Millipedes, mites and wingless insects appear.

350

**Carboniferous**

Insects now common. First reptile-like creatures appear. Amphibia develop quickly in warm, moist coal forests. Giant evergreens flourish.

250

**Permian**

Varied climate. Mountains form. Primitive reptiles become more common. Modern insects such as cicadas and true beetles develop.

230

MESOZOIC
(Age of
Reptiles)

**Triassic**

Widespread desert conditions. First mammals. First ichthyosaurs (carnivorous, fish-shaped reptiles) evolve. Early meat-eating dinosaurs appear. Procompsognathus and Saltoposuchus are common, as is the plant-eating Plateosaurus.

200

**Jurassic**

Lands swampy. The first true bird, Archaeopteryx, appears. Ichthyosaurs, reptiles that were completely adapted to life in the sea, surface to take air into their lungs. The Age of Dinosaurs: Megalosaurus, the first dinosaur to be named, and giants like Brachiosaurus, Diplodocus and Brontosaurus – and an early armoured dinosaur, Stegosaurus.                165

**Cretaceous**

Cool climates. Major mountain building – Rocky Mountains and Andes begin to emerge. Flowering plants and bees are new in the world. Primitive birds, Ichthyornis and Hesperornis, and the first snakes appear. Fish, similar to those we know today – herring, swordfish, sturgeon, pike, sharks – swim in the seas. The old dinosaurs have vanished. New armoured dinosaurs, Ankylosaurus, are seen. Duck-billed dinosaurs, Iguanodon, Trachodon, Corythosaurus and Parasaurolophus – live near water. Psittacosaurus (parrot lizard), and the horned dinosaurs, the last of the great dinosaur families – Protoceratops, Triceratops, Monoclonius and Styracosaurus – roam the land. Tyrannosaurus, the largest flesh-eating animal of all, walks the earth. Pterosaurs (flying reptiles) widespread.                130

CAINOZOIC
(The Age
of Mammals)

**Palaeocene
and Eocene**

Generally hot. Mountain ranges continue to grow. Rise of placental mammals (whose young are nourished directly by the mother's blood until birth). Ancestors of the elephant, rhinoceros, horse, pig and cow come into existence. Crocodiles, turtles and land tortoises evolve and all groups of insects we know today. Primitive monkeys and gibbons appear. Flowering plants widespread.

65

**Oligocene**

Land mass grows at the expense of the sea. Warm climate. Forests get smaller, grasslands spread and plant-eating animals increase – small elephants with short trunks and tusks in upper and lower jaws, giant rhinoceroses. New species of crabs, snails and sea-urchins evolve, as do ancestors of modern cats, dogs and bears. A primitive ape, possibly related to the ancestors of man, appears.

36

**Miocene**

Climate mild. Europe and Asian land masses finally join. Primitive manlike ape, Proconsul, spread from Africa to Asia and Europe. A gibbon-like ape, Pliopithecus, common in forests of southern Europe. Elephants steadily increasing in size, spread from Africa into Europe, Asia and north

America. Long-legged water birds, ducks and pelicans in rivers and lakes. Primitive penguins live in Antarctica.

26

**Pliocene**

Continents and oceans begin to take roughly their present shape. Climates cooling. Marine life – both plant and animal – much as it is today. Elephants, horses, other mammals more like modern types. Man-like apes continue to develop, not only the forest-dwellers but the species known as Australopithecus, which walk in open country and may be ancestral to man.

11

**Pleistocene**

Succeeding Ice Ages leave only harder varieties of plants in Europe – oak, willow, poplar, elm, hawthorn. Stone Age cave men. Mammoths and gigantic mammals.

1

**Holocene**

Ice-sheets disappear. (The Ice Age may not yet be over – we may be living in an inter-glacial, in which case the cold will return.) Britain is cut off from the Continent. Modern mammals and man dominant.

0·1

# Some Extinct Animals

1. PREHISTORIC ANIMALS (which lived long before Man appeared on earth):

| | |
|---|---|
| Coelacanth | (primitive fish) – lived 300 million years ago. It was presumed to have been extinct around 70 million years ago, yet specimens have been caught recently. |
| Meganeura | A giant insect with a wing span of up to 30 inches – similar to a dragonfly. |
| Pteranodon | Giant flying reptile with wing span of up to 25 feet. |
| Diplodocus | The 'long tailed' herbivorous dinosaur which lived in the United States and grew up to lengths in excess of 90 feet. |
| Iguanodon | This dinosaur (the term, derived from the Greek, means 'terrible lizard'), from the Early Cretaceous period reached about 15 feet in height when standing. Remains have been found on the Isle of Wight. |
| Tyrannosaurus | Literally 'tyrant lizard' and most famous of all the carnivorous reptiles. They had short, weak forelimbs and strong hind limbs and tails. |
| Moa | A huge flightless bird from New Zealand resembling vaguely ostriches and emus, except that the moas were perhaps three or four times larger. |
| Baluchitherium | Related to present-day rhinos, this huge mammal lived in Baluchistan and Mongolia and measured 18 feet at the shoulder. |
| Megatherium | Giant ground sloth – remains found in South America. |

Other prehistoric animals were: Eusthenopteron, Ichthyostega, Eryops, Gerrothorax, Diplocaulus, Seymouria, Stenaulorhynchus, Mosasaurus, Mandasuchus, Plateosaurus, Cetiosaurus, Coelophysis, Ornithomimus, Deinonychus, Scelidosaurus, Polacanthus, Hypsilophodon, Corythosaurus, Rhamphorhynchus, Phororhacos, Aepyornis, Cryptoclidus, Tanystropheus, Dimetrodon, Lystrosaurus, Cynognathus, Megazostrodon, Diprotodon, Sivatherium, Hyracotherium, Coelondonta, Deinotherium, Glyptodon.

2. Species that have become extinct since the age of Man – ie, in the last 200,000 years:

**Heath Hen**  (*Tympanuchus cupido cupido*) An extinct North American grouse which inhabited wooded districts. The last to survive was seen on the island of Martha's Vineyard, Massachusetts, in the early 1930s.

**Passenger Pigeon**  (*Ectopistes migratorius*) North American bird which nested in great colonies and wheeled in flocks dense enough to darken the sky. The last of the species, a bird hatched in captivity, died in the Cincinnati (Ohio) Zoo in 1914.

**Dodo**  The common name for two extinct species of large, clumsy, flightless birds which inhabited the islands of Mauritius and Réunion in the Indian Ocean. The Mauritius dodo (*Raphus Cucullatus*) was slightly larger than a turkey. The dodo has been extinct since about 1680.

**Great Auk**  (*Pinguinus impennis*) A large flightless sea bird, slightly smaller than a tame goose. The body was 30 inches long, the wings used in swimming under water being less than 6 inches long. It bred at St Kilda, the Faeroe Islands, Iceland and Funk Island off Newfoundland. The last reported sightings were in the early 1850s.

**Quagga**  (*Equus quagga*) A zebra-like animal formerly found in vast herds on the great plains of South Africa. The last died in the London Zoo in 1872.

**Steller's Sea Cow**  (*Hydro-damalis stelleri*) Reached a length of about 24 feet, with a relatively small head and broad, horizontal forked tail fluke. They browsed on the seaweed in the bays of the Bering and Copper Islands in the Bering Strait near Kamchatka. Less than thirty years after its discovery in 1741 by Georg W. Steller the animal was exterminated.

**Aurochs**  (*Bos taurus primi-genius*) The wild ox of Europe from which domestic cattle are descended. It survived in the Jaktorow forest of central Poland until 1627. It was six feet high at the shoulder, black in colour, with spreading, forwardly curved horns.

**Mammoth**  Broadly speaking, any extinct member of the elephant subfamily *Elephantinae*. Similar to living elephants in the body skeleton, mammoths differ from them, and each other, in the shape of the skull, tusk form and molar structure. One of the most complete mammoth carcasses was that unearthed in 1899 from the bed of a river in Siberia.

**Sabre-toothed Tiger**
(*Smilodon*) A large, short-limbed carnivore with immense canine teeth. Among living cats, only the lion approaches Smilodon in massiveness and even the largest lions do not reach the proportions of the largest sabre-tooths, which ranged in the Pleistocene period in North and South America. It became extinct not more than a few thousand years ago.

# 3 THE WORLD WE LIVE IN

## The Earth

| | |
|---|---|
| Total Surface Area (estimated) | 196,836,000 sq. miles |
| Land Area | 55,786,000 sq. miles |
| Water Area | 141,050,000 sq. miles |
| Equatorial Circumference | 24,901·8 miles |
| Equatorial Diameter | 7,926½ miles |
| Polar Diameter | 7,900 miles |
| Centre of the Earth | Almost 4,000 miles beneath our feet |
| Density | 5·52 |
| Atmosphere | 77·6 per cent nitrogen; 20·7 per cent oxygen |
| Temperature | Exceeds 4,000°F at the core |
| Weight (estimated) | 5,882,000,000,000,000,000,000 tons |
| Age (estimated) | 4,700 million years |
| Mean Orbital Speed | 185 miles per second (66,000 mph) or 584,000,000 miles in a year |
| Mean Distance to the Sun | 92,870,000 miles |
| Mean Distance to the Moon | 238,854 miles |

It is estimated that the Earth attracts 14·9 tons of cosmic dust annually.

| | |
|---|---|
| The Hottest Place on Earth | Dallol, Ethiopia, where the annual average temperature is 34·4°C (94° F). |
| The Coldest Place on Earth | The Pole of Cold, in Antarctica, which has an annual average temperature of −72°F, 16°F lower than the Pole. |

| | |
|---|---|
| **Highest Rainfall** | 73·62 in. fell in 24 hours at Cilaos, Réunion, Indian Ocean on March 15th–16th, 1952. This is equal to 7,435 tons of rain per acre. |
| **Most Rainy Days (Year)** | Bahia Felix, Chile, had 348 rainy days in 1916 (annual average 325 days). |
| **Longest Drought** | c. 400 years, Desierto de Atacama, Chile. |
| **Greatest Snowfall** | 76 in. of snow fell in 24 hours at Silver Lake, Colorado, USA on April 14th–15th, 1921. |
| **Highest Shade Temperature** | 136·4°F: Al' Aziziyah, Libya, recorded on September 13th, 1922. |
| **Lowest Screen Temperature** | —126·9°F: Vostok, Antarctica, on August 24th, 1960. |

# The Continents

A Continent is a vast tract of land not divided by the sea from other lands. The land surface of the Earth is made up of six Continents:

| | Area (sq. miles) |
|---|---|
| Europe | 1,903,000 |
| Asia | 16,661,000 |
| USSR | 8,649,000 |
| Africa | 11,683,000 |
| America | 16,241,000 |
| Oceania (Australia, New Zealand, New Guinea and the Islands of the Pacific) | 3,286,000 |

## Main Oceans

|  | Area of basin (in sq. miles) | Greatest depth (in feet) | Name of deepest area |
|---|---|---|---|
| Pacific | 64,186,300 | 36,198 | Mariana Trench |
| Atlantic | 31,814,640 | 30,246 | Puerto Rico Trench |
| Indian | 28,350,500 | 24,442 | Sunda Trench |
| Arctic | 5,427,000 | 17,880 | Eurasia Basin |

## Land Below Sea Level

| Lowest point | Approx. depth below sea level (in feet) |
|---|---|
| Dead Sea (Israel-Jordan) | 1,296 |
| Qattara Depression (Libyan Desert, Egypt) | 436 |
| Death Valley (California) | 282 |
| Lake Eyre (South Australia) | 52 |
| Netherlands coastal areas | 15 |

## The World's Highest Mountains

| | Peak | Country | Height (in feet) |
|---|---|---|---|
| EUROPE | | | |
| | ALPS. The highest peaks are: | | |
| | Mont Blanc | | 15,771 |
| | Monte Rosa | | 15,203 |
| | Dom | | 14,913 |
| | Matterhorn | | 14,690 |
| | Jungfrau | | 13,642 |
| | Eiger | | 13,025 |

ASIA

| | | |
|---|---|---|
| Everest | Nepal-Tibet | 29,028 |
| Godwin Austen (K2) | Kashmir | 28,250 |
| Kanchenjunga | Nepal-India | 28,208 |
| Nanga Parbat | Kashmir | 26,660 |
| Annapurna | Nepal | 26,504 |
| Nanda Devi | India | 25,645 |
| Kungur | Sinkiang | 25,325 |
| Minya Konka | China | 24,900 |

USSR

| | | |
|---|---|---|
| Communism Peak | USSR (Pamir range of Central Asia) | 24,590 |
| Mount Elbruz | Caucasus Range | 18,526 |
| Koshtan Tau | Caucasus Range | 17,096 |

AFRICA

| | | |
|---|---|---|
| Kilimanjaro | Tanzania | 19,340 |
| Kenya | Kenya | 17,058 |
| Margherita | Uganda – Republic of Congo | 16,763 |
| Ras Dashan | Ethiopia | 15,158 |

AMERICA (South)

| | | |
|---|---|---|
| Aconcagua | Argentina | 22,834 |
| Sargantay | Peru | 22,542 |
| Ojos del Salado | Argentine-Chile | 22,539 |
| Tupungato | Argentine-Chile | 22,310 |
| Huascarán | Peru | 22,205 |

AMERICA (North)

| | | |
|---|---|---|
| McKinley | Alaska | 20,320 |
| Logan | Canada | 19,850 |
| Citlaltepao | Mexico | 18,700 |
| St Elias | Alaska | 18,008 |
| Popocatapetl | Mexico | 17,887 |

OCEANIA

| | | |
|---|---|---|
| Sukarno | New Guinea | 16,500 |

# Some Volcanoes of the World

| Volcano | Location | Height (in feet) |
|---|---|---|
| **ACTIVE** | | |
| Antofalla | Argentina | 20,103 |
| Volcán Guayatiri (or Guallatiri) | Chile | 19,882 |
| Cotopaxi | Ecuador | 19,612 |
| Kluchevskaya | USSR | 16,130 |
| Mount Wrangel | USA | 14,000 |
| Mauna Loa | Hawaii | 13,675 |
| Cameroons | W. Cameroon | 13,350 |
| Mount Erebus | Ross Island, Antarctica | 12,450 |
| Nyiragongo | Congo | 11,560 |
| Etna | Sicily | 11,121 |
| Chillan | Chile | 10,500 |
| Nyamuragira | Congo | 10,150 |
| Villarica | Chile | 9,325 |
| Paricutin | Mexico | 9,000 |
| Asama | Japan | 8,200 |
| Ngauruhoe | New Zealand | 7,515 |
| Beeren Berg | Jan Mayen Island, Greenland Sea | 7,470 |
| Hecla | Iceland | 5,100 |
| Vesuvius | Italy | 3,700 |
| Stromboli | Lipari Island, Italy | 3,000 |
| **BELIEVED EXTINCT** | | |
| Aconcagua | Chile – Argentina | 22,976 |
| Chimborazo | Ecuador | 20,500 |
| Kilimanjaro | Tanganyika | 19,340 |
| Antisana | Ecuador | 18,850 |
| Elbruz | Caucasus | 18,526 |
| Popocatapetl | Mexico | 17,540 |
| Orizaba | Mexico | 17,400 |
| Karisimbi | Congo | 15,020 |
| Mikeno | Congo | 14,780 |
| Fujiyama | Japan | 12,395 |

DORMANT

| | | |
|---|---|---|
| Volcan Llullaillaco | Chile – Argentina | 22,058 |
| Demavend | Iran | 18,600 |
| Pico de Teyde | Teneriffe | 12,180 |
| Semerou | Indonesia | 12,050 |
| Haleakala | Hawaii | 10,032 |
| Guntur | Indonesia | 7,300 |
| Tongariro | New Zealand | 6,458 |
| Tristan da Cunha | South Atlantic | 6,000 |
| Pelée | Martinique, W. Indies | 4,430 |
| Krakatoa | Sunda Strait, S. Pacific | 2,600 |

# The World's Biggest Deserts

| Desert | Location | Approx. area (in sq. miles) |
|---|---|---|
| Sahara | Northern Africa | 3,000,000 to 3,500,000 |
| Libyan | Eastern part of the Sahara | 650,000 |
| Australian | Interior of Australia | 600,000 |
| Arabian | Arabian Peninsula, South-west Asia | 500,000 |
| Gobi | Central Asia, Mongolia | 450,000 |
| Patagonian | Argentina | 260,000 |
| Kalahari | Botswana | 200,000 |
| Great Sandy | North-western Australia | 160,000 |
| Great Victoria | South-west Central Australia | 125,000 |
| Syrian | Northern Saudi Arabia, South-eastern Syria, Western Iraq and North-eastern Jordan | 125,000 |
| Kara Kum | South Soviet Union | 110,000 |
| Nubian | North-eastern Sudan | 100,000 |
| Thar | North-western India and adjacent Pakistan | 100,000 |

# The World's Biggest Lakes

| Name | Location | Area (sq. miles) |
|---|---|---|
| Caspian Sea* | Asia | 170,000 |
| Superior | North America | 31,820 |
| Victoria Nyanza | Africa | 26,200 |
| Aral Sea* | USSR | 24,400 |
| Huron | North America | 23,010 |
| Michigan | North America | 22,400 |
| Malawi | Africa | 14,200 |
| Tanganyika | Africa | 12,700 |
| Great Bear | Canada | 11,660 |
| Baikal | USSR | 11,580 |
| Great Slave | Canada | 11,170 |
| Erie | North America | 9,940 |
| Winnipeg | Canada | 9,398 |
| Maracaibo | South America | 8,296 |
| Ontario | North America | 7,540 |
| Balkhash | USSR | 7,050 |
| Ladoga | USSR | 7,000 |
| Chad | Africa | 6,000 |
| Nettiling | Baffin Land | 5,000 |
| Eyre | Australia | 3,700 |

* Classified as lakes as they are completely landlocked.

# The World's Most Famous Rivers

| River | Outflow | Length (in miles) |
|---|---|---|
| Amazon | South Atlantic Ocean | 4,195 |
| Nile | Mediterranean | 4,145 |
| Mississippi-Missouri | Gulf of Mexico | 3,710 |
| Ob-Irtysh | Gulf of Ob | 3,460 |
| Yangtze | North Pacific | 3,400 |
| Congo | Atlantic Ocean | 3,000 |

| | | |
|---|---|---|
| Mekong | China Sea | 2,800 |
| Hwang-Ho (Yellow) | Yellow Sea (Pacific) | 2,600 |
| Niger | Gulf of Guinea | 2,600 |
| Volga | Caspian Sea | 2,400 |
| Mackenzie | Beaufort Sea | 2,350 |
| Yukon | Bering Sea | 2,000 |
| St Lawrence | Gulf of St Lawrence | 1,800 |
| Rio Grande | Gulf of Mexico | 1,800 |
| Orinoco | Atlantic Ocean | 1,800 |
| Danube | Black Sea | 1,725 |
| Indus | Arabian Sea | 1,700 |
| Euphrates | Persian Gulf | 1,700 |
| Brahmaputra | Bay of Bengal | 1,680 |
| Zambesi | Indian Ocean | 1,633 |
| Ganges | Bay of Bengal | 1,560 |
| Don | Sea of Azov | 1,210 |
| Rhine | North Sea | 820 |
| Seine | English Channel | 482 |
| Shannon | Limerick | 240 |
| Thames | North Sea | 210 |

FOOTNOTE: When, in 1969, the National Geographic Society re-measured the length of the Amazon, they found it to be 4,195 miles. This figure dismisses the long-held claim of the Nile to be the world's longest river.

# Great Ship Canals

| Name | Country | Opened | Length (in miles) |
|---|---|---|---|
| Gota | Sweden | 1832 | 115 |
| Suez | Egypt | 1869 | 100 |
| Kiel | Germany | 1895 | 61 |
| Panama | USA | 1914 | 50·5 |
| Elbe and Trave | Germany | 1900 | 41 |

# Longest Bridges

| Bridge | Location | Length (in feet of waterway) |
|---|---|---|
| Oosterschelde Road Bridge | Netherlands | 16,476 |
| Lower Zambesi | Africa | 11,322 |
| Storsstromsbroen | Denmark | 10,499 |
| Tay Railway Bridge | Scotland | 10,289 |
| Upper Sone | India | 9,839 |

# Longest Railway Tunnels

| Name | Country | Miles | Yards |
|---|---|---|---|
| Simplon | Switzerland–Italy | 12 | 560 |
| Apennine | Italy | 11 | 880 |
| St Gothard | Switzerland | 9 | 550 |
| Lötschberg | Switzerland | 9 | 130 |
| Mont Cenis | Italy | 8 | 870 |

(The London Underground *Northern Line* between East Finchley and Morden, via the Bank, uses tunnels totalling 17 miles 528 yards in length.)

# Distance of the Horizon

The limit of distance to which one can see varies with the height of the spectator.

| At a height of: | The range is: |
|---|---|
| 5 ft. | 2·9 miles |
| 50 ft. | 9·3 miles |
| 100 ft. | 13·2 miles |
| 1,000 ft. | 41·6 miles |
| 5,000 ft. | 93·1 miles |
| 20,000 ft. | 186·2 miles |

T–B

# The Seven Wonders of the Ancient World

The Pyramids of Egypt
The Hanging Gardens of Babylon
The Statue of Zeus at Olympia
The Temple of Artemis at Ephesus
The Tomb of Mausolus at Halicarnassus
The Colossus of Rhodes
The Pharos of Alexandria

# The Seven Wonders of the Middle Ages

The Colosseum, Rome
The Catacombs of Alexandria
The Great Wall of China
Stonehenge
The Leaning Tower of Pisa
The Porcelain Tower of Nankin
The Mosque of St Sophia at Constantinople

# 4 POPULATION

## World Population

The estimated total population of the world in mid-1972 was 3,782,000,000.
Progressive mid-year estimates:

| Date | Millions | Date | Millions |
|------|----------|------|----------|
| AD 1 | c. 200–300 | 1968 | 3,483 |
| 1650 | c. 500–550 | 1969 | 3,538 |
| 1750 | 750 | 1970 | 3,610 |
| 1850 | 1,240 | 1971 | 3,706 |
| 1950 | 2,517 | 1972 | 3,782 |
| 1966 | 3,353 | 1975 | 4,022 |
| 1967 | 3,420 | 1985 | 4,933 |

Approximately one-half of the world population is accounted for by the
population of four countries – China (mainland), India, the Union of
Soviet Socialist Republics and the United States of America.

The world population has doubled in the last 63 years. It is expected to
double again in the next forty years. It is now estimated that the world's
population in the year 2000 will be more than 6,000 million and possibly
closer to 7,000 million.

If the present 'population explosion' continues it is calculated that there
will be one person to each square yard by AD 2600 and humanity would
weigh more than the Earth itself by AD 3700.

In the last 600,000 years it has been estimated that 74,000,000,000
humans have been born and have died.

# Estimated Population of the Continents (mid-1970)

|  | Population (in millions) |
|---|---|
| Europe | 462 |
| Asia | 2,056 |
| USSR | 243 |
| Africa | 344 |
| America | 511 |
| Oceania | 19·4 |

# Estimated Population of the United Kingdom

The estimated population of the United Kingdom in 1971 was 55,347,000.

|  | Males | Females |
|---|---|---|
| England and Wales | 23,608,000 | 24,986,000 |
| Scotland | 2,515,000 | 2,713,000 |
| N. Ireland | 748,000 | 777,000 |
| Total | 26,872,000 | 28,475,000 |

# Ten Largest Cities in Britain (by Population)

|  | Estimated Total |
|---|---|
| Greater London | 7,418,020 |
| Birmingham | 1,013,420 |
| Glasgow | 907,672 |
| Liverpool | 603,210 |
| Manchester | 542,430 |

| | |
|---|---|
| **Sheffield** | 515,950 |
| **Leeds** | 501,080 |
| **Edinburgh** | 464,764 |
| **Bristol** | 426,170 |
| **Belfast** | 360,000 |

# Countries of the World and their Population (mid-1970)

| Europe | *Estimated Population (in millions)* |
|---|---|
| Albania | 2·17 |
| Andorra | 0·02 |
| Austria | 7·42 |
| Belgium | 9·68 |
| Bulgaria | 8·49 |
| Channel Islands | 0·12 |
| Czechoslovakia | 14·47 |
| Denmark | 4·92 |
| Faeroe Islands | 0·04 |
| Finland | 4·70 |
| France | 50·77 |
| Germany: | |
|    Federal Republic of Germany | 59·55 |
|    German Democratic Republic | 16·18 |
|    East Berlin | 1·07 |
|    West Berlin | 2·13 |
| Gibraltar | 0·03 |
| Greece | 8·89 |
| Hungary | 10·33 |
| Iceland | 0·21 |
| Ireland | 2·94 |
| Isle of Man | 0·05 |
| Italy | 53·67 |
| Liechtenstein | 0·02 |
| Luxembourg | 0·34 |
| Malta | 0·33 |
| Monaco | 0·02 |

| | |
|---|---|
| Netherlands | 13·02 |
| Norway | 3·88 |
| Poland | 32·81 |
| Portugal | 9·63 |
| Rumania | 20·25 |
| Spain | 33·29 |
| Sweden | 8·05 |
| Switzerland | 6·28 |
| Yugoslavia | 20·53 |

## Asia

| | |
|---|---|
| Afghanistan | 17·12 |
| Bahrain | 0·22 |
| Bhutan | 0·84 |
| Brunei | 0·12 |
| Burma | 27·58 |
| China (mainland) | 759·62 |
| China (Taiwan) | 14·04 |
| Hong Kong | 4·09 |
| India | 550·38 |
| Indonesia | 121·20 |
| Iran | 28·66 |
| Iraq | 9·44 |
| Israel | 2·89 |
| Japan | 103·54 |
| Jordan | 2·32 |
| Korea | 45·69 |
| Kuwait | 0·71 |
| Laos | 2·96 |
| Lebanon | 2·79 |
| Macau | 0·31 |
| Maldives | 0·11 |
| Mongolia | 1·29 |
| Muscat and Oman | 0·66 |
| Philippines | 38·49 |
| Portuguese Timor | 0·60 |
| Qatar | 0·08 |
| Saudi Arabia | 7·74 |
| Sikkim | 0·19 |
| Singapore | 2·05 |
| Syria | 6·10 |

| | |
|---|---|
| Turkey | 35·23 |
| Viet-Nam | 39·48 |
| Yemen | 5·73 |
| Yemen, People's Democratic Republic of, | 1·28 |
| | |
| **USSR** | 242·77 |
| Byelorussian S S R | 9·04 |
| Ukrainian S S R | 47·32 |

**Africa**

| | |
|---|---|
| Algeria | 14·01 |
| Botswana | 0·65 |
| Burundi | 3·60 |
| Cameroon | 5·84 |
| Cape Verde Islands | 0·25 |
| Congo – Democratic Republic of, | 17·42 |
| Congo – People's Republic of, | 0·94 |
| Dahomey | 2·69 |
| Equatorial Guinea | 0·29 |
| Ethiopia | 25·05 |
| Ghana | 9·03 |
| Guinea | 3·92 |
| Kenya | 10·90 |
| Liberia | 1·17 |
| Madagascar | 6·75 |
| Malawi | 4·53 |
| Mauritania | 1·17 |
| Mauritius | 0·83 |
| Morocco | 15·53 |
| Niger | 4·02 |
| Nigeria | 55·07 |
| Réunion | 0·45 |
| São Tomé and Príncipe | 0·06 |
| Senegal | 3·93 |
| Seychelles | 0·05 |
| Somalia | 2·79 |
| South Africa | 20·11 |
| Southern Rhodesia | 5·27 |
| Sudan | 15·70 |
| Tunisia | 5·14 |
| Uganda | 9·76 |

| | |
|---|---|
| United Arab Republic | 33·33 |
| United Republic of Tanzania | 13·27 |
| Upper Volta | 5·38 |
| Zambia | 4·30 |

## America (North)

| | |
|---|---|
| Antigua | 0·06 |
| Bermuda | 0·05 |
| British Honduras | 0·13 |
| Canada | 21·41 |
| Cuba | 8·39 |
| Dominica | 0·07 |
| Dominican Republic | 4·32 |
| El Salvador | 3·53 |
| Greenland | 0·05 |
| Grenada | 0·10 |
| Guadeloupe | 0·33 |
| Guatemala | 5·11 |
| Haiti | 4·87 |
| Honduras | 2·58 |
| Jamaica | 2·00 |
| Martinique | 0·34 |
| Mexico | 50·67 |
| Montserrat | 0·02 |
| Netherlands Antilles | 0·22 |
| Panama (not including Canal Zone) | 1·46 |
| St Vincent | 0·10 |
| Trinidad and Tobago | 1·07 |
| United States | 205·40 |

## America (South)

| | |
|---|---|
| Argentina | 24·35 |
| Bolivia | 4·93 |
| Brazil | 95·31 |
| Colombia | 21·12 |
| Ecuador | 6·09 |
| French Guiana | 0·05 |
| Guyana | 0·76 |
| Paraguay | 2·39 |

| | |
|---|---|
| Peru | 13·59 |
| Surinam | 0·39 |
| Uruguay | 2·89 |
| Venezuela | 10·40 |

**Oceania**

| | |
|---|---|
| Australia | 12·55 |
| Cook Islands | 0·02 |
| Fiji | 0·52 |
| Gilbert and Ellice Islands | 0·06 |
| New Guinea | 1·75 |
| New Hebrides | 0·08 |
| New Zealand | 2·82 |
| Papua | 0·67 |
| Tonga | 0·09 |
| Western Samoa | 0·14 |

# Main Languages of the World

| Language | Speakers (in millions) | Language | Speakers (in millions) |
|---|---|---|---|
| Mandarin (China) | 493 | Italian | 58 |
| English | 291 | Urdu (Pakistan and India) | 54 |
| Russian | 167 | Cantonese (China) | 45 |
| Hindi | 162 | Javanese (Indonesia) | 42 |
| Spanish | 155 | Ukrainian (mainly USSR) | 41 |
| German | 123 | | |
| Japanese | 98 | Telegu (India) | 41 |
| Bengali (India, Pakistan) | 85 | Wu (China) | 39 |
| | | Tamil (India and Ceylon) | 37 |
| Arabic | 82 | | |
| Portuguese | 80 | Min (China) | 36 |
| French | 73 | Korean | 35 |
| Malay | 71 | | |

# Expectation of Life at Birth

This table shows how many years men and women can expect to live if born in a particular country in the year stated.

| | | | |
|---|---|---|---|
| China (Mainland) | 1965–70 | Both sexes: | 50·0 |
| Japan | 1968 | Male 69·05 | Female 74·30 |
| Austria | 1969 | Male 66·46 | Female 73·34 |
| Czechoslovakia | 1966 | Male 67·33 | Female 73·57 |
| Denmark | 1967–68 | Male 70·6 | Female 75·4 |
| UK (England and Wales) | 1970 | Male 69·0 | Female 75·0 |
| (Estimated figure for 2010) | | Male 72·0 | Female (More than 79) |
| France | 1968 | Male 68·0 | Female 75·5 |
| Australia | 1960–1962 | Male 67·92 | Female 74·18 |
| Greece | 1960–1962 | Male 67·46 | Female 70·70 |
| USSR | 1967–1968 | Both sexes: | 70·0 |
| Hungary | 1964 | Male 67·0 | Female 71·83 |
| Italy | 1960–1962 | Male 67·24 | Female 72·27 |
| Canada | 1965–1967 | Male 68·75 | Female 75·18 |
| Spain | 1960 | Male 67·32 | Female 71·90 |
| United States | 1968 | Male 66·6 | Female 74·0 |
| India | 1972 | Male 49·0 | Female 53·0 |
| Sweden | 1967 | Male 71·85 | Female 76·54 |

# The Seven Ages of Man

'All the world's a stage,
And all the men and women merely players:
They have their exits and their entrances;
And one man in his time plays many parts,
His acts being seven ages'.

Shakespeare *As You Like It*,
Act II, Sc. vii.

| | | |
|---|---|---|
| Quadragenarian | = | 40–49 years old |
| Quinquagenarian | = | 50–59 years old |
| Sexagenarian | = | 60–69 years old |

| | | |
|---|---|---|
| Septuagenarian | = | 70–79 years old |
| Octogenarian | = | 80–89 years old |
| Nonagenarian | = | 90–99 years old |
| Centenarian | = | aged 100 or more |

# Wedding Anniversaries

Wedding anniversaries are named from the custom of giving a distinctive anniversary gift. The three most important are known as the silver wedding (after 25 years), the golden (after 50 years), and the diamond (after 60, 70 or 75 years).

Not all anniversaries have symbolic names – but here are a few of the most usual ones:

| | | | | | |
|---|---|---|---|---|---|
| 1st | cotton | 7th | woollen | 30th | pearl |
| 2nd | paper | 8th | bronze | 35th | coral |
| 3rd | leather | 9th | pottery | 40th | ruby |
| 4th | silk | 10th | tin | 45th | sapphire |
| 5th | wooden | 15th | crystal | 50th | gold |
| 6th | sweets | 20th | china | 55th | emerald |
| | | 25th | silver | 60th | diamond |

# 5 THE WONDERS OF NATURE

## The Animal Kingdom

All living things are either animals or plants. The Animal Kingdom consists of mammals, birds, reptiles, amphibians, fishes, insects and other invertebrates. It includes man as well as tiny one-celled organisms – animals so small that sometimes even the experts have difficulty in distinguishing them.

The Animal Kingdom can be easily divided into two – animals with backbones (vertebrates) and those without (invertebrates). Birds, reptiles, amphibians, fishes and mammals make up the vertebrate animals. Mammals and birds, unlike the other vertebrates, are warmblooded. They maintain a constant temperature. A rise in the temperature of Man is usually a sign of illness. Fishes, amphibians and reptiles have no regular body temperature – it changes with the temperature of the surroundings.

All mammals, except for a few primitive ones which lay eggs, bear their young alive. Even the ones that lay eggs suckle their young.

If we trace back the history of the various classes of vertebrates we find that the fishes gave rise to the first amphibians, the amphibians to the first reptiles and so on. The changes took place gradually.

MAN SHARES THE EARTH with an estimated 3,000,000,000,000,000,000,000,000,000,000,000 (3,000 quintillion) other living things.

THE LARGEST LIVING ANIMAL known today in the world is the Blue or Sulphur Bottom Whale (*Balaenoptera Musculus*), which grows to a maximum of 100 feet long.

THE LARGEST LIVING LAND MAMMAL is the African bush elephant (*Loxodonta Africana Africana*). The average adult bull weighs $5\frac{3}{4}$ tons, and often stands 10 or 11 feet high.

THE SMALLEST? Of all free-living organisms the smallest is a pleuro-pneumonia-like organism known as *Mycoplasma Laidlawii* which has a diameter of 0·000004 of an inch in its early life. The strain of *Mycoplasma* known as H 39 weighs an estimated $1·0 \times 10^{-16}$ of a gramme. Thus a 174-ton blue whale would weigh 177,000 trillion times as much!

# Collective Nouns

| | | | |
|---|---|---|---|
| Ants | Colony | Locusts | Plague |
| Apes | Shrewdness | Magpies | Tidings |
| Badgers | Cete | Nightingales | Watch |
| Bass | Shoal | Owls | Parliament |
| Bears | Sloth | Partridges | Covey |
| Caterpillars | Army | Peacocks | Ostentation |
| Cats | Clowder | Pheasants | Covey |
| Cattle | Drove | Plovers | Congregation |
| Chickens | Peep | Ponies | String |
| Crows | Murder | Pups | Litter |
| Doves | Dule | Rabbits | Nest |
| Ducks | Balding | Ravens | Unkindness |
| (on water) | Paddling | Rhinoceroses | Crash |
| Eggs | Clutch | Rooks | Building |
| Fish | School | Seals | Pod |
| Foxes | Skulk | Sheep | Flock |
| Geese (on water) | Gaggle | Sparrows | Host |
| (in flight) | Skein | Squirrels | Dray |
| Hares | Husk | Starlings | Mummuration |
| Hawks | Cast | Storks | Mustering |
| Hens | Brood | Swallows | Flight |
| Herons | Siege | Toads | Knot |
| Horses | Harras | Trout | Hover |
| Jellyfish | Smack | Turkeys | Rafter |
| Kittens | Kindle | Turtles | Bale |
| Lapwings | Deceit | Turtledoves | Pitying |
| Larks | Exaltation | Whales | Gam |
| Leopards | Leap | Wolves | Route |
| Lions | Pride | Woodpeckers | Descent |

# Well-known Animals of the World

| | |
|---|---|
| Antelopes | Africa, Southern Asia, India. |
| Bears | North and South America, Europe, Northern Asia. |
| Buffaloes | (Water) India, Ceylon, Indo-China, Egypt, Philippine Islands. |
| | (African or Cape) Southern and Central Africa. |
| Camels | (Bactrian) The two-humped camels are found from China to Turkestan. |
| | (Dromedary) The one-humped camels live in the desert regions of Arabia and Egypt. |
| Chimpanzees | The forests of tropical Africa. |
| Elephants | India, Africa. |
| Giraffes | The tallest animals in the world. Africa. |
| Gorillas | Gorillas are the largest of the apes. They live in the forested areas of Central Africa. |
| Foxes | (Red) Northern Europe, Asia and North America. |
| | (Grey) United States. |
| | (Arctic) Alaska, Greenland, northern Eurasia. |
| Hippopotamuses | The deep rivers of Africa. |
| Hyenas | (Striped) From India to North Africa. |
| | (Brown) Southern Africa. |
| | (Spotted) Central and southern Africa. |
| Kangaroos | Australia and New Guinea. |
| Koalas | Bear-like marsupial mammals of Australia. |
| Lions | Africa, Asia. Mountain lions (often called Cougars or Pumas) live in North and South America. |
| Llamas | South America. |
| Musk-Oxen | North America and Greenland. |
| Orang-Utans | Forests and jungles of Borneo and Sumatra. |
| Pandas | China and Tibet. |
| Reindeer | The Arctic regions of Europe and western Asia. |
| Rhinoceroses | (Black) Africa. |
| | (White) Africa. |
| | (Great One-horned) Northern Bengal, Assam and Nepal. |
| Skunk | (Spotted) From Central America to central United States. |
| Tapirs | Central America, northern South America, Burma, Siam, Malaya and Sumatra. |
| Tigers | Asia – from India to Siberia and Java. |
| Wolves | Found in the cold regions throughout the Northern Hemisphere. |
| Zebras | Africa. |

# Periods of Gestation and Incubation

| Species | Usual Period | Species | Usual Period |
|---|---|---|---|
| Ass | 365–374 days | Guinea Pig | 63–70 days |
| Bitch | 63 days | Hen | 21 days |
| Canary | 14 days | Human | 273 days |
| Camel | 45 weeks | Mare | 336 days |
| Cat | 56 days | Mouse | 18–19 days |
| Cow | 280 days | Pigeon | 18 days |
| Duck | 28 days | Rabbit | 32 days |
| Elephant | 2 years | Rat | 21–24 days |
| Ewe | 147–150 days | Sow | 112 days |
| Goat | 151 days | Turkey | 28 days |
| Goose | 30 days | Zebra | 56 weeks |

# Points of a Horse

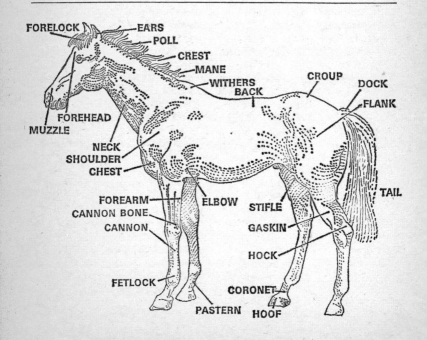

# Horse Talk

| | |
|---|---|
| **Colt** | Male horse under the age of four. |
| **Filly** | Female horse under the age of four. |
| **Foal** | A colt or filly up to the age of 12 months. |
| **Gelding** | Castrated stallion. |
| **Mare** | The female. |
| **Stallion** | A horse capable of reproducing the species. |

# Life Cycles of Mammals

| | Maximum recorded life (in years) | | Maximum recorded life (in years) |
|---|---|---|---|
| Antelope | 15 | Horse | 20 |
| Badger | 14 | Kangaroo | 17 |
| Bear (Brown) | 34 | Lion | 20-30 |
| Camel | 40 | Monkey (Marmoset) | 16 |
| Cat | 21 | Mouse | 2 |
| Chimpanzee | 25 | Otter (European) | 11 |
| Cow | 20 | Pig | 15 |
| Dog | 20 | Porcupine | 20 |
| Elephant (Indian) | 70 | Rabbit | 6 |
| Ewe | 12 | Reindeer | 15 |
| Fox | 12 | Rhinoceros | 40 |
| Gerbil | 5 | Sea-Lion | 23 |
| Giraffe | 27 | Shrew (Common) | $1\frac{1}{2}$ |
| Guinea-pig | 6 | Squirrel | 10 |
| Hamster (Golden) | 1–2 | Tiger | 20 |
| Hedgehog | 3 | Whale | 24 |
| Hippopotamus | 40 | | |

# British Birds

Birds form a very large branch of the Animal Kingdom. The sequence of Orders is as follows:

1. **Passeriformes** (Perching Birds) – Crow, Raven, Rook, Jackdaw, Magpie, Jay, Chough, Starling, Hawfinch, Greenfinch, Goldfinch, Siskin, Linnet, Bullfinch, Crossbill, Chaffinch, Brambling, Corn-Bunting, Yellow-Bunting (or Yellow-Hammer), Reed-Bunting, House Sparrow, Tree Sparrow, Skylark, Woodlark, Meadow-Pipit, Tree-Pipit, Pied Wagtail, Grey Wagtail, Yellow Wagtail, Nuthatch, Great Tit, Blue Tit, Coal Tit, Long-tailed Tit, Red-backed Shrike, Spotted Flycatcher, Goldcrest, Firecrest, Chiffchaff, Willow-Warbler, Reed-Warbler, Blackcap, Whitethroat, Mistle-Thrush, Song Thrush, Blackbird, Redwing, Wheatear, Stonechat, Redstart, Nightingale, Robin, Hedge-Sparrow, Wren, House Martin, Sand-Martin.
2. **Apodiformes** – Swifts.
3. **Caprimulgiformes** – Nightjars.
4. **Coraciiformes** – Bee-eaters, Hoopoe, Kingfisher.
5. **Piciformes** – Woodpeckers, Wrynecks.
6. **Cuculiformes** – Cuckoos.
7. **Strigiformes** – Owls.
8. **Falconiformes** (Birds of Prey) – Peregrine Falcon, Merlin, Kestrel, Golden Eagle, Common Buzzard, Sparrow-Hawk, Goshawk, Kite, Osprey.
9. **Ciconiiformes** – Storks, Spoonbills, Ibises, Herons, Bitterns, Flamingos.
10. **Anseriformes** – Swans, Geese, Ducks.
11. **Pelecaniformes** – Gannets, Cormorants.
12. **Procellariiformes** – Petrels.
13. **Podicipitiformes** – Grebes.
14. **Colymbiformes** – Divers.
15. **Columbiformes** – Pigeons, Doves.
16. **Charadriiformes** – Curlew, Whimbrel, Woodcock, Common Snipe, Dunlin, Sandpiper, British Redshank, Plover, Oyster-Catcher, Gulls, Terns, Skuas, Auks, Puffins.
17. **Gruiformes** – Bustards, Cranes, Rails, Moorhens, Coots.
18. **Galliformes** (Game Birds) – Grouse, Ptarmigan, Pheasant, Partridge, Quail.

# Parts of a Bird

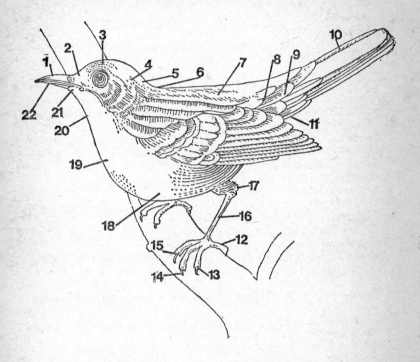

1. Upper Part (Bill)
2. Forehead
3. Crown
4. Ear Coverts
5. Nape
6. Neck
7. Back
8. Rump
9. Upper Tail Coverts
10. Tail Feathers
11. Under Tail Coverts
12. Hind Toe
13. Outer Toe
14. Middle Toe
15. Inner Toe
16. Tarsus (Elongated Ankle)
17. Tibia (Shin Bone)
18. Belly
19. Breast
20. Throat
21. Chin
22. Lower Part (Bill)

## Some Bills of Birds

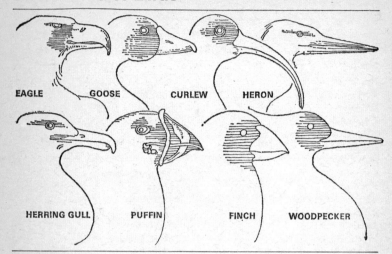

EAGLE   GOOSE   CURLEW   HERON

HERRING GULL   PUFFIN   FINCH   WOODPECKER

## Some Feet of Birds

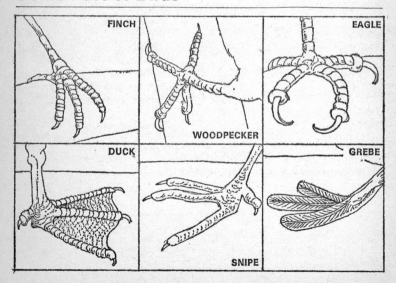

FINCH   WOODPECKER   EAGLE

DUCK   SNIPE   GREBE

# Life Cycles of Birds

The average life expectancy of a bird in the wild is very short. These figures show the maximum recorded life-span for an individual of each species to the nearest year.

| | | | |
|---|---|---|---|
| Blackbird | 9 | Black Headed Gull | 30 |
| Black Cap | 5 | Herring Gull | 32 |
| Bullfinch | 8 | Jackdaw | 14 |
| Chaffinch | 10 | Jay | 18 |
| Tree Creeper | 4 | Kestrel | 16 |
| Collared Dove | 3 | Magpie | 15 |
| Stock Dove | 8 | Mallard | 20 |
| Dunnock | 8 | House-Martin | 6 |
| Fieldfare | 5 | Moorhen | 11 |
| Spotted Flycatcher | 8 | Nuthatch | 9 |
| Canada Goose | 11 | Barn Owl | 15 |
| Greenfinch | 10 | Little Owl | 16 |
| Wood Pigeon | 14 | Song Thrush | 14 |
| Rock-Pipit | 5 | Blue Tit | 10 |
| Redstart | 7 | Coal Tit | 5 |
| Redwing | 19 | Great Tit | 10 |
| Robin | 11 | Long-tailed Tit | 4 |
| Rook | 20 | Marsh Tit | 10 |
| Starling | 20 | Turnstone | 20 |
| House Sparrow | 11 | Grey Wagtail | 3 |
| Tree Sparrow | 10 | Pied Wagtail | 6 |
| Swallow | 16 | Great Spotted Woodpecker | 9 |
| Mute Swan | 19 | Green Woodpecker | 5 |
| Swift | 21 | Wren | 5 |
| Mistle-Thrush | 10 | Yellow-Hammer | 7 |

(There are 8,600 known living species of birds. The flightless North African ostrich – *Struthio Camelus Camelus* – is the largest, reaching a height of nine feet and a weight of 345 lb.)

# Freshwater Fishes

This list gives the names of some of the many freshwater fishes that inhabit the waters of the British Isles. The Families are as follows:

1. **Petromyzonidae** – the Lampreys.
2. **Acipenseridae** – the Sturgeon.
3. **Clupeidae** – the Shads.
4. **Salmonidae** – the Salmon, Trout, Char, Whitefish, Grayling.
5. **Osmeridae** – Smelt (or Sparling).
6. **Esocidae** – the Pike.
7. **Cyprinidae** – Carp, Barbel, Gudgeon, Tench, Minnow, Chub, Dace (or Dart), Roach, Rudd, the Breams, the Bleak.
8. **Cobitidae** – the Loaches.
9. **Anguillidae** – the Common Eel.
10. **Gadidae** – the Burbot.
11. **Serranidae** – the Bass or Sea Perch.
12. **Percidae** – the Perch, Pope (or Ruffe).
13. **Mugilidae** – the Mullets.
14. **Cottidae** – the Bullhead (or Miller's Thumb).
15. **Gasterosteidae** – the Sticklebacks.
16. **Pleuronectidae** – the Flounder.

# Parts of a Fish

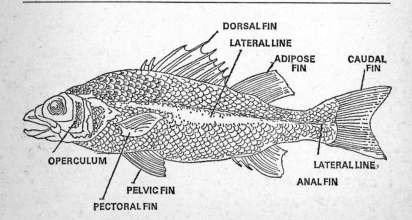

# Life Cycles of Fishes

|  | Maximum length of life (in years) |  | Maximum length of life (in years) |
|---|---|---|---|
| Cod | 13 | Pike | 15 |
| Goldfish | 10 | Plaice | 22 |
| Haddock | 14 | Salmon | 13 |
| Herring | 18 | Sturgeon | 25 |
| Perch | 10 | | |

THE LARGEST OF BRITISH FRESHWATER FISHES is the common sturgeon. The heaviest recorded sturgeon (caught in the River Esk, Yorkshire in 1810), weighed 460 lb.

THE SHORTEST RECORDED FRESHWATER FISH and the smallest of all vertebrates is the dwarf pygmy goby. It measures only 7·5–11 millimetres long, and was first identified in 1927. It is found in the lakes of Luzon, Philippines.

# Arthropoda

The Arthropoda is the largest division of the Animal Kingdom, forming about three-quarters of the known species. This is the class to which the Insects belong. Arthropoda comes from two Greek words meaning 'having jointed feet' but, in fact, it is the legs rather than the feet which are jointed.

The most important groups of Arthropoda are: Insecta, Arachnida, Crustacea, Diplopoda and Chilopoda.

1 – Insecta. It is estimated that about five out of every six animal species in the world are insects. There are about 20,000 named species in Britain alone and about 3 million species or more in the world – and more are being discovered each year. There are twenty-five Orders of British Insects. The best-known of the very small, primitive, wingless insects are the Silverfish and the Firebrat, which are common in buildings in the British Isles. Of the winged insects the following are the ones we see most:

Dragonfly
Mayfly

Cockroach
Stonefly
Earwig
Cricket
Grasshopper
Bugs (there are about 1,630 known species in Britain including Bedbug, Water Scorpion, Water Boatman, Froghoppers, Leaf-hoppers and Aphids – Greenfly and Blackfly)
Alder-fly
Snake-fly
Scorpion-fly
Caddis-fly (there are nearly 200 species of Caddis-fly. Fishermen use them as lures and some popular names for them are: the Great Red Sedge, Silverhorns and the Grannom)
Butterflies and Moths (c. 2,190 British species)
House Fly, Gnat, Mosquito (c. 5,200 British species)
Fleas
Ants, Bees, Wasps (over 6,000 British species)
Beetles and Weevils (c. 3,690 British species)

2. **Arachnida** – The majority of this group are land animals. They range in size from tiny mites no more than 0·1 mm long to the enormous black spider of Africa which is 180 mm long. They are chiefly predators, and live on other insects.

The best-known dwellers in our surroundings are:
*Spiders
Mites
Ticks
Tail-less Whip Scorpions
Whip Scorpions
Daddy Longlegs (or Harvestmen)
Sun Spiders (solpugids)

*There are 603 known British species of spider, covering an estimated population of more than 500,000,000,000,000. The longest is the Cardinal spider among which males sometimes have a leg span over 5 in. (body length, 19 mm. or 0·75 of an inch).

The world's largest known spider is the mygale or 'bird-eating' spider – a male specimen, collected in French Guinea in 1925, had a body length of 3½ in. and a leg span of 10 in. when fully extended.

The rarest in Britain is the black and crimson Eresus Niger which has been recorded less than a dozen times. The smallest known spiders found in Britain are Saloca Diceros, which have a body span of 1 mm. (or 1/25th of an inch).

3. **Crustacea** – Crustacea are sometimes known as the 'insects of the sea'. There is scarcely a ditch or pond where some, at least, of the more minute forms cannot be found. On land they are less common. They play a part in the seas and oceans similar to that played by insects on land. There is a multitude of crustacea that do not have popular names. Among the most familiar are:
   Crabs
   Lobsters
   Woodlice
   Crayfish
   Prawns
   Shrimps
   Sandhoppers
   Barnacles
   Water fleas

4. **Diplopoda** – These are the Millipedes. They have two pairs of legs to each segment of the body, with the exception of the first three segments.

5. **Chilopoda** – or Centipedes. The word 'Centipede' means 'hundred-footed' but the number of legs varies from 15–173 pairs, depending on the species. Centipedes have only one pair of legs to a segment.

THE OLDEST RECORDED INSECT is a wood-boring beetle which has been known to live for up to 37 years. Some queen termites are believed to live for as long as 40 years. A Russian bird flea is reported to have lived for 1,487 days.

THE LARGEST of the 21,000 species of insects found in the British Isles is the rare death's-head hawk moth. It has a wing-span of up to 5·25 in., a body length of about 2·36 in. and an abdomen girth of 1·57 in.

THE LARGEST NATIVE BUTTERFLY is the swallowtail, which has a wing-span of 3–3½ in. and weighs 0·017 of an ounce.

# Parts of an Insect

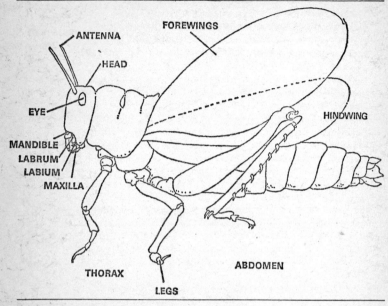

FOREWINGS

ANTENNA

HEAD

EYE

HINDWING

MANDIBLE
LABRUM
LABIUM
MAXILLA

ABDOMEN

THORAX

LEGS

# Some British Wild Flowers

This list gives the names of some British wild flowers, arranged in their botanical families:

1. **Buttercup Family** – Buttercup, Marsh Marigold, Wood Anemone, Lesser Celandine, Traveller's Joy, Water Crowfoot, Monkshood, Columbine, Adonis.
2. **Pink and Cranesbill Families** – Ragged Robin, Red Campion, Maiden Pink, Greater Stitchwort, Meadow Cranesbill, Hemlock Storksbill.
3. **Forget-me-not and Parsley Families** – Forget-me-not, Hound's Tongue, Bugloss, Sea Holly, Hemlock.
4. **Figwort Family** – Ivy-Leaved Toadflax, Eyebright, Germander Speedwell, Yellow Toadflax, Foxglove.
5. **Rose Family** – Dog Rose, Herb Bennet, Wild Strawberry, Bramble, Agrimony, Cinquefoil, Crab Apple, Meadowsweet.
6. **Mint Family** – Red Dead Nettle, Water Mint, Marjoram, Ground Ivy, Hedge Woundwort.

7. **Wallflower and Primrose Families** – Wild Wallflower, Jack-by-the-Hedge, Shepherd's Purse, Lady's Smock, Primrose, Cowslip, Yellow Loosestrife, Scarlet Pimpernel.

8. **Pea Family** – Kidney Vetch, Red Clover, Broom, Bird's Foot Trefoil, Furze, Sainfoin.

9. **Daisy Family** – Daisy, Hemp Agrimony, Fleabane, Ox-Eye Daisy, Yarrow, Coltsfoot, Chicory, Nipplewort, Ragwort, Cat's Ear, Carline Thistle, Groundsel, Tansy, Cornflower, Dandelion, Burdock, Goat's Beard, Bristly Ox-Tongue.

10. **Various Families** – Red Poppy, Wood Sorrel, Sweet Violet, Wild Heartsease, Flax, Rose-Bay, Willow-Herb, Milkwort, Ivy, Field Scabious, Teasel, Goose-Grass, Honeysuckle, Lesser Periwinkle, Harebell, Lamb's-Tongue Plantain, Sea Lavender, Thrift, Heather, Bluebell, Cuckoo-Pint, Vernal Grass.

# Parts of a Flower

BUTTERCUP

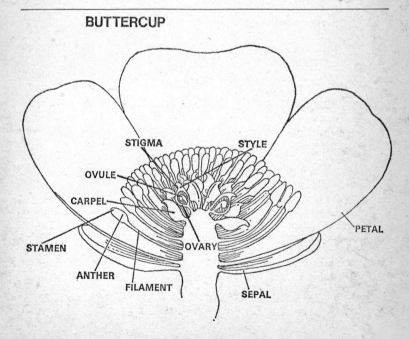

# The Rarest Flowers in Britain

Specimens of many plants are only known in a single locality, so it is rather difficult to determine which is the rarest flower in Britain. But the following three may well qualify for the title:

    The adder's-tongue spearwort
    The flecked pink spurred coral-root (a British orchid)
    The rose purple Alpine coltsfoot

# Main Trees in Britain

The trees which grow in Great Britain are divided into two main groups: the *Angiosperms*, broad-leaved trees which can be deciduous or evergreen, and *Gymnosperms*, which comprise mainly coniferous trees and are, with few exceptions, evergreen.

**Angiosperms**

| | |
|---|---|
| Alder | Lime (or Linden) |
| Almond | Magnolia |
| Apple | Maple |
| Ash | Mulberry |
| Aspen | Oak |
| Beech | Pear |
| Birch | Plane |
| Box | Plum |
| Buckthorn | Poplar |
| Cherry | Quince |
| Damson | Sloe |
| Elder | Sweet Bay (the true Laurel) |
| Elm | Sycamore |
| Hawthorn (or May) | Tamarisk |
| Hazel | Tulip Tree |
| Holly | Walnut |
| Hornbeam | White Beam |
| Horse Chestnut | Willow |
| Laburnum | Wistaria |

**Gymnosperms**

Cedar
Common Spruce (Norway Spruce)
Cypress
Douglas Fir
Larch

Maidenhair Tree
Monkey Puzzle (or Chile Pine)
Scots Pine
Silver Fir
Yew

# Tallest Trees in Great Britain

|  | Location | Height (in feet) |
|---|---|---|
| **Douglas Fir** | Powis Castle Montgomery | 180 |
| **Grand Fir** | Strong Argyllshire | 177 |
| **Wellingtonia** | Endsleigh Devon | 165 |
| **Spruce (Sitka)** | Murthly Perth | 164 |
| **Spruce (Sitka)** | Shelton Abbey Co. Wicklow | 162 |
| **Hemlock (Western)** | Benmore Argyllshire | 157 |
| **Lime** | Duncombe Park Yorkshire | 154 |
| **Silver Fir** | Dupplin Castle Perthshire | 154 |
| **Ash** | Duncombe Park Yorkshire | 148 |
| **Pine (Corsican)** | Stanage Park Radnor | 147 |
| **Larch (European)** | Parkhatch Surrey | 142 |
| **Beech** | Yester House East Lothian | 142 |

# Some Trunks and Leaves

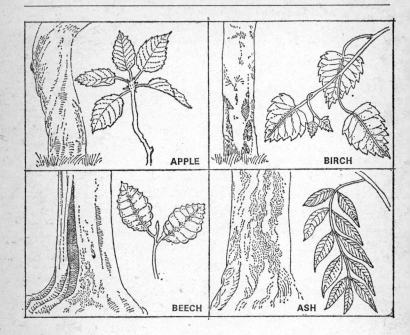

# 6 CODES

## The Country Code

Damage done to the countryside every year, particularly at holiday seasons, is frightening. Most of it is unintentional; all the same, one thoughtless or careless action can ruin someone's livelihood. To keep visitors aware of this, and to guide their behaviour the Countryside Commission prepared, in 1951, a Country Code, consisting of ten maxims based on common sense – and common failings. It runs like this:

1. Guard against all risk of fire.
2. Fasten all gates.
3. Keep dogs under proper control.
4. Keep to paths across farm land.
5. Avoid damaging fences, hedges and walls.
6. Leave no litter.
7. Safeguard water supplies.
8. Protect wild life, wild plants, and trees.
9. Go carefully on country roads.
10. Respect the life of the countryside.

## The Dog Owners' Code

**Do** keep him well under control in the country, and always on the lead if there is livestock about. Even well-behaved dogs may chase and savage livestock unless restrained, and an animal savaged by a dog suffers pain and terror beyond description. (In one year, dogs killed 6,000 sheep and 20,000 poultry.)

**Do** exercise him regularly. He needs a good run, off the lead – but not where he can run on to a road, and not near livestock.

**Do** keep him clean – frequent brushing is the best way and gives you a chance to look for pests, cuts, sores or bad ears.

**Do** see that he has somewhere to sleep that is dry and out of draughts. If he has a kennel, it should be raised off the ground and protected against both heat and cold.

**Do** feed him regularly – one or two good meals every day at the same time. He needs fresh water too.

**Do** have your name and address marked on his collar, so that he can be brought home if he strays.

**Don't** let him run loose on the road. Dogs let loose on the highway are a danger to themselves and a menace to road users. In one year alone, 75,000 dogs suffered in road accidents and 3,000 people were killed or injured in road accidents in which dogs were involved.

**Don't** keep him tied up or shut up by himself for long periods – it will make him cross and snappy and too excited to control when he is released. Never leave him in a car with all the windows closed.

**Don't** delay before obtaining skilled attention if he seems ill. Meanwhile keep him warm. See that he has a drink and something to eat if he wants it, but don't fuss him.

**Don't** let the children tease him when they are playing together.

**Don't** let him worry the neighbours by barking unchecked, and don't let him foul pavements or grass verges.

**Don't** keep a dog unless you are prepared to take the trouble to look after him properly and to train him in obedience.

*A dog that is not healthy and well-trained is a misery to himself, an annoyance to neighbours, a danger to livestock and traffic and a nuisance to his owner. A healthy, well-trained dog is a contented dog, a trusty friend and guardian, and a companion who spreads happiness all round.*

# The Green Cross Code

**1. First find a safe place to cross, then stop.**
It is safer to cross at some places than others. Subways. Footbridges. Zebra and Pelican crossings. Traffic lights. Where there is a policeman, or a lollipop man, or a traffic warden. If you can't find any good crossing places like these choose a place where you can see clearly along the roads in all directions. Don't try to cross between parked cars. Move to a clear space and always give drivers a chance to see you clearly.

# WRONG                    RIGHT

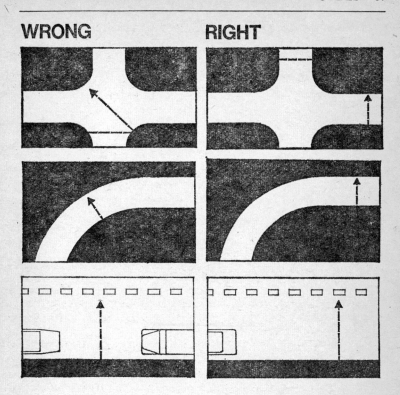

**2. Stand on the pavement near the kerb.**

Don't stand too near the edge of the pavement. Stop a little way back from the kerb where you'll be away from traffic, but you can still see if anything is coming.

**3. Look all round for traffic and listen.**

Traffic may be coming from all directions, so take care to look along every road. And listen too, because you can sometimes hear traffic before you can see it.

**4. If traffic is coming, let it pass. Look all round again.**

If there's any traffic near let it go past. Then look round again and listen to make sure no other traffic is coming.

**5. When there is no traffic, walk straight across the road.**
When there is no traffic near it's safe to cross. If there is something in the distance do *not* cross unless you're certain there's plenty of time. Remember, even if traffic is a long way off it may be coming very fast. When it's safe, walk straight across the road – don't run.

**6. Keep looking and listening for traffic while you cross.**
Once you're in the road, keep looking and listening in case you didn't see some traffic or in case other traffic suddenly appears.

# 7 THE WEATHER

---

## Clouds

---

The proper study of clouds began when an English chemist, Luke Howard, gave Latin names to a few obviously different cloud forms in 1803. The terms he gave to the three main forms, which became the basis of the internationally accepted cloud classification, are: *cumulus* (Latin for 'heap'); *cirrus* ('curl' or 'hair'); and *stratus* ('layer').

Meteorologists now divide clouds into ten types.

**A.** The **HIGH CLOUDS** (mean heights 16,500 to 45,000 – 5 to 13 km) are called '*Cirrus*', '*Cirrocumulus*' and '*Cirrostratus*'.

*Cirrus* clouds, which look rather like curly white wisps of hair drawn out in plumes across a blue sky, are also known as 'Mare's-tail' or 'paint-brush'. They are the highest clouds in the sky. The temperature where they lie is below freezing point and the particles are really clouds of ice crystals. Sailors believe *cirrus* in a blue sky foretells windy weather.

*Cirrocumulus* looks rather like the white caps on the ocean or the ripples in the sand on the sea-shore. These small cloud patches are often seen after a depression at the approach of fair weather.

The appearance in the sky of *Cirrostratus*, a transparent, whitish cloud veil, which does not obscure the sun or moon, usually means that rain is on the way. The refraction of the sun's rays by the ice crystals often causes a halo round the sun or moon.

**B.** The **MIDDLE CLOUDS** (mean heights 6,500 to 23,000 – 2 to 7 km) are known as '*Altocumulus*', '*Altostratus*' and '*Nimbostratus*'.

*Altocumulus* are large rounded white or greyish masses of clouds with shadows, often arranged in wavy lines, sometimes broken into 'popples' by the intersection of two sets of waves. The wave form is caused by the flow of one air-layer over another differing in temperature, density or humidity. In summer they can often be seen in the early morning or late evening.

*Altostratus*, a sure sign of rain, gives a thin, continuous grey or bluish cloud sheet through which the sun barely shines. This 'watery-sky' is caused by a current of warm moist air flowing up over a cold front.

*Nimbostratus*, dark grey and threatening clouds, are thick enough to blot out the sun. The base and edges are usually ragged and separate fragments ('scud') are torn from the base by strong winds.

**C. The LOW CLOUDS** (mean heights 0 to 6,500 – 0 to 2 km) are '*Stratocumulus*', '*Stratus*', '*Cumulus*' and '*Cumulonimbus*'.

The first of these, *Stratocumulus*, are large lumpy masses of dark grey or whitish cloud – a lower and heavier form of the Middle Cloud, *Altocumulus*.

*Stratus*, uniform layers of grey cloud with a fairly uniform base, often thickens and turns to fog, drizzle or rain. It is the lowest type of cloud, and when the sun is visible its outline is clearly seen through the cloud.

*Cumulus* are heavy, detached, dome or cauliflower-shaped clouds with sharp outlines and flat bases. The sunlit parts are brilliant white.

*Cumulonimbus* clouds tower up to a far greater height than the cumulus. They are the massive, lowering thunderclouds that can stretch through all cloud levels. Powerful ascending currents carry the cloud to heights where rain, snow and hail are formed.

# The Colours of the Rainbow

Violet, Indigo, Blue, Green, Yellow, Orange, Red.

# Coastal Weather Forecast Areas

*The map opposite is Crown Copyright, reproduced with the permission of the Controller of Her Majesty's Stationery Office*

This map shows the boundaries of the coastal sea areas referred to in the shipping forecasts.

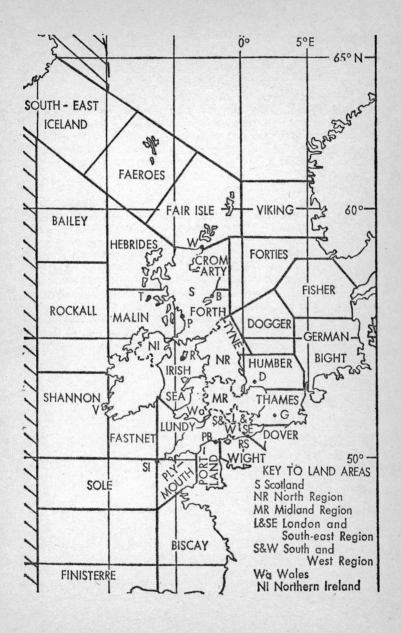

65° N

0°  5°E

SOUTH - EAST
ICELAND

FAEROES

BAILEY

FAIR ISLE — VIKING

60°

HEBRIDES    W

CROM-
ARTY

FORTIES

ROCKALL    MALIN

S

T

FORTH    B

FISHER

P

DOGGER

GERMAN

NI

TYNE

R

NR

HUMBER

BIGHT

IRISH

D

SHANNON    SEA    MR    THAMES

V

Wa

S&    L&    • G

W    SE

LUNDY

DOVER

FASTNET    PB    RS

WIGHT

SI

50°

SOLE    PLY-
MOUTH    PORT-
LAND

KEY TO LAND AREAS
S Scotland
NR North Region
MR Midland Region
L&SE London and
        South-east Region
S&W South and
        West Region
Wa Wales
NI Northern Ireland

BISCAY

FINISTERRE

# The Beaufort Scale

The Beaufort Scale is a series of numbers from 0 to 17, to designate the force of the wind. The numbers 0 to 12 were arranged by Admiral Sir Francis Beaufort in 1806 to indicate the strength of the wind from a calm, force 0, to a hurricane, force 12 – 'that which no canvas could withstand'. The Beaufort numbers 13 to 17 were added by the US weather bureau in 1955.

| Beaufort Number | Miles Per Hour | Description | Observation |
|---|---|---|---|
| 0 | 0–1 | Calm | Smoke rises vertically |
| 1 | 1–3 | Light Air | Smoke drifts slowly |
| 2 | 4–7 | Slight breeze | Leaves rustle |
| 3 | 8–12 | Gentle breeze | Leaves and twigs move |
| 4 | 13–18 | Moderate breeze | Small branches move |
| 5 | 19–24 | Fresh breeze | Small trees sway |
| 6 | 25–31 | Strong breeze | Large branches sway |
| 7 | 32–38 | Moderate gale | Whole trees move |
| 8 | 39–46 | Fresh gale | Twigs break off trees |
| 9 | 47–54 | Strong gale | Branches break |
| 10 | 55–63 | Whole gale | Trees snap and are blown down |
| 11 | 64–75 | Storm | Widespread damage |
| 12 | More than 75 | Hurricane | Extreme damage |
| 13 | 83–92 | ⎫ | |
| 14 | 93–103 | ⎪ | |
| 15 | 104–114 | ⎬ Hurricane | |
| 16 | 115–125 | ⎪ | |
| 17 | 126–136 | ⎭ | |

# Fahrenheit and Centigrade Temperatures

Gabriel Daniel Fahrenheit (1688–1736) was a German physicist who made important improvements in the construction of thermometers and introduced the thermometric scale known by his name. It had a boiling point at 212° and a freezing point at 32°.

The Centigrade thermometer was invented by Anders Celsius (1701–1744), a Swedish astronomer. This Celsius scale had a boiling point at 100° and a freezing point at 0° (zero).

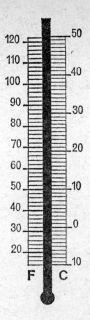

To convert Fahrenheit into Centigrade: subtract 32, multiply by 5 and divide by 9.
To convert Centigrade into Fahrenheit: multiply by 9, divide by 5 and add 32.

# 8 TIME

## The Seasons of the Year

> 'Four seasons fill the measure of the year;
> There are four seasons in the mind of man'.
> (Sonnet *The Human Seasons*, Keats)

The year is divided into four seasons – Spring, Summer, Autumn and Winter – each associated with a stage of vegetation and a type of weather. The seasons are defined astronomically to begin about the 21st day of March, June, September and December.

*Spring*, the first season of the year, begins at the Vernal Equinox – the time at which the Sun crosses the Equator and day and night are of equal length all over the world.

*Summer*, the second and warmest season, begins at the Summer Solstice, the time at which the Sun is farthest from the Equator and seems to stay still before returning. Sunrise and sunset show no variation for several days. The longest day is June 21st or 22nd.

*Autumn*, the third season, begins astronomically at the Autumnal Equinox, when the Sun crosses from North to South of the Equator and causes night and day to be of equal length.

*Winter*, the fourth and coldest season of the year, begins at the Winter Solstice and ends at the Vernal Equinox. Midwinter is marked by the shortest day – usually December 22nd.

# The Months

**January**      (Lat. *Ianuarius*) Although named for Janus, the two-faced Roman god of beginnings, January was the eleventh month, not the first, until about 153 BC.

**February**      (Lat. *Februarius*) The twelfth month of the early Roman calendar primarily devoted to ceremonies of purification, in anticipation of the New Year, hence its name derived from the root of Februare, 'to purify'.

**March**      (Lat. *Martius*) Originally the first month and the beginning of the annual cycle of religious festivals. Named for the god Mars, the god of war.

**April**      (Lat. *Aprilis*) The month considered by the Romans sacred to Venus. Its name is thought to originate either from that of Aphrodite, her Greek equivalent, or from the Lat. *aperire* ('to open'), referring to the unfolding of buds and blossoms at this season.

**May**      (Lat. *Maius*) The origin is uncertain: some derive it from Maiores meaning 'elders'; others from Maia, a goddess, whose name meant 'increase'.

**June**      (Lat. *Iunius*) The name is possibly connected with that of the goddess, Juno, though some Roman authorities preferred to think that this month honoured the young and favoured the derivation 'iuniores' – the opposite of 'maiores' (see May).

**July**      (Lat. *Iulius*) The fifth month in the early Roman calendar, originally called Quintilis. It was renamed in honour of Julius Caesarin 44 BC, the year of his death.

**August**      (Lat. *Augustus*) The sixth month in the early Roman calendar, originally called Sextilis. It was renamed after the Emperor Augustus in 8 BC.

**September**      (Lat. *Septem*) As is shown by its Latin name, it was the seventh month in the early Roman calendar. *Septem* means seven, and *imber* a shower of rain, from the rainy season usually beginning at this time of year.

**October**      (Lat. *Octo*) The eighth month in the early Roman calendar. Ghosts, hobgoblins and witches of Halloween are relics of a pre-Christian Celtic feast of the dead held at this season.

**November**      (Lat. *Novem* 'nine') The ninth month in the ancient Roman calendar, when the year began in March. The old Saxon name was *Wind-monath* (wind month) when the fishermen drew their boats ashore and ceased fishing until the next spring.

**December** (Lat. *Decem* 'ten') Some features survive in the traditional observances connected with Christmas of both the Roman Saturnalia which was celebrated in December and a great mid-winter festival held by the ancient Teutonic peoples.

# The Days of the Week

**Sunday** (Old English: *Sunnendaeg*) The first day of the week, anciently dedicated to the Sun.

**Monday** The second day of the week: called by the Anglo-Saxons *Monandaeg*, i.e, the day of the Moon.

**Tuesday** The third day of the week. Named after Tiu, son of Odin, and a younger brother of Thor.

**Wednesday** The fourth day of the week, Woden's (or Odin's) Day.

**Thursday** The day of the god Thor. The French call it '*jeudi*', Jove's day. Both Jove and Thor were gods of thunder and formerly Thursday was sometimes called Thunderday.

**Friday** The sixth day of the week: in ancient Rome called *dies Veneris*, the day dedicated to Venus, hence the French *vendredi*. Northern nations adopted the same naming system and the nearest equivalent to Venus was Frigg or Freyja, hence Friday.

**Saturday** The seventh day of the week: called by the Anglo-Saxons *Saeterdaeg*, after the Latin *Saturni Dies*, the day of Saturn.

# The Date Line

*The Date Line*, where each calendar day begins, is a zig-zag line that coincides approximately with the 180th meridian. The date must be set back one day when crossing in an easterly direction, and put forward one day when crossing in a westerly direction.

It is indicated by joining up the following nine points:

| Lat. | Long. | Lat. | Long. | Lat. | Long. |
|------|-------|------|-------|------|-------|
| 60°S. | 180° | 15°S. | 172½°W. | 53°N. | 170°E. |
| 51°S. | 180° | 5°S. | 180° | 65½°N. | 169°W. |
| 45°S. | 172½°W. | 48°N. | 180° | 75°N. | 180° |

# World Time Chart

| Area | Standard time (difference from GMT in hours) |
|---|---|
| Afghanistan | $+4\frac{1}{2}$ |
| Albania | +1 |
| Aleutian Islands | −11 |
| Andaman Islands | $+6\frac{1}{2}$ |
| Angola | +1 |
| Antigua | −4 |
| Argentina | −4 |
| Australia | |
| (a) Victoria, New South Wales, Queensland, Tasmania | +10 |
| (b) N. Territory, S. Australia | $+9\frac{1}{2}$ |
| (c) West Australia | +8 |
| Austria | +1 |
| Azores | −2 |
| Bahamas | −5 |
| Bahrein | +3 |
| Barbados | −4 |
| Bermuda | −4 |
| Bolivia | −4 |
| Botswana | +2 |
| Brazil | |
| (a) East including all coast and Brasilia | −3 |
| (b) West | −4 |
| (c) Territory of Acre | −5 |
| British Honduras | −6 |
| Brunei | +8 |
| Bulgaria | +2 |
| Burma | $+6\frac{1}{2}$ |
| Canada | |
| (a) Newfoundland | $-3\frac{1}{2}$ |
| (b) Atlantic Zone: Labrador, New Brunswick, | |

| Area | Standard time (difference from GMT in hours) |
|---|---|
| Nova Scotia, Prince Edward Is., Quebec (East of Pte. des Monts) | −4 |
| (c) Eastern Zone: North-West Territory (East), Ottawa, Ontario, Quebec (West of Pte. des Monts) | −5 |
| (d) Central Zone: Manitoba, North-West Territory (Central) | −6 |
| (e) Mountain Zone: Alberta, North-west Territory (Mountain) Saskatchewan | −7 |
| (f) Pacific Zone: British Columbia, North-west Territory (West) | −8 |
| (g) Yukon Territory: White-horse and Watson Lake Dawson City and Mayo | −9 |
| Cape Verde Islands | −2 |
| Central African Republic | +1 |
| Ceylon | $+5\frac{1}{2}$ |
| Chile | −4 |
| China | |
| (a) Chungking, Lanchow | +7 |
| (b) Peking, Shanghai | +8 |
| Christmas Island (Indian Ocean) | +7 |
| Congo Republic | |
| (a) Kinshasa | +1 |
| (b) Kivu, Katanga, Kasai | +2 |
| Congo, Republic of (Brazzaville) | +1 |
| Cook Islands | $-10\frac{1}{2}$ |
| Costa Rica | −6 |
| Cuba | −5 |

| Area | Standard time (difference from GMT in hours) | Area | Standard time (difference from GMT in hours) |
|---|---|---|---|
| Cyprus | +2 | Italy | +1 |
| Czechoslovakia | +1 | Jamaica | −5 |
| Denmark | +1 | Japan | +9 |
| Dominica | −4 | Jordan | +2 |
| Dominican Republic | −5 | Kenya | +3 |
| Ecuador | −5 | Korea | |
| Egypt | +2 | (a) North Korea | +9 |
| Ethiopia | +3 | (b) Republic of Korea | |
| Falkland Islands | −4 | (South) | +9 |
| Fiji | +12 | Kuwait | +3 |
| Finland | +2 | Laos | +7 |
| French Guiana | −4 | Latvia, USSR | +2 |
| Germany | +1 | Lebanon | +2 |
| Greece | +2 | Leeward Islands | −4 |
| Greenland | | Lesotho | +2 |
| (a) Scoresby Sound | −2 | Libya | +1 |
| (b) Angmagssalik, West | | Lithuania | +1 |
| Coast except Thule | −3 | Luxembourg | +1 |
| (c) Thule area | −4 | Madeira | −1 |
| Grenada | −4 | Malawi | +2 |
| Guinea | −1 | Malaysia, Federation of | |
| Guyana | −3¾ | (a) West Malaysia | |
| Haiti | −5 | (Malaya) | +7½ |
| Honduras | −6 | (b) East Malaysia (Sabah, | |
| Hong Kong | +8 | Sarawak) | +8 |
| Hungary | +1 | Maldive Islands | +5 |
| India | +5½ | Malta | +1 |
| Indonesia | | Mauritania | −1 |
| (a) Western Zone: Java, | | Mauritius | +4 |
| Sumatra, Bali, Madura | +7 | Mexico | |
| (b) Central Zone: Borneo, | | (a) Mexico City | −7 |
| Celebes, Timor | +8 | (b) Baja California Sur, | |
| (c) Eastern Zone: Molucca | | States of Sonora, Sinaloa | |
| Islands, Kai, Aroe, West | | and Nayarit | −7 |
| Irian | +9 | (c) Baja California Norte | −7 |
| Iran | +3½ | Mozambique | +2 |
| Iraq | +3 | Nepal | +5½ |
| Ireland | +1 | New Guinea | +10 |
| Israel | +2 | New Zealand | +12 |

| Area | Standard time (difference from GMT in hours) |
|---|---|
| Nicaragua | $-5\frac{3}{4}$ |
| Nigeria | +1 |
| Norway | +1 |
| Pakistan | |
| (a) West | +5 |
| (b) East (East Bengal) | +6 |
| Panama | -5 |
| Papua | +10 |
| Paraguay | -4 |
| Peru | -5 |
| Philippine Islands | +8 |
| Poland | +1 |
| Puerto Rico | -4 |
| Rhodesia | +2 |
| Salvador | -6 |
| Santa Cruz Islands | +11 |
| Saudi Arabia | +3 |
| Senegal | -1 |
| Seychelles | +4 |
| Singapore | $+7\frac{1}{2}$ |
| Solomon Islands | +11 |
| Somalia | +3 |
| South Africa, Republic of | +2 |
| Sudan | +2 |
| Sweden | +1 |
| Switzerland | +1 |
| Syria | +2 |
| Tahiti | -10 |
| Taiwan | +8 |
| Tanzania (Tanganyika and Zanzibar) | +3 |
| Thailand | +7 |

| Area | Standard time (difference from GMT in hours) |
|---|---|
| Tonga (Friendly Islands) | +13 |
| Trinidad and Tobago | -4 |
| Tunisia | +1 |
| Turkey | +2 |
| Uganda | +3 |
| United Kingdom | +1 |
| | |
| United States of America | |
| (a) Eastern Zone | -5 |
| (b) Central Zone | -6 |
| (c) Mountain Zone | -7 |
| (d) Pacific Zone | -8 |
| (e) Alaska: | |
| Ketchikan to Skagway | -8 |
| (f) Hawaiian Islands | -10 |
| USSR | |
| (a) Kiev, Leningrad, Moscow, Odessa | +3 |
| (b) Archangel, Volgograd | +4 |
| (c) Omsk | +6 |
| (d) Vladivostok | +10 |
| Uruguay | $-3\frac{1}{2}$ |
| Venezuela | $-4\frac{1}{2}$ |
| Vietnam | |
| (a) North Vietnam | +7 |
| (b) Republic of Vietnam (South) | +8 |
| Virgin Islands | -4 |
| Windward Islands | -4 |
| Yemen | +3 |
| Yugoslavia | +1 |
| Zambia | +2 |

# 9 COMMUNICATIONS

## The Post Office

There are 24,371 Post Offices in the UK (including 22,672 sub-Post Offices). In 1971–72 the Post Office handled some 4,260 million 1st class, 5,698 million 2nd class inland letters, 453 million overseas letters and postcards, 1,767 million inland parcels and 7·5 million overseas parcels.

Postage stamps to the value of approximately £183·5 million were sold.

342·3 million postal orders were issued, totalling £451·8 million; 4·1 million inland money orders, totalling £107·7 million; and 2·3 million overseas money orders, totalling £21·6 million.

LETTER POST SINCE 1897:

| | | |
|---|---|---|
| After | June 22nd, 1897 | 4 oz for 1d |
| | Nov. 1st, 1915 | 1 oz for 1d; 2 oz for 2d; 4 oz for 2½d |
| | June 3rd, 1918 | 4 oz for 1½d; 6 oz for 2d |
| | June 1st, 1920 | 3 oz for 2d |
| | May 29th, 1922 | 1 oz for 1½d; 3 oz for 2d |
| | May 14th, 1923 | 2 oz for 1½d |
| | May 1st, 1940 | 2 oz for 2½d |
| | Oct. 1st, 1957 | 1 oz for 3d; 2 oz for 4½d |
| | May 17th, 1965 | 2 oz for 4d; 4 oz for 6d |
| | Sept. 16th, 1968 | Two-Tier Letter Service introduced |

## INLAND POSTAL RATES FROM MARCH 6th, 1972: LETTER POST

| *Not over* | *First Class* | *Second Class* |
|---|---|---|
| 2 oz | 3p | 2½p |
| 4 oz | 4p | 3½p |
| 6 oz | 6p | 5½p |
| 8 oz | 8p | 6½p |
| 10 oz | 10p | 7½p |
| 12 oz | 13p | 8½p |
| 14 oz | 15p | 9½p |
| 1 lb 0 oz | 17p | 11½p |
| 1 lb 8 oz | 24p | 13½p |
| 2 lb 0 oz | 34p | maximum |
| each additional 1 lb | 17p | |

The Post Office has some 6,168 telephone exchanges and 16,025,000 telephones. There are over 75,000 public call offices, most of them in the streets. In 1914 there were less than 1,000 automatic telephones in the country: today there are more than 12,500,000 and the number is increasing rapidly.

|  | TOTAL *(Provisional figures for period 1.4.71–31.3.72)* |
|---|---|
| Trunk calls | 1,699,000,000 |
| Local calls | 10,330,000,000 |
| Overseas calls (originating in this country) | 22,223,000 |
| Radio calls from ships | 263,000 |
| Telephone connexions (auto) | 9,929,000 |
| Telephone connexions (manual) | 99,000 |

# Talking With Deaf People

1. Face them directly.
2. Don't shout – speak slowly and distinctly.
3. Try to give a visual indication of what you are saying.
4. Use short sentences – each with a single thought.

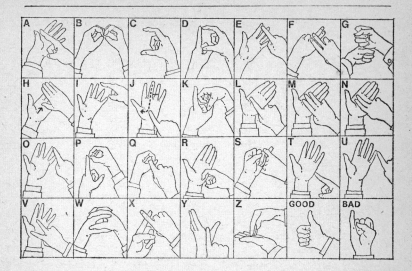

Finger Spelling Alphabet
(Reproduced by courtesy of the British Deaf Association).

# International Morse Code

The Morse Code was invented by Samuel Morse in 1838 as a means of sending messages by telegraph. The following are the rules for spacing:

**1.** A long is equal to three shorts.
**2.** The space between elements which form the letter, figure or symbol is equal to one short.
**3.** The space between 2 letters, figures, or symbols is equal to three shorts (i.e. one long).
**4.** The space between two words is equal to five shorts.

| Letter | Character | Letter | Character | Letter | Character | Letter | Character |
|--------|-----------|--------|-----------|--------|-----------|--------|-----------|
| A | · — | D | — · · | G | — — · | 1 | · — — — — |
| B | — · · · | E | · | H | · · · · | 2 | · · — — — |
| C | — · — · | F | · · — · | I | · · | 3 | · · · — — |

| | | | | | | | | | |
|---|---|---|---|---|---|---|---|---|---|
| J | ·--- | P | ·--· | V | ···- | 4 | ····- |
| K | -·- | Q | --·- | W | ·-- | 5 | ···· |
| L | ·-·· | R | ·-· | X | -··- | 6 | -···· |
| M | -- | S | ··· | Y | -·-- | 7 | --··· |
| N | -· | T | - | Z | --·· | 8 | ---·· |
| O | --- | U | ··- | | | 9 | ----· |
| | | | | | | 10 | ----- |

| | | | |
|---|---|---|---|
| Preliminary Call | -·-·- | Oblique Stroke | -··-· |
| Full Stop | ·-·-·- | Brackets | -·--·- |
| Comma | --··-- | Underline | ··--·- |
| Apostrophe | ·----· | Long Break Sign | -···- |
| Hyphen | -····- | Error | ········· |
| Inverted Commas | ·-··-· | End of Message | ·-·-· |
| Question | ··--·· | Finish of Transmission for an indefinite period | ···-·- |

# Distress Signals

1. The best-known emergency signal is SOS, which some people take to mean 'Save Our Souls', made in Morse by radio or any available means. The Morse Code for SOS is ···-----···
2. A signal sent by radio of the word 'mayday', from the French *m'aidez*, 'help me'.
3. A gun or other explosive signal fired at intervals of a minute.
4. A continuous sounding of any fog-signal apparatus.
5. A signal consisting of a square flag having above or below it a ball, or anything resembling a ball.

# Wavebands Allocated to Broadcasting in the United Kingdom

| Band | Frequencies* | Remarks |
|---|---|---|
| Long-wave (LF) | 150–285 kHz (2,000–1,053 m.) | One frequency (200 kHz) assigned to BBC and used at Droitwich for Radio 2. |

| | | |
|---|---|---|
| Medium-wave (MF) | 525–1,605 kHz (571–187 m.) | Various frequencies assigned to the BBC and IBA for radio broadcasting in the UK. Two frequencies for the BBC's European Services. |
| Short-wave (HF) | 3,950–4,000 kHz (75–m. band) | Frequencies in these bands are used as required by the BBC's External Services for broadcasting to Europe and overseas. |
| | 5,950–6,200 kHz (49–m. band) | The order of frequency for particular service areas depends upon diurnal and seasonal conditions. |
| | 7,100–7,300 kHz (41–m. band) | |
| | 9,500–9,775 kHz (31–m. band) 11,700–11,975 kHz (25–m. band) 15,100–15,450 kHz (19-m. band) 17,700–17,900 kHz (16-m. band) 21,450–21,750 kHz (13–m. band) 25,600–26,100 kHz (11–m. band) | |
| Band I (vhf) | 41–68 MHz | Five channels each 5 MHz wide for BBC 405-line television. |
| Band II (vhf) | 87·5–100 MHz | Frequencies at present restricted to the sub-band 88–97·6 MHz and used for fm sound broadcasting Radios 2, 3 and 4 and local broadcasting, BBC and independent. |
| Band III (vhf) | 174–216 MHz | Eight channels each 5 MHz wide for BBC and IBA 405-line television. |
| Band IV (uhf) | 470–582 MHz | Fourteen channels each 8 MHz wide for BBC and IBA 625-line television. |

| | | |
|---|---|---|
| Band V (uhf) | 614–854 MHz | Thirty channels each 8 MHz wide for BBC and IBA 625-line television. |
| Band VI (shf) | 11,700–12,700 MHz | Allocated for both terrestrial and satellite broadcasting and likely to be the first band used for the latter service. |
| Band VII (ehf) | 41–43 GHz | Allocated for satellite broadcasting. |
| Band VIII (ehf) | 84–86 GHz | Allocated for satellite broadcasting. |

* The relationship between frequency and wavelength is as follows:

$$\text{Wavelength (in metres)} = \frac{300}{\text{Frequency (in MHz)}}$$

Thus the wavelength corresponding to a frequency of 60 MHz is

$$\frac{300}{60} = 5 \text{ metres}$$

The frequency corresponding to a wavelength of 1,500 metres is

$$\frac{300}{1,500} = 0{\cdot}2 \text{ MHz}$$

or 200 kHz (1 MHz = 1,000 kHz).

# Greenwich Time Signal

THE TIME SIGNALS which are broadcast all over the world throughout the day are received by land line from the Royal Observatory Time Station at Herstmonceux in Sussex. On January 1st, 1972, the familiar six short pips were replaced by, normally, five short pips followed by a long one. The correct time is indicated, to an accuracy of $\frac{1}{20}$ of a second, by the beginning of the last pip.

# Some Long-running Sound Radio Programmes

The longest-running sound radio programme is *The Week's Good Cause* which began on January 24th, 1926 and is still on the air.

The longest-running record programme? Roy Plomley's *Desert Island Discs* which began on January 29th, 1942.

Other long-running sound radio programmes:

| | First edition | Final edition |
|---|---|---|
| Workers' Playtime | 28.10.41 | 6.10.64 |
| Family Favourites | 1. 8.45 | (Still running) |
| Twenty Questions | 28. 2.47 | (Still running) |
| Mrs Dale's Diary (subsequently The Dales) | 5. 1.48 | 26. 4.69 |
| Sports Report | Jan. 1948 | (Still running) |
| Listen with Mother | 16. 1.50 | (Still running) |
| The Archers | 29. 5.50 | (Still running) |
| Five to Ten | 11.12.50 | 3. 4.70 |
| Sing Something Simple | 10. 7.59 | (Still running) |

# Some Long-running Television Programmes

The longest-running television programme – apart from the News – is *Panorama* which began on November 11th, 1953.

Other long-running television programmes:

| | First edition | Final edition |
|---|---|---|
| Take Your Pick | 23. 9.55 | July 1968 |
| Opportunity Knocks | 13. 6.56 | (Still running) |
| Tonight | 15. 2.57 | 18. 6.65 |
| Emergency–Ward 10 | 19. 2.57 | 2. 7.67 |
| Coronation Street | 9.12.60 | (Still running) |
| The Avengers | 22. 7.61 | 1969 |
| Z-Cars | 2. 1.62 | (Still running) |
| Dr Finlay's Casebook | 16. 8.62 | 3. 1.71 |
| The Virginian | 4. 5.64 | (Still running) |
| Horizon | 2. 5.64 | (Still running) |
| Crossroads | 2.11.64 | (Still running) |

THE LONGEST BROADCAST by the BBC was the coverage of the Coronation of Queen Elizabeth II on June 2nd, 1953. It lasted 7 hours 15 minutes – from 10.15 AM – 5.30 PM.

# Some Important Dates in the Story of British Broadcasting

**1922**
14 Nov    Daily broadcasting began from the London station of the British Broadcasting Company (2LO).

**1923**
28 Sep    First issue of the *Radio Times* published.
30 Dec    First Continental programme by landline from Radiola, Paris.
31 Dec    First broadcast of chimes of Big Ben to usher in the New Year.

**1924**
 4 Apr    Broadcasts for schools began.
23 Apr    First broadcast speech by King George V from the opening of the British Empire Exhibition, Wembley.

**1926**
31 Dec    The British Broadcasting Company dissolved.

**1927**
 1 Jan    The British Broadcasting Corporation constituted under Royal Charter for ten years.

**1929**
16 Jan    First issue of *The Listener* published.
21 Oct    Brookmans Park station brought into service marking the beginning of the regional scheme.

**1932**
 2 May    Broadcasting House, London, brought into service.
22 Aug    First experimental television programme from Broadcasting House, 30-line system (Baird process taken over by BBC).
25 Dec    First Round-the-Empire Christmas Day programme and broadcast message by King George V.

**1936**
 2 Nov    High-definition Television Service from Alexandra Palace officially inaugurated.
11 Dec    Abdication broadcast by H R H Prince Edward.

**1937**
12 May  King George VI Coronation: first TV Service outside broadcast.

**1938**
3 Jan  First foreign-language service began (in Arabic).

**1939**
24 May  First time Derby televised (scenes from course televised in 1938).
1 Sep  Television Service closed down for reasons of national defence.
1 Sep  Home Service replaced National and Regional Services.
3 Sep  Broadcasts by King George VI and the Prime Minister, Mr Neville Chamberlain, on the outbreak of war.

**1940**
7 Jan  Forces Programme began.

**1944**
27 Feb  General Forces Programme began, replacing Forces Programme.

**1945**
29 Jul  Light Programme introduced and Regional Home Services restarted.

**1946**
7 Jun  Television Service resumed.
29 Sept  Third Programme introduced.

**1947**
1 Jan  General Overseas Service began.

**1948**
11 Oct  First television outside broadcast from No 10 Downing Street: Commonwealth Conference.

**1950**
27 Aug  First television outside broadcast from the Continent (Calais).
30 Sep  First 'live' air to ground television broadcast (from an aircraft in flight).

**1952**
21 Apr  First direct television from Paris (experimental).
5 May  First schools television programme (4 weeks experiment).

**1953**

2 Jun   Coronation ceremony televised for the first time.

15 Jun  First television relay from ship at sea during the Royal Naval Review.

**1954**

6 Jun ⎫  First European exchange of television programmes with eight
4 Jul ⎭  countries taking part.

**1955**

2 May   First vhf radio broadcasting station brought into service at Wrotham.

20 Sep  First issue of *TV Times* published.

22 Sep  First ITV programmes transmitted in the London area.

**1956**

16 Jun  First 'live' television broadcast from a submarine at sea.

4 Aug   First television transmission from a helicopter.

5 Nov   The first series of experimental colour television transmissions to include 'live' pictures from Alexandra Palace studios and Crystal Palace transmitter began.

**1957**

24 Sep  BBC Television for schools began.

25 Dec  Her Majesty the Queen's Christmas broadcast televised for the first time (heard simultaneously on radio).

**1958**

28 Oct  State Opening of Parliament televised for the first time.

**1959**

17 Jun  First public demonstration of transmission of films for television by transatlantic cable; first programme use June 18th, 1959.

**1960**

26 Mar  Grand National televised for the first time.

**1961**

15 Feb  Eclipse of the sun televised for BBC viewers from France, Italy, and Yugoslavia through Eurovision.

14 Apr  First live television broadcast from Russia of welcome in Moscow of first 'space man', Major Gagarin.

1 May  Moscow May Day Parades seen 'live'.

10 Jun  The first live television broadcast from London to USSR – Trooping the Colour.

8 Jul  First television broadcast from London to Hungary – Wimbledon tennis.

**1962**

20 Feb  Transmission of first message from space from US astronaut Colonel John Glenn.

11 Jul  First exchange of 'live' transatlantic programmes by satellite Telstar.

16 Jul  First transmission of colour television by Telstar.

**1964**

Mar  First pirate radio station, Radio Caroline, began transmissions.

16 Apr  First 'live' television relay from Japan to Europe via Telstar.

20 Apr  First BBC-2 programmes on 625-lines transmitted from Crystal Palace.

**1966**

21 Apr  Television cameras allowed in the House of Commons for the first time.

**1967**

1 Jul  BBC-2 began regular colour television transmissions using PAL system on 625-lines (first in Europe).

15 Aug  Ban on pirate radio broadcasting came into force in Great Britain.

30 Sep  Radio 1 introduced on 247 m. Radio networks renamed Radio 1, 2, 3, and 4.

8 Nov  BBC local radio experiment began from Leicester.*

**1968**

6 Feb  First 'live' colour TV coverage of Olympic Games.

**1969**

16 May  Postmaster General announced start of colour television on ITV and BBC-1.

21 Jul  Man's first landing on the moon televised.

15 Nov  Colour television extended to BBC-1 and ITV on 625-lines vhf.

**1970**

2 Jul  State Opening of Parliament televised in colour for the first time.

**1971**
9 Jan     First issue of *Look In*, Junior TV Times, published.
10 Jan    Open University transmissions started on radio and BBC-TV.
16 Jun    Lord Reith died.

**1972**
20 Jan    Restrictions lifted on radio and television broadcasting hours.

14 Nov    50th anniversary of the first programmes broadcast by the British Broadcasting Company.

## *BBC LOCAL RADIO

There are 20 BBC local radio stations around Britain reaching more than 70% of the population:

| | | | | | |
|---|---|---|---|---|---|
| Radio Birmingham | vhf 95·6 | 206 m | Radio Manchester | vhf 95·1 | 206 m |
| Radio Bristol | vhf 95·4 | 194 m | Radio Newcastle | vhf 95·4 | 206 m |
| Radio Humberside | vhf 95·3 | 202 m | Radio Sheffield | vhf 88·6 & 95·05 | 290 m |
| Radio London | vhf 95·3 | 206 m | Radio Brighton | vhf 95·8 | 202 m |
| Radio Merseyside | vhf 95·85 | 202 m | Radio Carlisle* | vhf 95·6 | 202 m |
| Radio Oxford | vhf 95·0 | 202 m | Radio Leicester | vhf 95·2 | 188 m |
| Radio Stoke-on-Trent | vhf 94·6 | 200 m | Radio Medway | vhf 97·0 | 290 m |
| Radio Blackburn | vhf 96·4 | 351 m | Radio Nottingham | vhf 94·8 | 195 m |
| Radio Derby | vhf 96·5 | 260 m | Radio Solent | vhf 96·1 | 301 m |
| Radio Leeds | vhf 94·6 | 271 m | Radio Teesside | vhf 96·6 | 194 m |

*Opening during 1973.

# The Independent Broadcasting Authority

On July 12th, 1972, the Independent Television Authority was re-named the Independent Broadcasting Authority and had its functions extended to cover the provision of Independent Local Radio.

The Independent Broadcasting Authority builds, owns and operates the transmitting stations which radiate ITV programmes, allocating transmitters to carry programmes originated by the various programme contractors.

The original VHF network was started with the opening of ITV programmes in the London area on September 22nd, 1955. The first batch of four of the new UHF transmitters, radiating the duplicated 625-line combined colour/black-and-white pictures in the Pal colour system, came into programme service on November 15th, 1969. The UHF network will continue to build up for many years.

The Independent Broadcasting Authority does not itself produce programmes.

Fifteen programme companies are under contract with the Authority to provide the programme service in fourteen areas for the six-year contract period until the end of July 1974.

The programme companies obtain their revenue from the sale of advertising time in their own areas. Television advertisers can have nothing to do with programme production. They buy time in Independent Television just as they buy space in newspapers. They do not 'sponsor' programmes. The IBA controls the amount and distribution of advertising. The amount of advertising is limited to six minutes an hour, averaged over the day's programmes, with a maximum, normally, of seven minutes in any one clock hour. There is an average of three advertising intervals an hour.

On November 11th, 1971, the then Minister of Posts and Telecommunications, Mr Christopher Chataway, announced that the first five Independent Local Radio stations would be in London (two), Birmingham, Glasgow and Manchester. On June 19th, 1972, the present Minister, Sir John Eden, stated that the next stations were now expected to be at Liverpool, Tyneside, Swansea, Sheffield, Plymouth, Edinburgh, Portsmouth, Bradford, Ipswich and Nottingham. Subsequently, further stations are likely to be opened at Belfast, Blackburn, Bournemouth, Brighton, Bristol, Cardiff, Coventry, Huddersfield, Leeds, Teesside and Wolverhampton.

Under the provisions of the Television Act 1964 as amended by the Sound Broadcasting Act 1972 no programme sponsorship or advertising magazines will be permitted. Advertising time is to be sold for spot advertisements. These must be distinguishable as such and recognizably separate from one another and from the programme.

From the outset of Independent Local Radio, the provision of a reliable news service will be one of the most important elements in the programming.

# The IBA Companies

| Area | Company | ITV/BBC HOMES (JICTAR/ AGB) as at August 1972 |
|---|---|---|
| The Borders and Isle of Man | Border Television | 166,000 |
| Central Scotland | Scottish Television | 1,415,000 |
| Channel Islands | Channel Television | 32,000 |
| East of England | Anglia Television | 1,395,000 |
| Lancashire | Granada Television | 2,460,000 |
| London (Weekdays to 7 PM. Friday) | Thames Television | 4,180,000 |
| (Weekends from 7 PM. Friday) | London Weekend Television | 4,180,000 |
| Midlands | ATV Network | 2,730,000 |
| North-East England | Tyne Tees Television | 840,000 |
| North-East Scotland | Grampian Television | 289,000 |
| Northern Ireland | Ulster Television | 367,000 |
| South of England | Southern Independent Television | 1,270,000 |
| South-West England | Westward Television | 449,000 |
| Wales and West of England | Harlech | 1,275,000 |
| Yorkshire | Yorkshire Television | 1,770,000 |

INDEPENDENT TELEVISION NEWS is jointly owned by all the programme companies and is controlled by a board of directors representing those companies. It is a non-profit-making company which provides the daily programmes of national and international news to all stations throughout the Independent Television network.

# 10 TRAVEL

## A. Ships and the Sea

## Her Majesty's Fleet

STRENGTH OF THE FLEET, 1972–3

| Type/Class | Operational, Preparing for Service or Engaged on Trials and Training | Reserve or Undergoing Long Refit, Conversion, etc. |
|---|---|---|
| **Aircraft Carriers** | 1<br>*Ark Royal* | |
| **Commando Ships** | 2<br>*Bulwark, Albion* | 1<br>*Hermes* |
| **Submarines** | 23 | 12 |
| Polaris Submarines | *Resolution, Revenge* | *Repulse, Renown, Warspite* |
| Fleet Submarines | *Dreadnought, Churchill, Swiftsure\*, Conqueror, Courageous, Valiant* | |
| Oberon Class | *Oberon, Orpheus, Odin, Opossum, Olympus, Opportune, Onslaught* | *Otus, Onyx, Oracle, Otter, Osiris, Ocelot* |
| Porpoise Class | *Porpoise, Rorqual, Grampus, Sea Lion, Walrus* | *Narwhal, Cachalot, Finwhale* |
| A Class | *Aeneas, Alliance, Andrew* | |

| | | |
|---|---|---|
| **Assault Ships** | 2<br>*Fearless, Intrepid* | |
| **Cruisers** | 2<br>*Blake, Tiger* | |
| **Guided Missile**<br>    **Destroyers** | 6<br>*Devonshire, Fife, Glamorgan,<br>Antrim, Norfolk, Bristol\** | 3<br>*Kent, Hampshire,<br>London* |
| **Other Destroyers**<br>    CA Class<br><br>    Battle Class | <br>2<br>*Cavalier, Caprice*<br>1<br>*Matapan* | |
| **General Purpose**<br>    **Frigates**<br>    Leander Class<br><br><br><br><br><br><br><br>    Tribal Class | <br>25<br>*Dido, Aurora, Argonaut,<br>Andromeda, Jupiter, Minerva,<br>Charybdis, Achilles, Apollo\*,<br>Arethusa, Cleopatra, Juno,<br>Phoebe, Sirius, Scylla,<br>Danae, Hermione, Penelope,<br>Bacchante, Diomede,<br>Ariadne\*, Naiad*<br>*Mohawk, Gurkha, Ashanti,* | <br>8<br>*Leander, Ajax,<br>Galatea, Euryalus*<br><br><br><br><br><br><br>*Eskimo, Nubian,<br>Tartar, Zulu* |
| **Anti-Aircraft Frigates**<br>    Type 41 | 3<br>*Lynx, Leopard, Jaguar* | 1<br>*Puma* |
| **Aircraft Direction**<br>    **Frigates**<br>    Type 61 | <br>2<br>*Lincoln, Chichester* | <br>2<br>*Llandaff, Salisbury* |

**Anti-Submarine
Frigates**                23
                          *Tenby, Whitby, Eastbourne,*   1
                          *Torquay, Falmouth,*
                          *Londonderry, Plymouth,*
                          *Yarmouth, Lowestoft,*
                          *Rothesay, Berwick, Brighton,*
                          *Rhyl, Scarborough*


Blackwood Class
Type 14                   *Palliser, Russel, Hardy,*      *Dundas*
                          *Exmouth, Keppel*
Type 15                   *Rapid, Grenville, Ulster,*
                          *Undaunted*

**Fleet Maintenance Ships**                              2
                                                         *Triumph, Berry*
                                                         *Head*


**Submarine Depot Ship**                                 1
                                                         *Forth*


**MCM Support Ship**       1
                          *Abdiel*


**Diving Trials Ship**     1
                          *Reclaim*


**Mine Countermeasures
Forces**                  40                              4
Coastal Minesweepers/
Minehunters               *Bronington, Nurton,*          *Shavington, Ashton,*
                          *Bildeston, Lewiston, Upton,*  *Highburton,*
                          *Kellington, Kedleston,*       *Maxton*
                          *Wiston, Sheraton, Wotton,*
                          *Soberton, Kirkliston,*
                          *Hubberston, Bossington,*
                          *Brinton, Gavinton, Brereton,*
                          *Alfriston, Bickington,*
                          *Crichton, Wilton\*, Fittleton,*
                          *Hodgeston, Repton, Iveston,*
                          *Woolaston, Crofton, Laleston,*
                          *Stubbington, Shoulton,*

|  |  |  |
|---|---|---|
|  | *Glasserton, Walkerton, Pollington, Chawton* |  |
| Inshore Minesweepers | *Aveley, Isis, Dittisham, Thornham, Flintham, Arlingham* |  |
| **Coastal Patrol Vessels** | 5 *Wolverton, Beachampton, Monkton, Wasperton, Yarnton* |  |
| **Fast Training Boats/ Patrol Boats** | 3 *Scimitar, Sabre, Cutlass* | 2 *Dark Hero, Dark Gladiator* |
| **Seaward Defence Boats** | 2 *Droxford, Beckford* |  |
| **Royal Yacht/Hospital Ship** | 1 *Britannia* |  |
| **Ice Patrol Ship** | 1 *Endurance* |  |
| **Survey Ships/Vessels** | 12 *Hecla, Hecate, Hydra, Bulldog, Beagle, Fox, Fawn, Echo, Egeria, Enterprise, Woodlark, Waterwitch* |  |

* Under construction on March 31st, 1972 and due to come into service during the year. At that date 3 more Fleet submarines, 6 Type 42 Destroyers, 8 Type 21 Frigates, and 1 Survey Ship were also under construction.

# Naval Ranks and Ratings

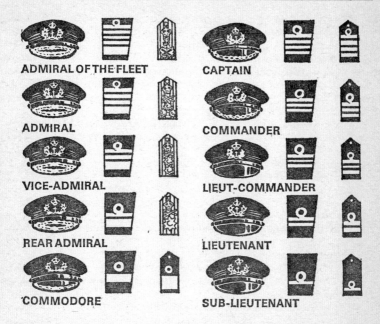

ADMIRAL OF THE FLEET

ADMIRAL

VICE-ADMIRAL

REAR ADMIRAL

COMMODORE

CAPTAIN

COMMANDER

LIEUT-COMMANDER

LIEUTENANT

SUB-LIEUTENANT

In addition to the above there are Midshipmen, Cadets, Warrant Officers, Chief Petty Officers and Petty Officers (the non-commissioned officers), leading seamen, able seamen and ordinary seamen.

The highest rank of Engineer Officers, Surgeon Officers and Accountant Officers or Paymasters, is that of Vice-Admiral, otherwise ranks are the same as those in the executive branch.

# Sea Terms

ABAFT – Nearer the stern than (an object), eg, abaft the gangway.
ADRIFT – Broken from moorings. Driven at random by tide and wind.
AVAST – To hold fast.
AWASH – Level with the surface of the water.

BELAY – To secure a rope to a cleat, belaying pin, or bollards.

BILGE – That part of a ship near the keel.

BROACH TO – Coming suddenly up to the wind.

BY THE HEAD – When a vessel is deeper in the water forward than aft she is said to be 'by the head'.

BY THE STERN – Opposite of 'by the head'.

CARRY AWAY – To break a spar or rope.

CHECK – To ease a rope a little. To stop progress.

CLAP ON – An order to get hold of a rope or purchase for the purpose of hauling on it.

DEAD WATER – The water in a vessel's wake close to her stern.

DRAG – A ship is said to be dragging when her anchor is not holding.

DRAUGHT – The depth of the lowest point of a ship or boat below the waterline.

EBB – The return of the tide-water towards the sea.

FLOW – The rise of the tide.

FREEBOARD – The height of a ship's upper deck above the waterline.

HAND OVER HAND – Hauling a rope quickly with alternate hands.

HANDSOMELY – Slowly and with care.

JACOB'S LADDER – A ladder made of rope or wire with wooden bars for steps.

LAND FALL – The first sight of land when at sea.

NEAP TIDES – Tides which rise least and fall least from the mean level.

SHEER – The rise of a ship's deck at the head and stern above the midship portion.

SHIPSHAPE – In proper seamanlike manner.

SMACK IT ABOUT – Get a move on.

STEERAGE WAY – When a vessel is moving with sufficient way to be steered.

TRIM – The condition of a ship with reference to how she floats on the water.

UNDER WAY – When a vessel is not at anchor or made fast to the shore or aground.

WEATHER TIDE – A tide that carries a vessel to windward.

WIND'S EYE – That point from which the wind blows.

YAW – When a ship does not steer a straight and steady course and her head moves from one side to the other, she is said to yaw about.

# Parts of a Ship

STEM – The extreme front or foremost part of the ship.

STERN – The extreme rear or aftermost part of the ship.

BOW – That part of the ship's side which is near the stem.

QUARTER – That part of the ship's side which is near the stern.

BEAM – That part of the ship's side which lies between the bow and quarter.

STARBOARD SIDE – The right-hand side of a ship looking forward.

PORT SIDE – The left-hand side of a ship looking forward.

FORE AND AFT LINE – The line between the stem and stern – ie, in line with the keel.

ATHWARTSHIPS – At right angles to the fore and aft line.

MIDSHIPS – Lying midway between stem and stern in a fore and aft line or midway between starboard and port in a thwartship line.

FORECASTLE (Also fo'c's'le) – The fore part of the upper deck.

QUARTERDECK – The after part of the upper deck.

WAIST – The midship part of the upper deck between the forecastle and quarter deck.

POOP – A short deck above the upper deck right aft in the stern.

TOPGALLANT FORECASTLE – A short deck above the upper deck, right forward over the forecastle.

# Ship's Time

| | |
|---|---|
| 8 AM to Noon | Forenoon Watch |
| Noon to 4 PM | Afternoon Watch |
| 4 PM to 6 PM } 6 PM to 8 PM } | Dog Watches |
| 8 PM to Midnight | First Watch |
| Midnight to 4 AM | Middle Watch |
| 4 AM to 8 AM | Morning Watch |

These times are kept by a bell being struck every half-hour, beginning with one at the first half-hour of the watch and ending with eight at the fourth hour of the watch except during the Dog Watches. During the Dog Watches, which are shorter in order to prevent the same watch having the same hours each day for duty, one bell is struck at 6.30 PM two bells at 7 PM, three bells at 7.30 PM and eight bells at 8 PM.

# Bends and Hitches

1. Bowline
2. Carrick Bend
3. Clove Hitch
4. Double Sheet Bend
5. Figure of Eight Knot
6. Fisherman's Bend
7. Reef Knot
8. Rolling Hitch
9. Running Bowline
10. Sheepshank
11. Single Sheet Bend
12. Timber Hitch

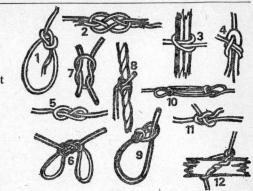

## Sea Measures

1 Fathom = 6 feet
1 Cable = One-tenth of a nautical or sea mile, and measures 608 feet, or roughly 200 yards
1 Nautical or Sea Mile = 6,080 feet, or roughly 2,000 yards
1 Knot = Speed of 1 nautical or sea mile per hour

## The Compass

*The Magnetic Compass* used for determining direction is operated by the magnetism of the earth.

A compass card is graduated in degrees clockwise from 000 (North) to 359, the circle being divided into 360 degrees. Directions are described as 'zero-four-five' (written 045°), 'three-two-eight' (328°) etc.

Magnetic compasses used to be graduated in points, each circle had 32 points, and each point represented 11¼ degrees. Some of these points are still used when referring to general directions:

| | |
|---|---|
| The 4 Cardinal Points | N., E., S., and W. |
| The 4 Half-Cardinal Points | N.E., S.E., S.W., and N.W. |
| The 8 Intermediate Points | N.N.E., E.N.E., E.S.E., S.S.E., S.S.W., W.S.W., W.N.W., N.N.W. |

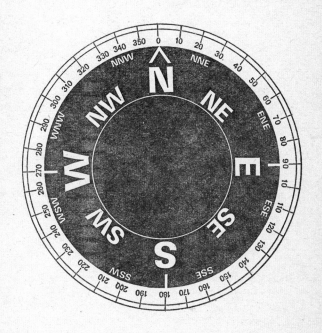

# How to Find South in Daytime by Means of Your Watch

Hold your watch flat in your hand with the hour hand pointing to the sun. A line drawn halfway between the hour hand and the figure 12 on your watch will point to the South.

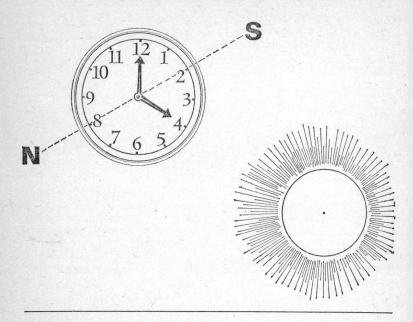

## The Cinque Ports

The Cinque Ports were originally five in number: Dover, New Romney, Sandwich, Hastings and Hythe. After the Norman Conquest Rye and Winchelsea were added. Other members, known as 'limbs' are – Deal, Margate, Ramsgate, Tenterden, Faversham and Folkestone. The present Lord Warden of the Cinque Ports is Sir Robert Menzies.

## Some Important Dates in the Story of the Sea

*c.* 1280 Mariner's Compass in general use.
**1492–3** Columbus' first voyage of exploration; Bahamas discovered.
**1495–6** First dry dock constructed at Portsmouth.
**1498** Vasco da Gama reaches India by sea.

| | |
|---|---|
| **1508** | First Marine Insurance in England. |
| **1546** | Henry VIII institutes the Navy Board for the maintenance of the Fleet. |
| **1577** | Drake sailed from Plymouth on his voyage round the world. |
| **1591** | The last fight of the *Revenge* (Aug. 31st). |
| **1600** | East India Company granted Charter. |
| **1620** | The *Mayflower* sails. Foundation of New England. |
| **1637** | Building of the *Sovereign of the Seas*, the first ship to carry 100 guns. |
| **1660** | The title General at Sea superseded by that of Admiral. |
| **1675** | Greenwich Observatory founded (Aug. 10th). |
| **1740** | Anson made his voyage round the world. |
| **1748** | Uniform for Officers adopted. |
| **1757** | Captain Campbell's Sextant supersedes the Quadrant. |
| **1765** | Launch of HMS *Victory*. |
| **1768** | Captain Cook's voyage to the Pacific in the *Endeavour*. |
| **1776** | Cook's voyage to find a navigable passage from the Pacific to the Atlantic over Canada. (He was killed in 1779.) |
| **1789** | Mutiny on the *Bounty*. |
| **1794** | Nelson loses the sight of his right eye at Calvi (July 10th). |
| **1797** | Mutiny at the Nore. |
| **1797** | Nelson loses his right arm at Santa Cruz (July 24th). |
| **1798** | Battle of the Nile (Aug. 1st). |
| **1799** | HMS *Lutine* wrecked. |
| **1805** | Battle of Trafalgar (Oct. 21st). |
| **1806** | Nelson buried in St Paul's (Jan. 9th). |
| **1812** | First steamboat, the *Comet*, plied on the Clyde. |
| **1815** | First steam vessel on the Thames. |
| **1817** | Present Custom House opened in London. |
| **1818** | First steamer crossed the Atlantic. |
| **1822** | Caledonian Canal opened. |
| **1824** | National Lifeboat Institution founded. |
| **1825** | First steam voyage to India. |
| **1837** | Shells, as substitute for Round Shot, made permissive in the British Navy. |
| **1838** | First regular Steamboat Service across Atlantic – voyage took 17 days. |
| | Screw propeller first used. |
| | The *Fighting Temeraire* is towed to her last berth. |
| **1840** | P & O Steam Navigation Company established. |
| **1843** | Gentlemen Volunteers rechristened Naval Cadets. |
| **1848** | North-West Passage discovered. |

| | |
|---|---|
| **1851** | First Submarine Telegraph. |
| **1854** | Napoleon III constructs 'Ironclads'. |
| **1857** | International Code of Signals established. |
| | Uniform for men adopted. |
| **1858** | *Great Eastern* steamer launched (Jan. 31st). |
| | First message by Atlantic Cable. |
| **1860** | First British sea-going steam ironclad battleship, *Warrior*, launched. |
| **1861** | Storm warnings first issued. |
| **1863** | Twin screws used. |
| **1866** | Atlantic cable laid by *Great Eastern*. |
| **1867** | The wooden three-decker *Victoria* was the flagship at the Review at Spithead, the last occasion on which a wooden ship of the line performed this office at a Review. |
| | Navigating Lieutenants substituted for Masters. |
| **1869** | Suez Canal opened (Nov. 17th). |
| **1873** | Royal Naval College, Greenwich, opened. |
| **1881** | Breech-loading principle accepted by Admiralty for big guns. |
| **1887** | Quick-firing principle applied to heavy guns. |
| **1894** | Manchester Ship Canal opened. |
| **1895** | Kiel Canal opened. |
| **1900** | Wireless Telegraphy adopted by Admiralty. |
| **1901** | New International Code of Signals in use. First wireless signals sent across Atlantic. First British submarine launched. |
| **1904** | First transatlantic turbine steamer *Victorian* launched. |
| **1905** | Wireless Telegraphy messages to ships at sea accepted by Post Offices. |
| **1906** | Launch of HMS *Dreadnought*. |
| **1907** | First British battle cruiser launched. |
| **1912** | Loss of *Titanic* – largest steamship afloat – and 1,513 lives. |
| **1915** | White Star liner *Lusitania* sunk by German submarine. |
| **1916** | Battle of Jutland – last great fleet action for gunners. |
| **1917** | Unrestricted German U-Boat warfare commenced. |
| **1918** | Naval Mutiny at Wilhelmshaven. Surrender of the German High Seas Fleet. |
| **1919** | German Fleet scuttled at Scapa Flow. |
| **1931** | The Invergordon Mutiny. |
| **1933** | Italian liner *Rex* won the Blue Riband of the Atlantic – Gibraltar to Ambrose Lightship: 3,181 m. in 4 days, 13 hours, 58 minutes. Average speed: 28·92 knots. |
| **1934** | Mersey tunnel opened. Cunard White Star liner *Queen Mary* launched at Clydebank. |

**1935**    French liner *Normandie* gained Blue Riband of the Atlantic. Southampton to Ambrose Light vessel: 4 days, 11 hours, 33 minutes. Average speed: 29·68 knots.

**1936**    *Queen Mary* won Blue Riband of the Atlantic. Bishop Rock to Ambrose Light Vessel: 2,907 m. in 4 days, and 27 minutes. Average speed: 30·14 knots.

**1938**    *Queen Mary*: Bishop Rock to Ambrose Light Vessel in 3 days, 21 hours, 48 minutes. Average speed: 30·99 knots.

**1941**    Attack by the Japanese on the US Fleet at Pearl Harbor resulting in the entry into the war of Japan and USA.

**1945**    Surrender of the German Fleet. 156 U-Boats surrendered and 221 scuttled themselves.

**1946**    *Queen Elizabeth* left Southampton for New York on maiden voyage as passenger liner.

**1947**    *Queen Mary* left Southampton for New York on her first post-war passenger voyage.

**1958**    US nuclear submarine *Nautilus* made first passage under North Pole. She went beneath the pack ice off Point Barrow, Alaska, on August 1st, was at the North Pole on the 4th, and emerged from pack ice on the Greenwich meridian at 70°N on August 5th.

        US nuclear submarine *Seawolf* remained submerged for 60 days during which she logged 13,700 miles.

**1959**    St Lawrence Seaway officially opened by Queen Elizabeth and President Eisenhower.

**1961**    Launch of nuclear submarine *Dreadnought*.

**1963**    Loss of US atomic submarine *Thresher* with 129 lives.

**1966**    Sir Francis Chichester left Plymouth on August 27th on the start of his single-handed, round-the-world voyage in *Gipsy Moth IV*. He arrived back in Plymouth Sound on May 28th, 1967.

        Britain's first Polaris submarine, HMS *Resolution*, launched at Barrow by Queen Elizabeth, the Queen Mother. She carries 16 Polaris missiles as well as conventional torpedoes. (Went into service October 3rd, 1967.)

**1967**    British nuclear submarine HMS *Valiant* completed her submerged homeward journey from Singapore to the Clyde; a distance of 12,000 miles in 27 days, mostly at a depth below 200 ft.

        Caning for juniors in the Royal Navy abolished. Wreck of Sir Cloudesley Shovel's flagship *Association*, sunk in 1707 found off the Isles of Scilly.

        *Queen Elizabeth II* launched.

        *Queen Mary* completed her last passenger voyage (later sold to US interests).

**1968**    Alec Rose completed his single-handed round-the-world voyage in his yacht *Lively Lady*.

Last passenger voyage of *Queen Elizabeth I* ended on Nov. 15th (sold to US then Hong Kong interests).

First Polaris missile to be fired from a British nuclear submarine launched from the *Resolution*.

**1970**    Prototype naval uniforms in radical new styles designed and tried out. Last issue of rum to the Royal Navy.

**1971**    HMS *Sheffield*, the Royal Navy's first Type 42 guided missile destroyer (its first warship to have all gas turbine propulsion) launched by HM the Queen at Barrow.

**1972**    *Queen Elizabeth I* capsized and sank in Hong Kong harbour.

Launching of HMS *Wilton*, a 153-ft. minehunter and the Royal Navy's first plastic warship.

# B. Motor Cars

THE TOTAL MILEAGE of public roads in Great Britain (as at September 1972) was approximately 209,925, of which 159,455 were in England, 29,493 in Scotland and 20,977 in Wales.

There were 20,304 miles of principal roads, 9,075 miles of trunk roads, and 180,546 miles of other roads. Trunk and principal road motorway amounted to 744 miles.

THE NUMBER OF MOTOR VEHICLES in Great Britain with current licences at December 1971 totalled 15,454,370, of which 12,058,580 were cars.

# Distances From London to Major Cities by Road

| | *Miles* | | *Miles* |
|---|---|---|---|
| Aberdeen | 492 | Exeter | 169 |
| Birmingham | 111 | Glasgow | 389 |
| Bristol | 113 | Gloucester | 104 |
| Cardiff | 149 | Holyhead | 261 |
| Dover | 74 | Inverness | 529 |
| Edinburgh | 372 | Leeds | 191 |

| Liverpool | 198 | Plymouth | 211 |
| Manchester | 184 | Sheffield | 160 |
| Newcastle upon Tyne | 273 | Southampton | 77 |
| Penzance | 281 | York | 193 |

# Registrations of New Vehicles

Figures issued by the Society of Motor Manufacturers list the numbers of people buying the following makes of car in Great Britain, N. Ireland and the Isle of Man, during the 12 months ended December 1971 as follows:

| *British* | *No.* | *Imported* | *No.* |
|---|---|---|---|
| BLMC | 516,264 | Volkswagen | 48,883 |
| Ford | 240,937 | Renault | 41,732 |
| Vauxhall | 138,199 | Fiat | 36,205 |
| Chrysler (UK) (covers | 135,229 | Chrysler France | 24,243 |
| Hillman, Sunbeam, Humber etc.) | | | |
| Lotus | 1,755 | Volvo | 15,476 |
| Reliant Group | 1,164 | Audi/NSU | 11,095 |
| Jensen | 422 | Opel | 8,701 |
| Other | 3,808 | DAF | 8,677 |
| | | Saab | 7,186 |
| | | Citroen | 6,482 |
| | | Peugeot | 5,980 |
| | | BMW | 4,949 |
| | | Mercedes Benz | 3,985 |
| | | Toyota | 3,982 |
| | | Skoda | 2,624 |
| | | Alfa Romeo | 1,462 |
| | | Other | 16,221 |

# Index Marks – Vehicle Registration Numbers

| A | London | AC | Warwickshire | AF | Cornwall |
|---|---|---|---|---|---|
| AA | Hampshire | AD | Gloucestershire | AG | Ayrshire |
| AB | Worcestershire | AE | Bristol | AH | Norfolk |

| | | | | | |
|---|---|---|---|---|---|
| AI | Meath | BT | Yorkshire | DF | Gloucestershire |
| AJ | Yorkshire | BU | Oldham | DG | Gloucestershire |
| AK | Bradford | BV | Blackburn | DH | Walsall |
| AL | Nottinghamshire | BW | Oxfordshire | DI | Roscommon |
| AM | Wiltshire | BX | Carmarthenshire | DJ | St. Helens |
| AN | London | BY | London | DK | Rochdale |
| AO | Cumberland | BZ | Down | DL | Isle of Wight |
| AP | Sussex (East) | | | DM | Flintshire |
| AR | Hertfordshire | C | Yorkshire | DN | York |
| AS | Nairnshire | CA | Denbighshire | DO | Lincolnshire |
| AT | Kingston-upon-Hull | CB | Blackburn | | (Holland) |
| AU | Nottingham | CC | Caernarvonshire | DP | Reading |
| AV | Aberdeenshire | CD | Brighton | DR | Plymouth |
| AW | Salop | CE | Cambridgeshire | DS | Peeblesshire |
| AX | Monmouthshire | CF | Suffolk (West) | DT | Doncaster |
| AY | Leicestershire | CG | Hampshire | DU | Coventry |
| AZ | Belfast | CH | Derby | DV | Devon |
| | | CI | Laoighis | DW | Newport (Mon.) |
| B | Lancashire | CJ | Herefordshire | DX | Ipswich |
| BA | Salford | CK | Preston | DY | Hastings |
| BB | Newcastle upon Tyne | CL | Norwich | DZ | Antrim |
| BC | Leicester | CM | Birkenhead | | |
| BD | Northampton-shire | CN | Gateshead | E | Staffordshire |
| | | CO | Plymouth | EA | West Bromwich |
| BE | Lincolnshire (Lindsey) | CP | Halifax | EB | Cambridge |
| BF | Staffordshire | CR | Southampton | EC | Westmorland |
| BG | Birkenhead | CS | Ayrshire | ED | Warrington |
| BH | Buckingham-shire | CT | Lincolnshire (Kesteven) | EE | Grimsby |
| | | | | EF | West Hartlepool |
| BI | Monaghan | CU | South Shields | EG | Huntingdon |
| BJ | Suffolk (East) | CV | Cornwall | EH | Stoke-on-Trent |
| BK | Portsmouth | CW | Burnley | EI | Sligo |
| BL | Berkshire | CX | Huddersfield | EJ | Cardiganshire |
| BM | Bedfordshire | CY | Swansea | EK | Wigan |
| BN | Bolton | CZ | Belfast | EL | Bournemouth |
| BO | Cardiff | | | EM | Bootle |
| BP | Sussex (West) | D | Kent | EN | Bury |
| BR | Sunderland | DA | Wolverhampton | EO | Barrow-in-Furness |
| BS | Orkney | DB | Stockport | EP | Montgomeryshire |
| | | DC | Middlesbrough | ER | Cambridgeshire |
| | | DD | Gloucestershire | ES | Perthshire |
| | | DE | Pembrokeshire | ET | Rotherham |

| | | | | | |
|---|---|---|---|---|---|
| EU | Breconshire | GF | London | HV | London |
| EV | Essex | GG | Glasgow | HW | Bristol |
| EW | Huntingdonshire | GH | London | HX | London |
| EX | Great Yarmouth | GJ | London | HY | Bristol |
| EY | Anglesey | GK | London | HZ | Tyrone |
| EZ | Belfast | GL | Bath | | |
| | | GM | Motherwell and | IA | Antrim |
| F | Essex | | Wishaw | IB | Armagh |
| FA | Burton-on-Trent | GN | London | IC | Carlow |
| FB | Bath | GO | London | ID | Cavan |
| FC | Oxford | GP | London | IE | Clare |
| FD | Dudley | GR | Sunderland | IF | Cork |
| FE | Lincoln | GS | Perthshire | IH | Donegal |
| FF | Merionethshire | GT | London | IJ | Down |
| FG | Fife | GU | London | IK | City and County |
| FH | Gloucester | GV | Suffolk (West) | | of Dublin |
| FI | Tipperary | GW | London | IL | Fermanagh |
| FJ | Exeter | GX | London | IM | Galway |
| FK | Worcester | GY | London | IN | Kerry |
| FL | Huntingdon | GZ | Belfast | IO | Kildare |
| FM | Chester | | | IP | Kilkenny |
| FN | Canterbury | H | London | IR | Offaly |
| FO | Radnorshire | HA | Warley | IT | Leitrim |
| FP | Rutland | HB | Merthyr Tydfil | IU | Limerick |
| FR | Blackpool | HC | Eastbourne | IW | Londonderry |
| FS | Edinburgh | HD | Dewsbury | IX | Longford |
| FT | Tynemouth | HE | Barnsley | IY | Louth |
| FU | Lincolnshire | HF | Wallasey | IZ | Mayo |
| | (Lindsey) | HG | Burnley | | |
| FV | Blackpool | HH | Carlisle | | |
| FW | Lincolnshire | HI | Tipperary | J | Durham |
| | (Lindsey) | HJ | Southend | JA | Stockport |
| FX | Dorset | HK | Essex | JB | Berkshire |
| FY | Southport | HL | Wakefield | JC | Caernarvonshire |
| FZ | Belfast | HM | London | JD | London |
| | | HN | Darlington | JE | Cambridge |
| G | Glasgow | HO | Hampshire | JF | Leicester |
| GA | Glasgow | HP | Coventry | JG | Canterbury |
| GB | Glasgow | HR | Wiltshire | JH | Hertfordshire |
| GC | London | HS | Renfrewshire | JI | Tyrone |
| GD | Glasgow | HT | Bristol | JJ | London |
| GE | Glasgow | HU | Bristol | JK | Eastbourne |

| | | | | | |
|---|---|---|---|---|---|
| JL | Lincolnshire (Holland) | KX | Buckingham-shire | MI | Wexford |
| JM | Westmorland | KY | Bradford | MJ | Bedfordshire |
| JN | Southend | KZ | Antrim | MK | London |
| JO | Oxford | | | ML | London |
| JP | Wigan | | | MM | London |
| JR | Northumber-land | L | Glamorgan | MN | Isle of Man |
| | | LA | London | MO | Berkshire |
| JS | Ross and Cromarty | LB | London | MP | London |
| | | LC | London | MR | Wiltshire |
| JT | Dorset | LD | London | MS | Stirlingshire |
| JU | Leicestershire | LE | London | MT | London |
| JV | Grimsby | LF | London | MU | London |
| JW | Wolverhampton | LG | Cheshire | MV | London |
| JX | Halifax | LH | London | MW | Wiltshire |
| JY | Plymouth | LI | Westmeath | MX | London |
| JZ | Down | LJ | Bournemouth | MY | London |
| | | LK | London | MZ | Belfast |
| K | Liverpool | LL | London | | |
| KA | Liverpool | LM | London | N | Manchester |
| KB | Liverpool | LN | London | NA | Manchester |
| KC | Liverpool | LO | London | NB | Manchester |
| KD | Liverpool | LP | London | NC | Manchester |
| KE | Kent | LR | London | ND | Manchester |
| KF | Liverpool | LS | Selkirkshire | NE | Manchester |
| KG | Cardiff | LT | London | NF | Manchester |
| KH | Kingston-upon-Hull | LU | London | NG | Norfolk |
| | | LV | Liverpool | NH | Northampton |
| KI | Waterford | LW | London | NI | Wicklow |
| KJ | Kent | LX | London | NJ | Sussex (East) |
| KK | Kent | LY | London | NK | Hertfordshire |
| KL | Kent | LZ | Armagh | NL | Northumberland |
| KM | Kent | | | NM | Bedfordshire |
| KN | Kent | | | NN | Nottinghamshire |
| KO | Kent | M | Cheshire | NO | Essex |
| KP | Kent | MA | Cheshire | NP | Worcestershire |
| KR | Kent | MB | Cheshire | NR | Leicestershire |
| KS | Roxburghshire | MC | London | NS | Sutherland |
| KT | Kent | MD | London | NT | Salop |
| KU | Bradford | ME | London | NU | Derbyshire |
| KV | Coventry | MF | London | NV | Northamptonshire |
| KW | Bradford | MG | London | NW | Leeds |
| | | MH | London | NX | Warwickshire |

| | | | | | |
|---|---|---|---|---|---|
| NY | Glamorgan | PL | Surrey | RL | Cornwall |
| NZ | Londonderry | PM | Sussex (East) | RM | Cumberland |
| | | PN | Sussex (East) | RN | Preston |
| O | Birmingham | PO | Sussex (West) | RO | Hertfordshire |
| OA | Birmingham | PP | Buckingham- | RP | Northamptonshire |
| OB | Birmingham | | shire | RR | Nottinghamshire |
| OC | Birmingham | PR | Dorset | RS | Aberdeen |
| OD | Devon | PS | Shetland | RT | Suffolk (East) |
| OE | Birmingham | | (Zetland) | RU | Bournemouth |
| OF | Birmingham | PT | Durham | RV | Portsmouth |
| OG | Birmingham | | (County) | RW | Coventry |
| OH | Birmingham | PU | Essex | RX | Berkshire |
| OI | Belfast | PV | Ipswich | RY | Leicester |
| OJ | Birmingham | PW | Norfolk | RZ | Antrim |
| OK | Birmingham | PX | Sussex (West) | | |
| OL | Birmingham | PY | Yorkshire | S | Edinburgh |
| OM | Birmingham | PZ | Belfast | SA | Aberdeenshire |
| ON | Birmingham | | | SB | Argyll |
| OO | Essex | | | SC | Edinburgh |
| OP | Birmingham | QA QJ | | SD | Ayrshire |
| OR | Hampshire | QB QK | London: | SE | Banffshire |
| OS | Wigtownshire | QC QL | for | SF | Edinburgh |
| OT | Hampshire | QD QM | vehicles | SG | Edinburgh |
| OU | Hampshire | QE QN | temporarily | SH | Berwickshire |
| OV | Birmingham | QF QP | imported | SJ | Bute |
| OW | Southampton | QG QQ | from | SK | Caithness |
| OX | Birmingham | QH QS | abroad | SL | Clackmannan- |
| OY | London | | | | shire |
| OZ | Belfast | R | Derbyshire | SM | Dumfriesshire |
| | | RA | Derbyshire | SN | Dunbartonshire |
| P | Surrey | RB | Derbyshire | SO | Moray |
| PA | Surrey | RC | Derby | SP | Fife |
| PB | Surrey | RD | Reading | SR | Angus |
| PC | Surrey | RE | Staffordshire | SS | East Lothian |
| PD | Surrey | RF | Staffordshire | ST | Inverness-shire |
| PE | Surrey | RG | Aberdeen | SU | Kincardineshire |
| PF | Surrey | RH | Kingston-upon- | SV | Kinross-shire |
| PG | Surrey | | Hull | SW | Kircudbright- |
| PH | Surrey | RI | City and County | | shire |
| PI | Cork | | of Dublin | SX | West Lothian |
| PJ | Surrey | RJ | Salford | SY | Midlothian |
| PK | Surrey | RK | London | SZ | Down |

| T | Devon |
| TA | Devon |
| TB | Lancashire |
| TC | Lancashire |
| TD | Lancashire |
| TE | Lancashire |
| TF | Lancashire |
| TG | Glamorgan |
| TH | Carmarthenshire |
| TI | Limerick |
| TJ | Lancashire |
| TK | Dorset |
| TL | Lincolnshire (Kesteven) |
| TM | Bedfordshire |
| TN | Newcastle upon Tyne |
| TO | Nottingham |
| TP | Portsmouth |
| TR | Southampton |
| TS | Dundee |
| TT | Devon |
| TU | Cheshire |
| TV | Nottingham |
| TW | Essex |
| TX | Glamorgan |
| TY | Northumberland |
| TZ | Belfast |
| U | Leeds |
| UA | Leeds |
| UB | Leeds |
| UC | London |
| UD | Oxfordshire |
| UE | Warwickshire |
| UF | Brighton |
| UG | Leeds |
| UH | Cardiff |
| UI | Londonderry |
| UJ | Salop |
| UK | Wolverhampton |

| UL | London |
| UM | Leeds |
| UN | Denbighshire |
| UO | Devon |
| UP | Durham (County) |
| UR | Hertfordshire |
| US | Glasgow |
| UT | Leicestershire |
| UU | London |
| UV | London |
| UW | London |
| UX | Salop |
| UY | Worcestershire |
| UZ | Belfast |
| V | Lanarkshire |
| VA | Lanarkshire |
| VB | London |
| VC | Coventry |
| VD | Lanarkshire |
| VE | Cambridgeshire |
| VF | Norfolk |
| VG | Norwich |
| VH | Huddersfield |
| VJ | Herefordshire |
| VK | Newcastle upon Tyne |
| VL | Lincoln |
| VM | Manchester |
| VN | Yorkshire |
| VO | Nottinghamshire |
| VP | Birmingham |
| VR | Manchester |
| VS | Greenock |
| VT | Stoke-on-Trent |
| VU | Manchester |
| VV | Northampton |
| VW | Essex |
| VX | Essex |
| VY | York |

| VZ | Tyrone |
| W | Sheffield |
| WA | Sheffield |
| WB | Sheffield |
| WC | Essex |
| WD | Warwickshire |
| WE | Sheffield |
| WF | Yorkshire |
| WG | Stirlingshire |
| WH | Bolton |
| WI | Waterford |
| WJ | Sheffield |
| WK | Coventry |
| WL | Oxford |
| WM | Southport |
| WN | Swansea |
| WO | Monmouthshire |
| WP | Worcestershire |
| WR | Yorkshire |
| WS | Edinburgh |
| WT | Yorkshire |
| WU | Yorkshire |
| WV | Wiltshire |
| WW | Yorkshire |
| WX | Yorkshire |
| WY | Yorkshire |
| WZ | Belfast |
| X | Northumberland |
| XA | London |
| XB | London |
| XC | London |
| XD | London |
| XE | London |
| XF | London |
| XG | Middlesbrough |
| XH | London |
| XI | Belfast |
| XJ | Manchester |
| XK | London |

| | | | | | |
|---|---|---|---|---|---|
| XL | London | Y | Somerset | YM | London |
| XM | London | YA | Somerset | YN | London |
| XN | London | YB | Somerset | YO | London |
| XO | London | YC | Somerset | YP | London |
| XP | London | YD | Somerset | YR | London |
| XR | London | YE | London | YS | Glasgow |
| XS | Paisley | YF | London | YT | London |
| XT | London | YG | Yorkshire | YU | London |
| XU | London | YH | London | YV | London |
| XV | London | YI | City and County | YW | London |
| XW | London | | of Dublin | YX | London |
| XX | London | YJ | Dundee | YY | London |
| XY | London | YK | London | YZ | Londonderry |
| XZ | Armagh | YL | London | | |

| | | | |
|---|---|---|---|
| A | City and County of Dublin | ZM | Galway |
| ZA | City and County of Dublin | ZN | Meath |
| ZB | Cork (County) | ZO | City and County of Dublin |
| ZC | City and County of Dublin | ZP | Donegal |
| ZD | City and County of Dublin | ZR | Wexford |
| ZE | City and County of Dublin | ZT | Cork (County) |
| ZF | Cork | ZU | City and County of Dublin |
| ZH | City and County of Dublin | ZW | Kildare |
| ZI | City and County of Dublin | ZX | Kerry |
| ZJ | City and County of Dublin | ZY | Louth |
| ZK | Cork (County) | ZZ | Dublin: for vehicles temporarily imported from abroad |
| ZL | City and County of Dublin | | |

# International Registration Letters

| | | | |
|---|---|---|---|
| A | Austria | BR | Brazil |
| ADN | Southern Yemen (formerly Aden) | BRG | Guyana (formerly British Guiana) |
| AL | Albania | BRN | Bahrain |
| AND | Andorra | BRU | Brunei |
| AUS | Australia | BS | Bahamas |
| B | Belgium | BUR | Burma |
| BDS | Barbados | C | Cuba |
| BG | Bulgaria | CDN | Canada |
| BH | British Honduras | CGO | Congo (Dem Rep) |

| | | | |
|---|---|---|---|
| CH | Switzerland | IL | Israel |
| CI | Ivory Coast | IND | India |
| CL | Ceylon | IR | Iran |
| CO | Colombia | IRL | Ireland (Republic of) |
| CR | Costa Rica | IRQ | Iraq |
| CS | Czechoslovakia | IS | Iceland |
| CY | Cyprus | J | Japan |
| D | Germany | JA | Jamaica |
| DK | Denmark | K | Cambodia |
| DOM | Dominican Republic | KWT | Kuwait |
| DY | Dahomey | L | Luxembourg |
| DZ | Algeria | LAO | Laos |
| E | Spain (incl. African localities and provinces) | LB | Liberia |
| | | LS | Lesotho (formerly Basutoland) |
| EAK | Kenya | | |
| EAT | Tanzania (formerly Tanganyika) | M | Malta |
| | | MA | Morocco |
| EAU | Uganda | MC | Monaco |
| EAZ | Tanzania (formerly Zanzibar) | MEX | Mexico |
| | | MS | Mauritius |
| EC | Ecuador | MW | Malawi (formerly Nyasaland) |
| ET | United Arab Republic (Egypt) | | |
| | | N | Norway |
| F | France (incl. overseas departments and territories) | NA | Netherlands Antilles |
| | | NIC | Nicaragua |
| | | NIG | Niger |
| FL | Liechtenstein | NL | Netherlands |
| GB | United Kingdom of Great Britain and Northern Ireland | NZ | New Zealand |
| | | P | Portugal (incl. Angola, Cape Verde Islands, Mozambique, Portuguese Guinea, Portuguese Timor, São Tomé and Príncipe) |
| GBA | Alderney ⎫ Channel | | |
| GBG | Guernsey ⎬ Islands | | |
| GBJ | Jersey ⎭ | | |
| GBM | Isle of Man | | |
| GBZ | Gibraltar | PA | Panama |
| GCA | Guatemala | PAK | Pakistan |
| GH | Ghana | PE | Peru |
| GR | Greece | PI | Philippines |
| H | Hungary | PL | Poland |
| HK | Hong Kong | PTM | Malaysia |
| HKJ | Jordan | PY | Paraguay |
| I | Italy | R | Rumania |

| | | | |
|---|---|---|---|
| RA | Argentina | SN | Senegal |
| RB | Botswana (formerly Bechuanaland) | SU | Union of Soviet Socialist Republics |
| RC | China (National Republic) (Formosa) | SUD | Sudan |
| | | SWA | South West Africa |
| RCA | Central African Republic | SY | Seychelles |
| RCB | Congo (Brazzaville) | SYR | Syria |
| RCH | Chile | T | Thailand |
| RH | Haiti | TG | Togo |
| RI | Indonesia | TN | Tunisia |
| RIM | Mauritania | TR | Turkey |
| RL | Lebanon | TT | Trinidad and Tobago |
| RM | Malagasy Republic (formerly Madagascar) | U | Uruguay |
| | | USA | United States of America |
| RMM | Mali | V | Vatican City (Holy See) |
| RNR | Zambia (formerly Northern Rhodesia) | VN | Viet-Nam (Republic of) |
| | | WAG | Gambia |
| ROK | Korea (Republic of) | WAL | Sierra Leone |
| RSM | San Marino | WAN | Nigeria |
| RSR | Rhodesia (formerly Southern Rhodesia) | WD | Dominica ⎫ Windward |
| | | WG | Grenada ⎬ Islands |
| RU | Burundi | WL | St. Lucia ⎭ |
| RWA | Rwanda | WS | Western Samoa |
| S | Sweden | WV | St. Vincent (Windward Islands) |
| SD | Swaziland | | |
| SF | Finland | YU | Yugoslavia |
| SGP | Singapore | YV | Venezuela |
| SME | Surinam (Dutch Guiana) | ZA | South Africa |

# Some Important Dates in the Story of Motoring

**1770** Nicholas Cugnot built a 3-wheeled steam wagon – the first real automobile in the sense that it moved under its own steam.

**1801** Richard Trevithick, a Cornishman, built Britain's first steam carriage. He later concentrated on steam locomotives (see p. 112).

**1835** The Highways Act largely superseded the Turnpike Acts. It created the offence of 'Riding or driving furiously so as to endanger the life or limb of any person'.

**1861** The Locomotives Act required all motor vehicles to be in the charge of two people and imposed a speed limit of 10 mph in the country and 5 mph in towns.

**1865** The Locomotives Act imposed a 4 mph speed limit (2 mph in towns) and required a crew of three for all mechanically-propelled vehicles, stipulating that one of the crew must walk not less than 6 yards in front carrying a red flag by day and a lantern by night.

**1878** The red flag was abolished but one member of the crew was required to walk in front to warn horsemen – at a distance of 20 yards.

**1885** Two German engineers – Gottlieb Daimler and Karl Benz – separately achieved the first practical results in the design of the horseless carriage which was to become the internal combustion motor car.

**1892** The first petrol-engined car – an 1888 Benz – is thought to have been imported into Britain.

**1894** Road racing started in France.
The *Petit Journal* inspired the 80-mile Paris-Rouen contest – the world's first open-road reliability trial.

**1895** The Automobile Club de France was formed.
Michelin of France produced the first practical motor-car tyre.
The Paris-Bordeaux there-and-back 732 mile race was won by a Panhard-Levassor at 14·9 mph.
Britain's first motor show was organized at Tunbridge Wells.

**1896** Dr Frederick Lanchester tested his four-wheeled, petrol-engined phaeton.
In the US Henry Ford built his first car – a quadri-cycle.
It became no longer necessary for a crew member to walk in front of the vehicle. Speeds of up to 14 mph were allowed. The passing of this Act was celebrated by the famous Emancipation Run from London to Brighton.

**1897** Frederick Richard Simms – described as the 'father' of the British motor industry – founded the Automobile Club of Great Britain and Ireland (to become the R A C on December 8th).

**1900** First of the Gordon Bennett races – the forerunners of the international Grand Prix races we know today.

**1903** The Motor Car Act 1903 was passed. It was called the Motorist's Charter, and lifted the speed limit from 14 to 20 mph, provided for driving licences, compulsory registration and number plates.
Henry Ford set up a new world speed record at 91·37 mph in an Arrow.

**1905** The Automobile Association was formed in June.
Herbert Austin founded the Austin Motor Co and produced the first Austin the following year.

The first Tourist Trophy race, in the Isle of Man, was won at 33·9 mph by Mr J. S. Napier in an Arrol-Johnston.

**1907**  The Rolls-Royce Silver Ghost made its first appearance. The 7,434 cc Ghost remained in production until 1925.
On June 17th Brooklands racing track was opened near Weybridge, Surrey. In July Selwyn Edge used it to set up a 24-hour record in a Napier, completing 1,582 miles at an average speed of close on 66 mph.

**1908**  Birth of the Model T Ford – the 'Tin Lizzie' with its 2,880 cc engine and 2–speed epicyclic gearbox.

**1910**  Petrol tax was introduced at 3d a gallon. A graduated scale of motor licence duties was introduced.

**1919**  First post-war Motor Show. Motorists were paying 4s a gallon for petrol which had cost 1s 9d before the war.

**1920**  Britain's first roadside petrol pump was installed at Aldermaston, near Newbury, Berks.

**1922**  Herbert Austin introduced his 747 cc Baby Austin with three-speed gearbox and four-wheel brakes.

**1923**  Henry Seagrave, in a Sunbeam, gained Britain's first Grand Prix victory.

**1930**  Abolition of the 20 mph speed limit.

**1934**  New Road Traffic Act imposed a 30 mph speed limit in built-up areas which came into operation the following year.
Driving licence tests introduced.

**1935**  Malcolm Campbell, in his Rolls-engined Bluebird, raised the land-speed record above the 300 mph mark for the first time (301·13 mph).

**1937**  London Motor Show held for the first time at Earl's Court.

**1938**  The number of motor vehicles on Britain's roads exceeded 3,000,000 for the first time.

**1939**  John Cobb in his car 'Railton' set up a new world land-speed record of 369·7 mph. Petrol rationing introduced.

**1942**  Basic petrol ration withdrawn.

**1947**  On Bonneville Salt Flats, Utah, John Cobb pushed the world land-speed record to 394·2 mph (Sept. 16th). On one of his runs he exceeded 400 mph on land – a record which remained unbeaten for 17 years.

**1950**  Petrol rationing abolished on July 1st. The tubeless tyre perfected in the USA.

**1955**  Britain's first Highway Code.

**1956**  The Road Traffic Act 1956 included a compulsory annual test for vehicles ten years old or more.

**1958** Britain's first stretch of motorway opened – the Preston By-Pass (Dec. 5th). First parking meter order made.

**1960** The Road Traffic and Roads Improvement Act 1960 provided for the appointment of Traffic Wardens by the Police. The start of motor vehicle testing on a voluntary basis at more than 14,000 testing stations.

**1964** On Lake Eyre, S. Australia, Donald Campbell in his wheel-driven car 'Bluebird' achieved a speed of 429·311 mph over 666·386 yards. Peak speed: c. 440 mph.

**1965** Craig Breedlove set up an official speed of 608.21 mph in four-wheeled jet-propelled car 'The Spirit of America' at Bonneville Salt Flats, Utah, on Nov. 15th.

**1967** The breath test introduced: motorists in Great Britain subject to a legal maximum limit to the amount of alcohol which they may have in their blood.

**1968** Introduction of tests for heavy goods vehicles.

**1969** Cars first registered on or after January 1st 1965, are required to have safety belts in front seats – later cars must already have seat belts.

# C. Railways

## Principal Gauges*

| English | Metric | Chief places where used |
|---|---|---|
| 5 ft. 6 in. | 1·676 m. | India, Pakistan, Ceylon, Spain, Portugal, Argentina, Chile |
| 5 ft. 3 in. | 1·600 m. | N. Ireland, Republic of Ireland, S. Australia, Victoria, Brazil |
| 5 ft. 0 in. | 1·524 m. | USSR, Finland |
| 4 ft. 8½ in. | 1·435 m. | Standard for Great Britain, Canada, USA, Mexico, European Continent (except Spain, Portugal, Finland and USSR), Algeria, Morocco, Tunisia, Saudi Arabia, Egypt, Turkey, Iraq, Iran, Australian Commonwealth, New South Wales, China, South Korea. Also used in Japan, Western Australia and Victoria |

| | | |
|---|---|---|
| 3 ft. 6 in. | 1·067 m. | Queensland, S. Australia, W. Australia, Tasmania, New Zealand, South & East Africa, Malawi, Rhodesia, Ghana, Nigeria, Sudan, Japan, Indonesia, Sweden, Norway |
| 3 ft. 5¼ in. | 1·05 m. | Algeria, Syria, Lebanon and Jordan |
| 3 ft. 3⅜ in. | 1 m. | India, Pakistan, Iraq, South America, East & West Africa, Burma, Malaysia, Thailand, Cambodia, Viet-Nam |
| 3 ft. 0 in. | 0·914 m. | Mexico, Central America, Colombia & Peru |
| 2 ft. 11 in. | 0·891 m. | Sweden |
| 2 ft. 6 in. | 0·762 m. | India, Ceylon |
| 23⅝/24 in. | 0·600/ 0·610 m. | Wales, India, Pakistan & S. America |

\* A gauge is the distance between a pair of wheels or rails.

# Fastest Individual Runs in Great Britain

| Year | Route | Engine | Max Speed (mph) | Average Speed (mph) |
|---|---|---|---|---|
| 1903 | Paddington-Plymouth (via Bristol) | City of Bath | 75 | 63·0 |
| 1904 | Plymouth-Bristol | City of Truro | 102¼ | 62·2 |
| 1904 | Bristol-Paddington | Duke of Connaught | — | 71·4 |
| 1932 | Swindon-Paddington | Tregenna Castle | 92 | 81·6 |
| 1935 | Newcastle-King's Cross | Papyrus | 108 | 70·8 |
| 1935 | King's Cross – Peterborough | Silver Link | 112½ | 83·3 |
| 1936 | Glasgow-Euston | Princess Elizabeth | — | 70·0 |
| 1937 | Crewe-Euston | Coronation Scot | 114 | 79·8 |
| 1954 | Bristol-Paddington | King Richard II | — | 74·4 |

THE FASTEST REGULAR RAILWAY RUN IN THE WORLD is the 'New Tokaido' service of Japanese National Railways, inaugurated in November 1965. The train covers the 320·2 miles from Tokyo to Osaka in 3 hours 10 minutes at an average speed of 101·16 mph and the 212·4 miles between Tokyo and Nagoya in 2 hours to average 106·2 mph.

THE LONGEST DAILY NON-STOP RUN IN THE WORLD is made by the 'Sud Express' between Paris and Bordeaux, France, a distance of 359·8 miles.

THE LONGEST RUN ON BRITISH RAIL without an advertised stop is the 'Motorail Service' from King's Cross to Aberdeen, a distance of 523½ miles.

THE COUNTRY WITH THE GREATEST LENGTH OF RAILWAY is the United States. It has over 200,000 miles of track. The total route mileage of railway system in the United Kingdom as at December 1971 was 11,643 miles.

THE STEEPEST GRADIENT IN THE WORLD worked by adhesion is inclined at 1 in 11 on the electrically-operated metre-gauge Chamonix line of the South-Eastern Region of the French National Railways between Chedde and Servoz.

# Some Important Dates in the Story of Railways in Britain

**1801, May 21st** – Incorporation of the Surrey Iron Railway, the first public goods line in the world to be sanctioned by Parliament. Opened from Wandsworth to Croydon on July 16th, 1803.

**1804, February 21st** – Steam locomotive traction successfully used (experimentally) by Trevithick on the Penydaran tramroad at Merthyr Tydfil.
**June 29th** – Incorporation of Oystermouth Railway or Tramroad Company, the first to convey fare-paying passengers. The line from Swansea to Oystermouth, opened in 1806, was worked successively by horse, steam and electricity.

**1814, July 25th** – George Stephenson's first locomotive, '*Blücher*', introduced on the Killingworth Colliery wagonway.

**1825, September 27th** – Ceremonial opening of Stockton and Darlington Railway. Stephenson's locomotive '*Locomotion*' reached 15 mph.

**1829, October 6th–14th** – Trials on the Rainhill Level (Liverpool and Manchester Railway): Stephenson's '*Rocket*' won first prize of £500.

**1830, September 15th** – Liverpool and Manchester Railway formally opened, the first public railway in the world to be worked entirely by steam locomotives. This day also marked the first railway accident. William Huskisson, MP, was run down by Stephenson's '*Rocket*' and died the same night.

**1836, April 20th** – Festiniog Railway (1 ft. 11½ in. gauge) opened for slate traffic. The first narrow gauge public railway in the world.

**1837, July 4th** – Grand Junction Railway opened throughout – the first British trunk railway.

**1842, June 13th** – First railway journey made by Queen Victoria – from Slough to Paddington.

**1845, August 6th** – Opening of the Gauge Commission. Decision in favour of 4 ft. 8½ in. gauge as British standard reached the next year, with the exception of GWR and associated lines.

**1854, January 16th** – Present Paddington station opened, Great Western Railway.

**1855, February 1st** – GWR inaugurated the first special postal train in the world between London and Bristol. One first-class carriage was attached for passengers in June 1869.

**1857** – First steel rail made (by Robert Forester Mushet) and laid experimentally at Derby Station, Midland Railway, early in 1857. It remained in service until June 1873, and steel rails came into general use a few years later.

**1863, January 10th** – First underground city railway in the world opened, on the Metropolitan Railway, from Bishop's Road to Farringdon Street.

**1868, October 1st** – St Pancras Station opened, Midland Railway.

**1874, February 2nd** – Liverpool Street Station opened, Great Eastern Railway.

**June 1st** – Pullman cars introduced to Great Britain by Midland Railway.

**1877, December** – Sleeping cars (1st class) introduced on GWR.

**1879, November 1st** – Dining-car introduced on Great Northern Railway, London–Leeds service.

**1883, August 4th** – First section of Magnus Volk's Brighton electric railway opened. Pioneer electric railway in Great Britain.

**September 28th** – Electric traction formally inaugurated on the Giant's Causeway Railway. The first line in the world to be run on hydro-electric power.

**1890, December 18th** – City and South London Railway opened. First underground electric railway in the world.

**1892, March 7th** – Corridor trains introduced on GWR services.

**1905, September 12th** – Electric traction inaugurated on Inner Circle.

**1921, August 19th** – Royal Assent given to the Railways Act 1921 which resulted in the formation of the four British main-line railway companies.

**1926, September 12th** – The 'Golden Arrow' all-Pullman service, Calais–Paris, introduced on the through London–Paris route.

**1933, January 1st** – The '*Southern Belle*' – the first all-steel, all-electric

Pullman train in the world, introduced by Southern Railway (re-named *Brighton Belle*' on June 29th, 1934).

**1935, September 27th** – Trial run of LNER *'Silver Jubilee'* (London–Newcastle express) the first streamlined train in Great Britain. Attained an average speed of 100 mph for 43 miles.

**1937, June 29th** – Trial run of LMSR *'Coronation Scot'* streamlined express (London–Glasgow). Maximum speed of 114 mph attained approaching Crewe. Public service began July 5th.

**1948, January 1st** – British Railways nationalized.

**1961, September 9th** – Last day of steam haulage of regular passenger service on the Metropolitan Line, London Transport.

**1963, March 27th** – Dr Richard Beeching's report on the re-shaping of British Railways published. Among the main proposals: 2,128 of Britain's 7,000 stations and halts to be closed; passenger train services to be completely withdrawn from about 5,000 route miles; and many stopping passenger services to be discontinued.

**April 8th** – First London Transport train fitted with automatic driving equipment entered experimental service on District Line.

**1964, January 5th** – London Transport began experimenting with electronic ticket barrier control on Underground.

**April 5th** – London Transport began full-scale trials of automatic train operation on Central Line.

**1965, June 11th** – The last regular booked steam passenger train left Paddington. This marked the end of steam at Paddington except for special workings: the last was on November 27th. The official title of British Railways is, in fact, still British Railways, but from 1965 onwards the normal usage became 'British Rail'.

**June 14th** – *'Flying Scotsman'* covered 393 miles in 355 minutes at 66·42 mph – the fastest time ever for this run.

**1966, July 5th** – Opening of British Railways *'Seaspeed'* hovercraft service between Southampton and Cowes.

**1968, October 14th** – Queen Elizabeth II formally opened the rebuilt Euston Station, London.

**1969, March 7th** – Victoria Line, London Transport, opened throughout from Walthamstow to Victoria by Queen Elizabeth II – the first new tube across central London for over half a centruy and the most highly automated Underground railway line in the world.

# D. Aircraft

## United Kingdom Airlines

BRITISH OVERSEAS AIRWAYS CORPORATION is the second biggest international airline in the world and it is also the oldest. It began life in 1919 and was then called Aircraft Transport and Travel. Various mergers in 1924 made it into Imperial Airways and an Act of Parliament in 1939 made it BOAC.

The operational fleet of British Overseas Airways Corporation (as at May 1972): twelve 747 Jumbo Jets; 27 VC10s; 27 Boeing 707s.

BRITISH EUROPEAN AIRWAYS was formed in 1946 and from that time has been responsible for operating the great majority of British scheduled passenger, mail and freight air services beween Britain and the Continent of Europe and within the British Isles.

The following types of aircraft are in service with BEA (as at May 1972): 20 Viscounts; 10 Vanguards; 18 BAC Super 1-11; 53 Tridents (The Trident III is the largest aircraft in the fleet with 140 seats); 7 Sikorsky S61N Helicopters; 1 Bell Jet Range Helicopter (available for shuttle service for special jobs, eg for businessmen who wish to get to a conference). BEA Air Tours are currently operating 9 Comet 4B jets and 2 Boeing 707s, and 2 other aircraft which operate entirely Scottish operations are Herons (prop. jet aircraft).

# Direct Flight Air Distances from London

| To | Air Mileage | To | Air Mileage |
|---|---|---|---|
| Paris | 215 | Helsinki | 1,190 |
| Amsterdam | 231 | Tripoli | 1,532 |
| Dublin | 279 | Istanbul | 1,562 |
| Zurich | 542 | Cairo | 2,228 |
| Copenhagen | 609 | Tel Aviv | 2,320 |
| Madrid | 775 | Boston | 3,370 |
| Stockholm | 899 | Montreal | 3,420 |
| Rome | 953 | Bermuda | 3,436 |
| Lisbon | 972 | New York | 3,490 |
| Reykjavik | 1,174 | Bahrein | 3,522 |

| To | Air Mileage | To | Air Mileage |
|---|---|---|---|
| Toronto | 3,685 | Rio de Janeiro | 6,110 |
| Chicago | 4,138 | San Francisco | 6,164 |
| Nassau | 4,357 | Montevideo | 7,600 |
| Karachi | 4,730 | Singapore | 7,680 |
| Montego Bay | 4,812 | Buenos Aires | 7,700 |
| Kingston | 4,894 | Hong Kong | 8,169 |
| Delhi | 5,148 | Darwin | 9,966 |
| Colombo | 5,901 | Tokyo | 10,082 |

# Badges of Rank of Officers of The Royal Air Force

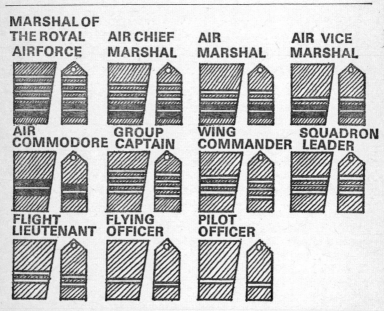

The principal non-commissioned ranks are: Warrant Officer, Flight Sergeant (Flt Sgt), Chief Technician (Chief Tech), Sergeant (Sgt), Corporal (Cpl), Junior Technician (Jnr Tech), Senior Aircraftman (SAC), Leading Aircraftman (LAC), Aircraftman (AC).

# Some Famous British Aircraft of World War II

**Spitfire** (fighter). Low-wing monoplane. The 'Spit' played a great part in defeating the Luftwaffe in the Battle of Britain.
  Max. speed: 375 mph at 20,250 ft.
  Span: 36 ft. 10 in.; Length: 30 ft. 4 in.
**Hurricane** (fighter-light bomber). Low-wing monoplane with single in-line engine. Played an outstanding role in the Battle of Britain. Hurricanes shot down more aircraft than all other types put together.
  Approx. speed: 335 mph at 22,000 ft.
  Span: 40 ft; Length: 31 ft. 5 in.
**Wellington** (medium bomber). Twin-engined, mid-wing monoplane. One of the most-used British bombers, known as the 'Wimpy'. The Wellington II had in-line engines; Wellington III, radial engines.
  Approx. max. speed: 244 mph at 17,000 ft.
  Span: 86 ft. 2 in.; Length: 61 ft. (II), 61 ft. 6 in. (III)
  Range: 3,240 miles.
**Stirling** (heavy bomber). Mid-wing monoplane with four radial engines. Inboard engines underslung. First of the big British four-engined bombers to go into service, becoming operational early in 1941. Carried over 8 tons of bombs.
  Approx. max. speed: 272 mph at 14,000 ft.
  Span: 99 ft; Length: 87 ft. 3 in.
**Halifax** (heavy bomber). Mid-wing monoplane with four in-line engines underslung. Pilots called it the 'Halibag'. Its 'block-busting' bombs caused considerable damage in Germany and the Middle East. Max. bomb load approx. 11,000 lb.
  Max. speed: 262 mph at 17,750 ft.
  Span: 99 ft; Length: 71 ft. 7 in.
**Lancaster** (heavy bomber). Mid-wing monoplane. Four in-line engines underslung. The 'dam-busters' bomber: carried a bomb load of over 6 tons.
  Max. speed: 280 mph.
  Span: 102 ft; Length: 69 ft. 6 in.
  Range: nearly 3,000 miles.
**Sunderland.** Four-engined flying boat nicknamed the 'Flying Porcupine' due to its many guns. Armed with power-operated turrets in the nose and in the tail; the tail turret carried 4 guns. Two flank gun positions each carried a single machine gun. Especially concerned with coastal

reconnaissance, convoying ships and in submarine patrol. Loaded weight: 44,600 lb.

**Mosquito** (light bomber-fighter). Twin engine, high mid-wing monoplane. Reconnaissance bomber. Constructed for the most part of plywood. Became operational at the end of 1942.

Span: 54 ft. 2 in.; Length: 40 ft. 9½ in.

**Swordfish** (torpedo bomber). Single radial engine biplane with fabric-covered wings, used by the British Fleet Air Arm for torpedo, spotter and reconnaissance work. Carried either a load of bombs or a single 18-inch torpedo slung between the divided undercarriage legs.

Max. speed: 144 mph at 5,500 ft.

Span: 45 ft. 6 in.; Length: 36 ft. 4 in.

**Blenheim** (medium bomber). Mid-wing monoplane with twin radial engines, used as a bomber and long-range fighter over France, in the North African campaigns and in the Middle East.

Max. speed: 260 mph at 12,000 ft.

Span: 56 ft; Length: 42 ft. 7 in.

# Some Important Dates in the History of Flying

**1783, October 15th** – Francois Pilâtre de Rozier became the world's first aeronaut when he ascended 84 feet above Paris in a hot-air balloon designed by Joseph and Etienne Montgolfier.

**1903, December 17th** – Orville and Wilbur Wright made the first sustained controlled flights in history in a powered aeroplane, the 'Flyer', at Kitty Hawk, N. Carolina, covering 120 feet in about 12 seconds.

**1908, October 16th** – Samuel F. Cody made the first officially-recognized aeroplane flight in Great Britain, at Farnborough, Hants.

**1909, July 25th** – Louis Bleriot of France crossed the English Channel in a Bleriot XI monoplane. He took off from Baraques, near Calais at 4.40 AM and landed at Dover at 5.20 AM.

**1912 (mid-August)** – F. K. McClean flew a Short pusher biplane under all the Thames bridges in London between Tower Bridge and Westminster, passing between the upper and lower spans of Tower Bridge.

**1913, August 20th** – Lt Nesterov, of the Imperial Russian Army first looped-the-loop in a Nieuport at Kiev.

**1913** – Appearance of the first four-engined aeroplane in the world – the Sikorsky '*Grand*'.

**1918, April 1st** – The Royal Air Force is formed.

**1919, June 14th–15th** – Capt John Alcock and Lt Arthur Whitten Brown made the first non-stop air crossing of the Atlantic in a Vickers Vimy bomber from St John's, Newfoundland to Clifden, Co Galway, Ireland.

**1919, November 12th–December 10th** – Two Australian brothers, Capt Ross Smith and Lt Keith Smith made the first flight from England to Australia – a distance of 11,294 miles.

**1925–6, November 16th–March 12th** – First flight from London to Cape Town and return by Alan Cobham in a de Havilland DH-50.

**1926, June 30th–October 1st** – First aeroplane flight from Britain to Australia and return made by Alan Cobham in a de Havilland DH-50. After this flight he was knighted.

**1927, May 20th–21st** – First solo non-stop crossing of the Atlantic by Capt Charles Lindbergh. New York to Paris – 33 hours 30 minutes.

**1928, May 15th** – The Australian Flying Doctor Service was inaugurated.

**1929, August 8th–29th** – First airship flight round the world. The Graf Zeppelin, commanded by Dr Hugo Eckener, flew from Lakehurst, New Jersey, to Friedrichshafen, Tokyo, Los Angeles and back to Lakehurst in 21 days, 7 hours, 34 minutes.

**1929, November 28th–29th** – Cdr R. E. Byrd made the first flight over the South Pole.

**1930, May 5th–24th** – First solo flight from England to Australia by a woman. Amy Johnson flew a de Havilland Moth from Croydon to Darwin in 19 days.

**1930, October 4th** – Airship R101 crashed in France on its maiden voyage, a disaster which put an end to airship development in Britain.

**1932, August 18th–19th** – First east to west crossing of the North Atlantic, by J. A. Mollison, in a de Havilland Puss Moth.

**1933, July 15th–22nd** – The first solo flight round the world. Wiley Post (American) flew a Lockheed monoplane from New York via Berlin, Moscow, Irkutsk, Alaska and back to New York – 15,596 miles in 7 days, 18 hours, 49 minutes.

**1936, June 26th** – The first prototype of the Focke-Wulf FW 61 twin-rotor helicopter made its first free flight – the first successful helicopter in the world.

**1937, May 6th** – The German Zeppelin 'Hindenburg', then the world's largest airship, caught fire and was destroyed when approaching its moorings at Lakehurst, America, with the loss of 35 lives. Before this it had completed ten transatlantic flights carrying up to 100 passengers each time. The crossing took 62 hours.

**1939, August 27th** – The first jet-propelled aeroplane to fly was the German Heinkel He 178.

**1940** (summer) – Fewer than 1,000 Hurricane and Spitfire fighters of the Royal Air Force met and defeated 3,500 aircraft of three Luftwaffe air fleets.

**1941, October 2nd** – A speed of 623 mph in level flight was recorded by Heini Dittmar in the Messerschmitt Me 163 '*Komet*' – the world's first operational rocket-powered fighter.

**1947, October 14th** – The first supersonic flight was made by Capt (now Lt-Gen) Charles E. Yeager, USAF, over Edwards Air Force Base, Muroc, California, USA. in a US Bell XS-I

**1950** – British European Airways commenced the first jet airliner service in the world – London-Le Bourget, in 57 minutes.

**1952, May 2nd** – The world's first jet airliner, a de Havilland Comet entered service (London-Johannesburg). Powered by four 4,450 lb. thrust turbojets. Cruising speed: 490 mph.

**1953** – The world's first turboprop airliner service opened by British European Airways using 48-seat Vickers Viscounts. Four 1,540 hp Rolls-Royce Dart engines gave the early Viscount a cruising speed of 320 mph.

**1957** – Russia puts first earth satellite, Sputnik 1, into orbit.

**1968** – Russia flies the world's first supersonic transport, the Tupolev Tu-144.

**1969** – French and British prototype of the Concorde supersonic transport flown.

**1970, January 12th** – The Boeing 747 'Jumbo Jet' arrived in London from New York on its first passenger carrying flight. It takes from 362–490 passengers in ten-abreast rows. Cruising speed, 595 mph: wingspan: 195·7 ft: length: 321·3 ft. Cost of each 747, £8¾m.

# The Airliner of the Future

The North American X-15 A-2 rocket-powered research aircraft, air-launched from modified Boeing B-52 bombers, has reached a speed of 4,534 mph (Mach 6·72) and an altitude of 67·08 miles.

# 11 SPACE

## Journey Into Space

Cape Canaveral was once an arrowhead of land jutting into the ocean – a wasteland inhabited by insects, snakes and alligators.

Then, one day, the scientists, engineers and technicians moved in and built gantry towers, blockhouses and roads. And on July 24th, 1950, the first missile shot from Cape Canaveral blasted off and dropped into the Atlantic.

But the Space Age can really be said to have begun on October 4th, 1957, when the USSR successfully launched a 'sputnik' into orbit. Twelve years later, on July 21st, 1969, American astronaut Neil Armstrong became the first man to walk on the surface of the Moon. His words 'That's one small step for a man, one giant leap for mankind' have gone down in history – and America's £10,000,000,000 programme for landing a man on the Moon was crowned with success.

The 12-day Apollo moon-shot – America's fifth moon-landing (the Apollo 13 landing mission had to be abandoned because of trouble with the spacecraft) cost £150 million.

Apollo 17, the last landing mission, is scheduled for December 1972. The total cost on manned spaceflight alone since the 1950s will be in the region of £11,000 million (this includes £150 million spent on the earlier Mercury and £500 million on the Gemini manned spaceflight programmes as well as varying amounts on unmanned space probes and satellites).

America is hoping to have a large station orbiting in space by the 1980s.

The first step in this direction is the Skylab, a spacecraft fitted out not only as a workshop but with living quarters as well. Unlike future platforms in space it will not be a permanent station. Skylab will be 'home' to three separate teams of astronauts for periods of 28–56 days in separate missions during 1973. The object of this $2,000 million project is to find out how useful man can be in space. Apollo spacecraft will serve as ferry boats from Earth.

The next step in this ambitious project will be a large manned Earth-orbital space station in which a dozen or so scientists and astronauts could live and carry out astronomical and Earth observations, and physics experiments. This would be built and supplied by large space shuttles. The Shuttle will, it is claimed, 'open the frontiers of space as railroads opened the wild west a century ago'.

The cost of the planned space station and shuttle service is estimated at around $14,000 million.

Manned orbits of planets are now rated almost as important as manned landings. Several unmanned attempts have been made by the Americans and Russians over the last ten years or so to reach Venus. The first 'official' Russian flight – Venus-1 – was launched in February 1961. Contact was lost and the flight was thought to have passed the planet. Another Soviet automatic spacecraft – Venus-7 – reached Venus on December 15th, 1970, after a flight lasting 120 days. It sent back signals to Earth for 23 minutes after landing before perishing in the intense heat of the planet's atmosphere. According to data relayed by the spacecraft the surface temperature in the landing area was about 887°F (475°C) and the density of the surface atmosphere was sixty times greater than that on Earth.

On March 27th, 1972, Russia launched another unmanned, one-ton spacecraft (code-named Venus-8) on the four-month journey to Venus.

America's Mariner-9 spacecraft, the first spacecraft in history to orbit another planet, began circling Mars, after a 248-million-mile journey from Cape Kennedy, on May 30th, 1971. It sent back invaluable data which is causing all previous scientific theories on the make-up and evolution of the planet to be drastically revised. The Russians, too, have launched unmanned spacecraft towards Mars to carry out scientific research around the planet.

In 1976 America expects to probe Mars with its Viking spacecraft. Inside the two Viking landers will be a bio-chemical laboratory which will send results automatically to Earth. It will also carry a soil-sampler and weather sensors.

Man's exploration of the solar system is advancing all the time.

# Man's Exploration of Space

| Date | Pilot | Country | Spacecraft | Flight Duration | |
|------|-------|---------|------------|------|------|
| | | | | hrs. | min. |
| **1961** | | | | | |
| April 12th | Yuri Gagarin (27) (First man in space) | USSR | Vostok 1 | 1 | 48 |
| May 5th | Alan B. Shepard (37) (First American in space) | USA | Freedom 7 | | 15 |
| July 21st | Virgil Grissom (34) | USA | Liberty Bell 7 | | 16 |
| Aug. 6th–7th | Gherman Stepanovich Titov (26) | USSR | Vostok 2 | 25 | 18 |
| **1962** | | | | | |
| Feb. 20th | John Glenn (40) (First American manned spacecraft to enter Earth orbit) | USA | Friendship | 4 | 55 |
| May 24th | Malcolm Scott Carpenter (37) | USA | Aurora 7 | 4 | 56 |
| Aug. 11th–15th | Andrian Grigoryevich Nikolayev (32) (First man-operated television from space) | USSR | Vostok 3 | 94 | 22 |
| Aug. 12th–15th | Pavel Romanovich Popovich (31) | USSR | Vostok 4 | 70 | 57 |
| Oct. 3rd | Walter Marty Schirra (39) | USA | Sigma 7 | 9 | 13 |
| **1963** | | | | | |
| May 15th–16th | Leroy Gordon Cooper (36) (Manual re-entry after failure of automatic control system) | USA | Faith 7 | 34 | 20 |
| June 14th–19th | Valeriy Fyodorovich Bykovsky (28) | USSR | Vostok 5 | 119 | 66 |
| June 16th–19th | Valentina Vladimirovna Tereshkova (26) (First woman in space) | USSR | Vostok 6 | 70 | 50 |

**1964**

| | | | | | |
|---|---|---|---|---|---|
| Oct. 12th–13th | Vladimir Mihailovich Komarov (37); Boris Borisovich Yegorov (37); Konstantin Petrovich Feoktiskov (38) | USSR | Voskhod 1 | 24 | 17 |

**1965**

| | | | | | |
|---|---|---|---|---|---|
| March 18th–19th | Aleksey Arkhipovich Leonov (30); Pavel Ivanovich Belyavev (39) (Leonov became first man to leave spacecraft and float in outer space) | USSR | Voskhod 2 | 26 | 2 |
| March 23rd | Virgil Ivan Grissom (38); John Watts Young | USA | Gemini 3 | 4 | 53 |
| June 3rd–7th | James McDivitt (35); Edward Higgins White (34); (White took first space walk by an American) | USA | Gemini 4 | 97 | 56 |
| Aug. 21st–29th | Leroy Gordon Cooper (38); Charles Conrad (35) | USA | Gemini 5 | 190 | 56 |
| Dec. 4th–18th | Frank Borman (37); James Lovell (37); (rendezvous with Gemini 6) | USA | Gemini 7 | 330 | 35 |
| Dec. 15th–16th | Walter Marty Schirra (43); Thomas P. Stafford (35) | USA | Gemini 6 | 25 | 51 |

**1966**

| | | | | | |
|---|---|---|---|---|---|
| March 16th | Neil Alden Armstrong (36); David Randolph Scott (36); (First docking between manned and unmanned spacecraft – Agena 7) | USA | Gemini 8 | 10 | 42 |
| June 3rd–6th | Thomas P. Stafford (36); Eugene Andrew Cernan (32) (Longest space walk to date – 129 minutes by Cernan) | USA | Gemini 9 | 72 | 21 |
| July 18th–21st | John Watts Young; Michael Collins (space walk by Collins) | USA | Gemini 10 | 70 | 74 |

| Sept.<br>12th–15th | Charles Conrad (36);<br>Richard F. Gordon<br>(space walk by Gordon) | USA | Gemini 11 | 71 | 17 |
|---|---|---|---|---|---|
| **1967** | | | | | |
| April<br>22nd–23rd | Vladimir Mikhailovich<br>Komarov (40)<br>(Killed when his landing<br>parachute tangled) | USSR | Soyuz 1 | 26 | 45 |
| Oct.<br>11th–22nd | Walter Marty Schirra<br>(45); Donn F. Eisele (38);<br>R. Walter Cunningham (36)<br>(First flight of capsule<br>designed ultimately for<br>7-day voyage to the moon) | USA | Apollo VII | 260 | 9 |
| Oct.<br>26th–30th | Georgiy T. Beregovoiy<br>(47)<br>(Rendezvous with<br>unmanned Soyuz 2) | USSR | Soyuz 3 | 94 | 51 |
| Dec.<br>21st–27th | Frank Borman (40); James<br>Lovell (40); William A.<br>Anders (35)<br>(First men to break free<br>from the Earth's<br>gravitational field. First<br>men to orbit the Moon.<br>Christmas radio greetings<br>sent from astronauts while<br>in Moon orbit) | USA | Apollo VIII | 147 | 0 |
| **1969** | | | | | |
| Jan.<br>14th–17th | Vladimir Shatalov (41);<br>Alexei Yeliseyev (34);<br>Yevgeny Khrunov (35) | USSR | Soyuz 4 | 71 | 14 |
| Jan.<br>15th–18th | Boris Volynov (34);<br>(Docked with Soyuz 4. First<br>joining of two manned<br>spacecraft in orbit.<br>Yeliseyev and Khrunov<br>transferred to – and<br>landed in – Soyuz 5) | USSR | Soyuz 5 | 72 | 46 |

| | | | | | |
|---|---|---|---|---|---|
| March 3rd–13th | James McDivitt (39); David Randolph Scott (36); Russell Louis Schweikart (33) (First trial of module – manned – in space. Crew transferred through interior connexion) | USA | Apollo IX | 241 | 1 |
| May 18th–26th | Thomas P. Stafford (38); John Watts Young (38); Eugene Andrew Cernan (35) | USA | Apollo X | 192 | 3 |
| July 16th–24th | Neil Alden Armstrong (38); Edwin Eugene Aldrin (39); Michael Collins (First Moon landing by man – Armstrong. Moon rock brought back to Earth) | USA | Apollo XI | 195 | 18 |
| Oct. 11th–16th | Giorgiy Shonin (34); Valery N. Kubasov (34); | USSR | Soyuz 6 | 118 | 42 |
| Oct. 12th–17th | Anatoly V. Filipchenko (41); Viktor V. Gorbatko (35); Vladislav N. Volkov (34) | USSR | Soyuz 7 | 118 | 41 |
| Oct. 13th–18th | Vladimir A. Shatalov (41); Alexei N. Yeliseyev (35) (Rendezvous and formation trials and experiments) | USSR | Soyuz 8 | 118 | 41 |
| Nov. 14th–24th | Charles Conrad (39); Richard F. Gordon (40); Alan L. Bean (37) (Second Moon landing by man – Conrad. Moon soil brought back to Earth) | USA | Apollo XII | 244 | 36 |
| **1970** April 11th | James Lovell (42); Fred Haise (36); John Swigert (38) (Landing on Moon abandoned after explosion in service module of spacecraft) | USA | Apollo XIII | 142 | 54 |

| June 1st | Andrian Nikolayev (33); Vitaly Sevastoyanov (35) | USSR | Soyuz 9 | 425 | 0 |
|---|---|---|---|---|---|

**1971**

| Jan. 31st | Alan Shepard (47); Edgar Mitchell (40); Stuart Roosa (37) | USA | Apollo XIV | 216 | 2 |
| April 23rd | Vladimir Shatalov (43); Alexei Yeliseyev (36); Nikolai Rukavishnikov (39) | USSR | Soyuz 10 | 47 | 45 |
| June 6th | Georgy Dobrovolsky (43); Vladislav Volkov (35); Viktor Patsayev (37) (Spent 24 days in space but when spacecraft returned to Earth the three cosmonauts were found dead in their seats) | USSR | Soyuz 11 | | |
| July 26th | David Scott (39); Alfred Worden (39); James Irwin (41) | USA | Apollo XV | 295 | 12 |

**1972**

| April 16th | John W. Young (41); Charles M. Duke (36); Thomas K. Mattingly (36) | USA | Apollo XVI | 265 | 51 |

1973-74 84 days in space
Gerald Carr
Edward Gibson
William Pogue

---

## Association Football

---

The Football Association is the ruling body of the game in England. It was formed in 1863. Professionalism entered the game around 1881, and was legalized in 1885. The present FA Cup competition was first held in 1871 and official international matches began the following year.

The Football League was founded in 1888 by twelve clubs.

| *Football League Champions* | *FA Challenge Cup Winners* |
|---|---|
| **1947** Liverpool | Charlton Athletic |
| **1948** Arsenal | Manchester United |
| **1949** Portsmouth | Wolverhampton Wanderers |
| **1950** Portsmouth | Arsenal |
| **1951** Tottenham Hotspur | Newcastle United |
| **1952** Manchester United | Newcastle United |
| **1953** Arsenal | Blackpool |
| **1954** Wolverhampton Wanderers | West Bromwich Albion |
| **1955** Chelsea | Newcastle United |
| **1956** Manchester United | Manchester City |
| **1957** Manchester United | Aston Villa |
| **1958** Wolverhampton Wanderers | Bolton Wanderers |
| **1959** Wolverhampton Wanderers | Nottingham Forest |
| **1960** Burnley | Wolverhampton Wanderers |
| **1961** Tottenham Hotspur | Tottenham Hotspur |
| **1962** Ipswich Town | Tottenham Hotspur |
| **1963** Everton | Manchester United |

| 1964 | Liverpool | West Ham United |
| 1965 | Manchester United | Liverpool |
| 1966 | Liverpool | Everton |
| 1967 | Manchester United | Tottenham Hotspur |
| 1968 | Manchester City | West Bromwich Albion |
| 1969 | Leeds United | Manchester City |
| 1970 | Everton | Chelsea |
| 1971 | Arsenal | Arsenal |
| 1972 | Derby County | Leeds United |

## SCOTTISH F.A. CUP WINNERS

The Scottish Cup competition came into being at the same time as the Scottish Football Association in 1873. Sixteen clubs took part in the first season's competition which was won by Queen's Park.

| 1947 | Aberdeen | 1956 | Heart of | 1964 | Rangers |
| 1948 | Rangers | | Midlothian | 1965 | Celtic |
| 1949 | Rangers | 1957 | Falkirk | 1966 | Rangers |
| 1950 | Rangers | 1958 | Clyde | 1967 | Celtic |
| 1951 | Celtic | 1959 | St. Mirren | 1968 | Dunfermline |
| 1952 | Motherwell | 1960 | Rangers | 1969 | Celtic |
| 1953 | Rangers | 1961 | Dunfermline | 1970 | Aberdeen |
| 1954 | Celtic | 1962 | Rangers | 1971 | Celtic |
| 1955 | Clyde | 1963 | Rangers | 1972 | Celtic |

## FOOTBALL LEAGUE CUP WINNERS

The Football League Cup was introduced in 1960. The competition is optional and it was not until the 1969–70 season that all 92 League clubs took part.

| 1961 | Aston Villa | 1965 | Chelsea | 1969 | Swindon Town |
| 1962 | Norwich City | 1966 | West Bromwich | 1970 | Manchester City |
| 1963 | Birmingham | | Albion | 1971 | Tottenham |
| | City | 1967 | Queen's Park | | Hotspur |
| 1964 | Leicester City | | Rangers | 1972 | Stoke City |
| | | 1968 | Leeds United | | |

# EUROPEAN CHAMPION CLUBS CUP WINNERS

The European Cup was inaugurated in 1955. Each season the champion club of each Association in the European Union of Football Associations is eligible to compete with the winner of the previous season's competition. Games are played at home and away and the total score of the two games decides the winner. Only one game is played in the final.

| 1957 | Real Madrid | 1964 | Inter Milan | 1969 | AC Milan |
|---|---|---|---|---|---|
| 1958 | Real Madrid | 1965 | Inter Milan | 1970 | Feyenoord |
| 1959 | Real Madrid | 1966 | Real Madrid | 1971 | Ajax |
| 1960 | Real Madrid | 1967 | Celtic | | (Amsterdam) |
| 1961 | Benfica | 1968 | Manchester | 1972 | Ajax |
| 1962 | Benfica | | United | | (Amsterdam) |
| 1963 | AC Milan | | | | |

# WORLD CUP WINNERS

The first World Cup competition was played in 1930. The Cup is sometimes called the Jules Rimet Cup, after Jules Rimet, a Frenchman who was Honorary President of FIFA (Federation Internationale de Football Association) from 1921–54. World championships are held every four years.

| 1930 | Uruguay | 1950 | Uruguay | 1962 | Brazil |
|---|---|---|---|---|---|
| 1934 | Italy | 1954 | West Germany | 1966 | England |
| 1938 | Italy | 1958 | Brazil | 1970 | Brazil |

# EUROPEAN CUP WINNERS' CUP

A competition between the winners (or runners-up) of each of the national cups.

| 1960–1 | A. C. Fiorentina | 1966–7 | Bayern Munich |
|---|---|---|---|
| 1961–2 | Atletico Madrid | 1967–8 | A. C. Milan |
| 1962–3 | Tottenham Hotspur | 1968–9 | Slovan Bratislava |
| 1963–4 | Sporting Lisbon | 1969–70 | Manchester City |
| 1964–5 | West Ham United | 1970–1 | Chelsea |
| 1965–6 | Borussia Dortmund | 1971–2 | Glasgow Rangers |

## EUROPEAN FAIRS' CUP WINNERS
(formerly INTER CITIES FAIRS' CUP)

| | | | | | |
|---|---|---|---|---|---|
| **1958** | Barcelona | **1964** | Real Madrid | **1969** | Newcastle United |
| **1960** | Barcelona | **1965** | Ferencvaros | | |
| **1961** | A. S. Roma | **1966** | Barcelona | **1970** | Arsenal |
| **1962** | Valencia | **1967** | Dynamo Zagreb | **1971** | Leeds United |
| **1963** | Valencia | **1968** | Leeds United | **1972** | Tottenham Hotspur |

THE HIGHEST SCORE recorded in a British first-class football match is 36. This was in 1885 when Arbroath beat Bon Accord by 36–0 in a Scottish Cup match.

In April 1936 Joe Payne scored a record 10 goals for Luton Town in a 3rd Division (South) match against Bristol Rovers.

THE GREATEST NUMBER OF GOALS scored in a career is 1,026 by Pelé, the Brazilian inside left, from 1957 to the World Cup final in June 1970. His real name is Edson Arantes do Nascimento.

Bobby Charlton, OBE, of Manchester United, has played in more internationals than any other British footballer. Between April 1958 and the World Cup in Mexico City in June 1970 he made 106 international appearances.

THE RECORD NUMBER of England amateur caps is 51, by Mike Pinner of Hendon, the former Pegasus goalkeeper, who played for England between 1955 and 1963.

THE LONGEST BRITISH MATCH on record was between Stockport County and Doncaster Rovers in the second leg of the 3rd Division (North) Cup in March 1946. It lasted 3 hours, 23 minutes.

# Athletics
as at September 27th, 1972

| MEN | WORLD RECORDS | | UK NATIONAL RECORDS | |
|---|---|---|---|---|
| *Event* | *Name* | *Performance* | *Name* | *Performance* |
| 100 yards | R. Hayes (USA) | 9·1 s. | P. Radford | 9·4 s. |
| | H. Jerome (Can) | | | |
| | J. Hines (USA) | | | |
| | C. Greene (USA) | | | |
| | J. Carlos (USA) | | | |
| 100 metres | J. Hines (USA) | 9·9 s. | B. Green | 10·1 s. |
| | R. R. Smith (USA) | | | |
| | C. Greene (USA) | | | |
| | E. Hart (USA)* | | | |
| | R. Robinson (USA)* | | | |
| 200 metres (turn) | T. Smith (USA) | 19·8 s. | D. Jenkins* | 20·3 s. |
| | D. Quarrie (Jam) | | | |
| 220 yards (turn) | T. Smith (USA) | 20·0 s. | P. Radford | 20·5 s. |
| 400 metres | L. Evans (USA) | 43·8 s. | D. Jenkins | 45·3 s. |
| 440 yards | J. Smith (USA) | 44·5 s. | R. Brightwell | 45·9 s. |
| 800 metres | P. Snell (NZ) | 1 min. 44·3 s. | C. Campbell | 1 min. 46·1 s. |
| | R. Doubell (Aus) | | | |
| | D. Wottle (USA) | | | |
| 880 yards | J. Ryun (USA) | 1 min. 44·9 s. | C. Carter | 1 min. 47·2 s. |
| 1,000 metres | J. May (E. Ger) | 2 min. 16·2 s. | J. Boulter | 2 min. 18·2 s. |
| | F. J. Kemper (W. Ger) | | | |
| 1,500 metres | J. Ryun (USA) | 3 min. 33·1 s. | P. Stewart | 3 min. 38·2 s. |
| | | | B. Foster | |
| 1 mile | J. Ryun (USA) | 3 min. 51·1 s. | P. Stewart | 3 min. 55·3 s. |
| 2,000 metres | M. Jazy (Fra) | 4 min. 56·2 s. | D. Bedford | 5 min. 03·2 s. |
| 3,000 metres | K. Keino (Ke) | 7 min. 39·6 s. | D. Bedford | 7 min. 46·4 s. |
| | E. Puttemans (Bel)* | 7 min 37·6 s. | | |
| 2 miles | L. Viren (Fin) | 8 min. 14·0 s. | I Stewart | 8 min. 22·0 s. |
| 3 miles | E. Puttemans (Bel) | 12 min. 47·8 s. | D. Bedford | 12 min. 52·0 s. |
| 5,000 metres | E. Puttemans (Bel) | 13 min. 13·0 s. | D. Bedford | 13 min. 17·2 s. |
| 6 miles | R. Clarke (Aus) | 26 min. 47·0 s. | D. Bedford | 26 min. 51·6 s. |
| 10,000 metres | L. Viren (Fin) | 27 min. 38·4 s. | D. Bedford | 27 min. 47·0 s. |
| 10 miles | W. Polleunis (Bel) | 46 min. 04·8 s. | R. Hill | 46 min. 44·0 s. |

| MEN | WORLD RECORDS | | UK NATIONAL RECORDS | |
|---|---|---|---|---|
| *Event* | *Name* | *Performance* | *Name* | *Performance* |
| 20,000 metres | G. Roelants (Bel) | 57 min. 44·4 s. | R. Hill | 58 min. 39·0 s. |
| 15 miles | R. Hill (GB) | 1 hr. 12 min. 48·2 s. | R. Hill | 1 hr. 12 min. 48·2 s. |
| 25,000 metres | R. Hill (GB) | 1 hr. 15 min. 22·6 s. | R. Hill | 1 hr. 15 min. 22·6 s. |
| 30,000 metres | J. Alder (GB) | 1 hr. 31 min. 30·4 s. | J. Alder | 1 hr. 31 min. 30·4 s. |
| 1 hour | G. Roelants (Bel) | 20,784 metres | R. Hill | 20,471 metres |
| Marathon (unofficial) | D. Clayton (Aus) | 2 hr. 08 min. 33·6 s. | R. Hill | 2 hr. 09 min. 28·0 s. |
| 3,000 metres steeplechase | A. Garderud (Swed) | 8 min. 20·8 s. | A. Holden | 8 min. 26·4 s. |
| | | 8 min. 20·8 s. | D. Hemery | 13·6 s. |
| 120 yards hurdles | R. Mulburn (USA | 13·0 s. | D. Hemery | 13·6 s. |
| 110 metres hurdles | M. Lauer (W. Ger) | 13·2 s. | | |
| | J. Calhoun (USA) | | | |
| | E. McCullough (USA) | | | |
| | R. Milburn (USA) | | D. Hemery | 48·1 s. |
| 400 metres hurdles | L. Akii-Bua (Uga) | 47·8 s. | D. Hemery | 50·2 s. |
| 440 yards hurdles | R. Mann (USA) | 48·8 s. | | |
| | | | G. Miller | |
| High Jump | P. Matzdorf (USA) | 7 ft. 6¼ in. (2·29m) | | 6 ft. 10 in. (2·08m) |
| | | | M. Campbell | |
| | | | D. Livesey | |
| Long Jump | R. Beamon (USA) | 29 ft. 2½ in. (8·90m) | L. Davies | 27 ft. 0 in. (8·23m) |
| Triple Jump | P. Perez (Cuba) | 57 ft. 1 in. (17·40m) | F. Alsop | 54 ft. 0 in. (16·46m) |
| Pole Vault | R. Seagren (USA) | 18 ft. 5¾ in. (5·63m) | M. Bull | 17 ft. 1¼ in. (5·21m) |
| Shot | R. Matson (USA) | 71 ft. 5½ in. (21·78m) | G. Capes | 66 ft. 2½ in. (20·18m) |
| Discus | J. Silvester (USA | 224 ft. 5 in. (68·40m) | W. Tancred | 203 ft. 2 in. (61·94m) |
| | R. Bruch (Swed) | 225 ft. 0 in.* (68·58m) | | |

| MEN | WORLD RECORDS | | UK NATIONAL RECORDS | |
|---|---|---|---|---|
| *Event* | *Name* | *Performance* | *Name* | *Performance* |
| Hammer | W. Schmidt (W. Ger) | 250 ft. 8 in. (76·40m) | B. Williams | 227 ft. 9 in. (69·42m) |
| Javelin | J. Lusis (USSR) | 307 ft. 9 in. (93·80m) | D. Travis | 273 ft. 9 in. (83·44m) |
| Decathlon | N. Avilov (USSR) | 8,454 pts. | P. Gabbett | 7,903 pts. |

| WOMEN | WORLD RECORDS | | UK NATIONAL RECORDS | |
|---|---|---|---|---|
| *Event* | *Name* | *Performance* | *Name* | *Performance* |
| 100 yards | Chi Cheng (Tai) | 10·0 s. | H. Young D. Hyman M. Rand D. Arden | 10·6 s. |
| 100 metres | W. Tyus (USA) Chi Cheng (Tai) R. Meissner-Stecher (E. Ger) E. Stropahl (E. Ger)* E. Glenskova (Cz)* | 11·0 s. | D. Hyman D. James V. Peat | 11·3 s. |
| 200 metres | Chi Cheng (Tai) R. Stecher (E. Ger) | 22·4 s. | D. Hyman M. Critchley | 23·2 s. |
| 220 yards | Chi Cheng (Tai) | 22·6 s. | D. Arden | 23·6 s. |
| 400 metres | M. Neufville (Jam) M. Zehrt (E. Ger)* | 51·0 s. | L. Board | 52·1 s. |
| 440 yards | J. Pollock (Aus) | 52·4 s. | D. Watkinson | 54·1 s. |
| 800 metres | H. Falck (W. Ger) | 1 min. 58·5 s. | R. Stirling | 2 min. 00·2 s. |
| 880 Yards | D. Willis (Aus) J. Pollock (Aus) | 2 min. 02·2 s. | A. Smith | 2 min. 04·2 s. |
| 1,500 metres | L. Bragina (USSR) | 4 min. 01·4 s. | S. Carey | 4 min. 04·8 s. |
| 1 mile | E. Tittel (W. Ger) | 4 min. 35·3 s. | A. Smith | 4 min. 37·0 s. |
| 3,000 metres | L. Bragina (USSR) | 8 min. 53·0 s. | J. Smith | 9 min. 05·8 s. |
| 100 metres hurdles | A. Ehrhardt (E. Ger) P. Ryan (Aus) | 12·5 s. | J. Vernon | 13·2 s. |
| 200 metres hurdles | P. Kilborn-Ryan (Aus) | 25·7 s. | S. Colyear | 26·7 s. |
| High Jump | I. Gusenbauer (Aut) | 6 ft. 3½ in. (1·92m) | B. Inkpen | 6 ft. 1¼ in. (1·86m) |

| WOMEN | WORLD RECORDS | | UK NATIONAL RECORDS | |
|---|---|---|---|---|
| Event | Name | Performance | Name | Performance |
| | U. Meyfarth (W. Ger) | | | |
| | J. Blagoyeva (Bulg)* | | | |
| | | 6 ft. 4¼ in. | | |
| | | (1·94m) | | |
| Long Jump | H. Rosendahl (W. Ger) | | M. Rand | |
| | | 22 ft. 5¼ in. | | 22 ft. 2¼ in. |
| | | (6·84m) | | (6·76m) |
| Shot | N. Chizhova (USSR) | | M. Peters | |
| | | 69 ft. 0 in. | | 53 ft. 6¼ in. |
| | | (21·03m) | | (16·31m) |
| Discus | F. Melnik (USSR) | | R. Payne | |
| | | 219 ft. 0 in. | | 190 ft. 4 in. |
| | | (66·76m) | | (58·02m) |
| | A. Menis (Rum)* | 220 ft. 10 in. | | |
| | | (67·32m) | | |
| Javelin | R. Fuchs (E. Ger) | 213 ft. 5 in. | S. Platt | 182 ft. 5 in. |
| | | (65·06m) | | (55·60m) |
| Pentathalon | M. Peters (GB) | 4,801 pts | M. Peters | 4,801 pts. |

* Subject to confirmation

# The Olympic Games

The first recorded Olympiad is that of Choroebus, 776 BC. Ancient Greek chronology was reckoned in cycles of four years corresponding with the periodic Olympic Games held once in four years on the plain of Olympia in Elis. The intervening years were the first, second and third of the Olympiad which received the name of the victor at the Games.

The modern Olympic Games were revived in Athens in 1896 and meetings have been held as follows:

| | | | |
|---|---|---|---|
| Athens | 1896 | Berlin | 1916* |
| Paris | 1900 | Antwerp | 1920 |
| St Louis | 1904 | Paris | 1924 |
| Athens | 1906 | Amsterdam | 1928 |
| London | 1908 | Los Angeles | 1932 |
| Stockholm | 1912 | Berlin | 1936 |

| | | | |
|---|---|---|---|
| Tokyo, then | | Melbourne | 1956** |
| Helsinki | 1940* | Rome | 1960 |
| London | 1944* | Tokyo | 1964 |
| London | 1948 | Mexico | 1968 |
| Helsinki | 1952 | Munich | 1972 |

* cancelled due to World Wars
** equestrian events held at Stockholm, Sweden

THE WINTER OLYMPICS were inaugurated in 1924 and meetings have been held as follows:

| | | | |
|---|---|---|---|
| France | 1924 | Italy | 1956 |
| Switzerland | 1928 | USA | 1960 |
| USA | 1932 | Austria | 1964 |
| Germany | 1936 | France | 1968 |
| Switzerland | 1948 | Japan | 1972 |
| Norway | 1952 | | |

# The Olympic Oath

The Olympic Oath is pronounced on behalf of all the assembled athletes by a contestant from the country where the Games are taking place. It runs:

'In the name of all competitors I promise that we will take part in these Olympic Games, respecting and abiding by the rules which govern them, in the true spirit of sportsmanship, for the glory of sport and for the honour of our teams.'

# Boxing

The British Boxing Board of Control (the BBBC) was formed in 1929.

In the old days of prize fighting there were no weight divisions. Indeed, weight divisions only began to be talked about in the 1850s and 1860s and there was no standardization until after the Queensberry Rules, compiled by the Marquess of Queensberry, Lord Lonsdale and Arthur Chambers (who later became lightweight champion of the world) had been widely adopted in the 1880s.

## WORLD CHAMPIONS
(as at September 22nd, 1972)

| | |
|---|---|
| **Heavyweight** | Joe Frazier |
| **Light Heavyweight** | Bob Foster |
| **Middleweight** | Carlos Monzon |
| **Welterweight** | Jose Napoles |
| **Lightweight** | Roberto Duran |
| **Featherweight** | Clemente Sanchez |
| **Bantamweight** | Enrique Pinder |
| **Flyweight** | Betulio Gonzales |

## BRITISH CHAMPIONS
(as at September 22nd, 1972)

| | | Weight limit |
|---|---|---|
| **Heavyweight** | Dan McAlinden | no upper limit |
| **Light Heavyweight** | Chris Finnegan | 12 st. 7 lb. |
| **Middleweight** | Bunny Sterling | 11 st. 6 lb. |
| **Welterweight** | Vacant | 10 st. 7 lb. |
| **Lightweight** | Vacant | 9 st. 9 lb. |
| **Featherweight** | Evan Armstrong | 9 st. |
| **Bantamweight** | Vacant | 8 st. 6 lb. |
| **Flyweight** | John McCluskey | 8 st. |

## COMMONWEALTH CHAMPIONS
(as at September 22nd, 1972)

| | | | |
|---|---|---|---|
| **Heavyweight** | Dan McAlinden | **Lightweight** | Percy Hayles |
| **Light Heavyweight** | Chris Finnegan | **Featherweight** | Toro George |
| **Middleweight** | Bunny Sterling | **Bantamweight** | Paul Ferrari |
| **Welterweight** | Ralph Charles | **Flyweight** | Henry Nissen |

## EUROPEAN CHAMPIONS
(as at September 22nd, 1972)

| | | | |
|---|---|---|---|
| **Heavyweight** | Joe Bugner | **Lightweight** | Antonio Puddu |
| **Light Heavyweight** | Chris Finnegan | **Featherweight** | Jose Legra |
| **Middleweight** | Jean Claude Bouttier | **Bantamweight** | Augustin Senin |
| **Welterweight** | Roger Menetrey | **Flyweight** | Fritz Chervet |

## WORLD HEAVYWEIGHT CHAMPIONS
(as at September 22nd, 1972)

| | | | | | |
|---|---|---|---|---|---|
| **1949** | Ezzard Charles | USA | **1952** | Rocky Marciano | USA |
| **1951** | Jersey Joe Walcott | USA | **1956** | Floyd Patterson | USA |

| 1959 | Ingemar Johansson | Sweden | 1964 | Cassius Clay | USA |
|------|-------------------|--------|------|--------------|-----|
| 1960 | Floyd Patterson | USA | 1970 | Joe Frazier | USA |
| 1962 | Sonny Liston | USA | | | |

Only two men have held British titles at three different weights. Len Harvey – middleweight champion 1929–33, light heavyweight 1933–34 and 1938–42, heavyweight 1933–34 and 1938–42. And Ted 'Kid' Lewis who was featherweight champion 1913–14, welterweight 1920–24, and middleweight 1920 (unofficial) and 1921–23.

The greatest purse in boxing has been £1,041,667 guaranteed to Joe Frazier and Cassius Clay (Muhammad Ali Haj) for their 15-round fight at Madison Square Gardens on March 8th, 1971.

# Cricket

Summarized results of 707 TEST MATCHES from 1877 to 1972: (as at September 30th, 1972)

| Australia v | W | D | L | New Zealand v | W | D | L |
|-------------|-----|-----|-----|---------------|-----|-----|-----|
| England | 82 | 62 | 70 | England | 0 | 22 | 20 |
| South Africa | 29 | 13 | 11 | Australia | 0 | 0 | 1 |
| West Indies | 17* | 7 | 6 | South Africa | 2 | 6 | 9 |
| New Zealand | 1 | 0 | 0 | West Indies | 2 | 7 | 5 |
| India | 16 | 6 | 3 | India | 2 | 7 | 7 |
| Pakistan | 2 | 3 | 1 | Pakistan | 1 | 7 | 4 |
| **England v** | | | | **Pakistan v** | | | |
| Australia | 70 | 62 | 82 | England | 1 | 11 | 9 |
| South Africa | 46 | 38 | 18 | Australia | 1 | 3 | 2 |
| West Indies | 20 | 22 | 16 | West Indies | 3 | 1 | 4 |
| New Zealand | 20 | 22 | 0 | New Zealand | 4 | 7 | 1 |
| India | 18 | 18 | 4 | India | 1 | 12 | 2 |
| Pakistan | 9 | 11 | 1 | **South Africa v** | | | |
| Rest of the World | 1 | 0 | 4 | England | 18 | 38 | 46 |
| | | | | Australia | 11 | 13 | 29 |
| **Rest of the World v.** | | | | New Zealand | 9 | 6 | 2 |
| England | 4 | 0 | 1 | | | | |
| **India v** | | | | **West Indies v** | | | |
| England | 4 | 18 | 18 | England | 16 | 22 | 20 |
| Australia | 3 | 6 | 16 | Australia | 6 | 7* | 17 |
| West Indies | 1 | 15 | 12 | New Zealand | 5 | 7 | 2 |
| New Zealand | 7 | 7 | 2 | India | 12 | 15 | 1 |
| Pakistan | 2 | 12 | 1 | Pakistan | 4 | 1 | 3 |

*Including one tie.

## HIGHEST INNINGS TOTAL
903 – 7 dec. by England at the Oval, 1938.

## LOWEST INNINGS TOTAL
36 by Australia at Birmingham, 1902.

## HIGHEST TEST WICKET PARTNERSHIPS

**413 for 1st**    V. Mankad (231) and P. Roy (173) for India v N. Zealand at Madras, 1955–6.

**451 for 2nd**    W. H. Ponsford (226) and D. G. Bradman (244) for Australia v England at The Oval, 1934.

**370 for 3rd**    W. J. Edrich (189) and D. C. S. Compton (208) for England v S. Africa at Lord's, 1947.

**411 for 4th**    P. B. H. May (285)* and M. C. Cowdrey (154) for England v West Indies at Birmingham, 1957.

**405 for 5th**    S. G. Barnes (234) and D. G. Bradman (234) for Australia v England at Sydney, 1946–7.

**346 for 6th**    J. H. Fingleton (136) and D. G. Bradman (270) for Australia v England at Melbourne, 1936–7.

**347 for 7th**    D. Atkinson (219) and C. Depeiza (122) for West Indies v Australia at Bridgetown, 1954–5.

**246 for 8th**    L. E. G. Ames (137) and G. O. Allen (122) for England v N. Zealand at Lord's, 1931.

**190 for 9th**    Asif Iqbal (146) and Intikhab Alam (51) for Pakistan v England at The Oval, 1967.

**130 for 10th**    R. E. Foster (287) and W. Rhodes (40)* for England v Australia at Sydney, 1903–4.

*Indicates not out.

## MOST WICKETS IN A TEST SERIES

| | Tests | Runs | Wkts. | Av. | |
|---|---|---|---|---|---|
| S. F. Barnes | 4 | 536 | 49 | 10·93 | England v S. Africa 1913–14 |
| J. C. Laker | 5 | 442 | 46 | 9·60 | England v Australia 1956 |
| C. V. Grimmett | 5 | 642 | 44 | 14·59 | Australia v S. Africa 1935–6 |
| A. V. Bedser | 5 | 682 | 39 | 17·48 | England v Australia 1953 |
| M. W. Tate | 5 | 881 | 38 | 23·18 | England v Australia 1924–5 |
| W. J. Whitty | 5 | 632 | 37 | 17·08 | Australia v S. Africa 1910–11 |
| H. J. Tayfield | 5 | 636 | 37 | 17·18 | S. Africa v England 1956–7 |
| A. E. E. Vogler | 5 | 783 | 36 | 21·75 | S. Africa v England 1909–10 |
| A. A. Mailey | 5 | 946 | 36 | 26·27 | Australia v England 1920–21 |
| G. A. Lohmann | 3 | 203 | 35 | 5·80 | England v S. Africa 1895–6 |

## TEST HAT TRICKS
(since the 1939-45 war)

| | | |
|---|---|---|
| **P. J. Loader** | England v West Indies, Leeds | 1957 |
| **L. F. Kline** | Australia v S. Africa, Cape Town | 1957–8 |
| **W. W. Hall** | West Indies v Pakistan, Lahore | 1958–9 |
| **G. M. Griffin** | S. Africa v England, Lord's | 1960 |
| **L. R. Gibbs** | W. Indies v Australia, Adelaide | 1960–1 |
| **E. J. Barlow** | Rest of World v England, Leeds | 1970 |

## WICKET KEEPING FEATS
(Most victims in a Test career)

| | | |
|---|---|---|
| **T. G. Evans** | England | 219 in 91 matches |
| **A. T. W. Grout** | Australia | 187 in 51 matches |
| **J. H. B. Waite** | S. Africa | 141 in 50 matches |
| **W. A. Oldfield** | Australia | 130 in 54 matches |

## COUNTY CHAMPIONSHIPS

| | | | |
|---|---|---|---|
| **1946** Yorkshire | **1953** Surrey | **1959** Yorkshire | **1965** Worcestershire |
| **1947** Middlesex | **1954** Surrey | **1960** Yorkshire | **1966** Yorkshire |
| **1948** Glamorgan | **1955** Surrey | **1961** Hampshire | **1967** Yorkshire |
| **1949** Middlesex and Yorks tie | **1956** Surrey | **1962** Yorkshire | **1968** Yorkshire |
| | | **1963** Yorkshire | **1969** Glamorgan |
| **1950** Lancs and Surrey tie | **1957** Surrey | **1964** Worcestershire | **1970** Kent |
| **1951** Warwickshire | **1958** Surrey | | **1971** Surrey |
| **1952** Surrey | | | **1972** Warwickshire |

## GILLETTE 'KNOCK OUT' CUP

| | | |
|---|---|---|
| **1963** Sussex | **1968** Warwickshire |
| **1964** Sussex | **1969** Yorkshire |
| **1965** Yorkshire | **1970** Lancashire |
| **1966** Warwickshire | **1971** Lancashire |
| **1967** Kent | **1972** Lancashire |

Highest total in Gillette Cup: 327-7 (60 overs), Gloucestershire versus Berkshire at Reading, 1966

## JOHN PLAYER LEAGUE WINNERS

| | | |
|---|---|---|
| **1969** Lancashire | **1971** Worcestershire |
| **1970** Lancashire | **1972** Kent |

Highest total in John Player League: 288–6, Sussex versus Middlesex at Hove, 1969

**YOUNGEST TEST PLAYER**
Mushtaq Mohamed (13 years 124 days) for Pakistan v West Indies, Lahore 1958

**OLDEST TEST PLAYER**
J. Southerton (49 years 119 days) for England v Australia, Melbourne 1876

**FASTEST TEST FIFTY**
J. J. Brown in 28 minutes for England v Australia 1894–5

**FASTEST TEST CENTURY**
J. M. Gregory in 70 minutes for Australia v South Africa at Johannesburg 1920–21

**FASTEST DOUBLE CENTURY**
D. G. Bradman in 214 minutes for Australia v England 1930

**MOST RUNS IN A DAY BY ONE BATSMAN**
D. G. Bradman (309) for Australia v England 1930

# Golf

The earliest mention of the game of golf is in 1457 when the Scottish Parliament passed a law under which 'golfe be utterly cryed downe'.

The oldest Club is the Honourable Company of Edinburgh Golfers, formed in 1744, ten years before the Royal and Ancient Club at St. Andrews, Fife.

## OPEN CHAMPIONS

The Open Championship was inaugurated in 1860 at Prestwick, Ayrshire, Scotland.

| | | | | | |
|---|---|---|---|---|---|
| 1946 | Sam Snead | USA | 1959 | Gary Player | S. Africa |
| 1947 | Fred Daly | Balmoral | 1960 | Ken Nagle | Australia |
| 1948 | Henry Cotton | Royal mid-Surrey | 1961 | A. Palmer | USA |
| | | | 1962 | A. Palmer | USA |
| 1949 | Bobby Locke | S. Africa | 1963 | Bob Charles | N. Zealand |
| 1950 | Bobby Locke | S. Africa | 1964 | A. Lema | USA |
| 1951 | Max Faulkner | unattached | 1965 | Peter Thomson | Australia |
| 1952 | Bobby Locke | S. Africa | 1966 | J. Nicklaus | USA |
| 1953 | Ben Hogan | USA | 1967 | R. de Vincenzo | Argentine |
| 1954 | Peter Thomson | Australia | 1968 | Gary Player | S. Africa |
| 1955 | Peter Thomson | Australia | 1969 | A. Jacklin | Potters Bar |

| **1956** | Peter Thomson | Australia | **1970** | J. Nicklaus | USA |
| **1957** | Bobby Locke | S. Africa | **1971** | L. Trevino | USA |
| **1958** | Peter Thomson | Australia | **1972** | L. Trevino | USA |

## WORLD CUP

The World Cup, first competed for in 1953, was originally called the Canada Cup. It has been won most often by the USA.

| **1956** | USA | **1962** | USA | **1967** | USA |
| **1957** | Japan | **1963** | USA | **1968** | Canada |
| **1958** | Ireland | **1964** | USA | **1969** | USA |
| **1959** | Australia | **1965** | South Africa | **1970** | Australia |
| **1960** | USA | **1966** | USA | **1971** | USA |
| **1961** | USA | | | | |

THE HIGHEST GOLF COURSE in the world is the Tuctu Golf Club in Peru which at its lowest point above sea-level is 14,335 ft.

THE LONGEST HOLE in the world is the 17th of 745 yards at the Black Mountain Golf Club, North Carolina, USA.

THE LONGEST HOLE on a championship course in Great Britain is the 6th at Troon, Ayrshire. It stretches 580 yards.

THE LONGEST RECORDED DRIVE – a distance of 445 yards – was made by Edward C. Bliss at Herne Bay, Kent, in 1931.

THE LONGEST HOLE EVER HOLED IN ONE was the 10th hole (440 yards) at Miracle Hills Golf Club, Omaha, Nebraska, USA. Robert Mitera achieved the feat on October 7th, 1965.

# Lawn Tennis

The All England Croquet and Lawn Tennis Club staged the first tournament in 1877. The rules laid down then remain the basic rules of the game today.

The oldest and most outstanding individual lawn tennis tournament of the world is Wimbledon. The Wimbledon Championships have always been played on grass. The first Championship was held at Wimbledon in June 1877. Professionals first played in 1968.

The outstanding team event is the contest for the Davis Cup, which began as a challenge match between Great Britain and the United States in 1900. The Davis Cup, more properly called the International Lawn Tennis Championship, is competed for on a knock-out principle and is divided into three zones – European, American and Eastern.

The Wightman Cup – officially called the Ladies' International Lawn Tennis Championship – is competed for every year in alternate countries between Great Britain and the United States. It was begun in 1923.

## WIMBLEDON CHAMPIONS

|  | Men's Singles | Women's Singles |
|---|---|---|
| 1946 | Y. Petra | Miss P. Betz |
| 1947 | J. A. Kramer | Miss M. Osborne |
| 1948 | R. Falkenburg | Miss A. Brough |
| 1949 | F. R. Schroeder | Miss A. Brough |
| 1950 | J. E. Patty | Miss A. Brough |
| 1951 | R. Savitt | Miss D. Hart |
| 1952 | F. A. Sedgman | Miss M. Connolly |
| 1953 | E. V. Seixas | Miss M. Connolly |
| 1954 | J. Drobny | Miss M. Connolly |
| 1955 | M. A. Trabert | Miss A. Brough |
| 1956 | L. A. Hoad | Miss S. Fry |
| 1957 | L. A. Hoad | Miss A. Gibson |
| 1958 | A. J. Cooper | Miss A. Gibson |
| 1959 | A. Olmedo | Miss M. Bueno |
| 1960 | N. Fraser | Miss M. Bueno |
| 1961 | R. Laver | Miss A. Mortimer |
| 1962 | R. Laver | Miss K. Susman |
| 1963 | E. McKinley | Miss M. Smith |
| 1964 | R. Emerson | Miss M. Bueno |
| 1965 | R. Emerson | Miss M. Smith |
| 1966 | M. Santana | Mrs L. W. King |
| 1967 | J. D. Newcombe | Mrs L. W. King |
| 1968 | R. Laver* | Mrs L. W. King* |
| 1969 | R. Laver* | Mrs P. F. Jones* |
| 1970 | J. D. Newcombe* | Mrs B. M. Court |
| 1971 | J. D. Newcombe* | Miss E. F. Goolagong* |
| 1972 | S. Smith | Mrs L. W. King* |

73 (* = Professional)          KING

# University Boat Race

Rowed on the River Thames from Putney to Mortlake – a distance of 4 miles, 374 yards. It began in 1829 as the result of a challenge issued to Oxford 'that the University of Cambridge hereby challenge the University of Oxford to row a match at or near London each in an eight-oared boat during the Easter vacation'. Cambridge have won 66 times, Oxford 51, and there has been one dead-heat.

74 Jimi Connors + Chris Everet.

# Motor Racing

The first motor race took place in France in 1894. It was won by Count de Dion who drove a de Dion steam vehicle from Paris to Rouen at a speed of 11·6 mph.

The International Gordon Bennet races began in 1900 and were later replaced by the French Grand Prix, a contest between manufacturers rather than nations.

The British Grand Prix originated at Brooklands, Surrey, in 1926.

The Monaco Grand Prix, a 'round-the-houses' race usually opens the European season. It was first run in 1929.

Sportscar racing, which more or less began with the 24-hour Grand Prix d'Endurance at Le Mans in 1923 is very popular. The Le Mans 24-hour Sports Car Race is one of the world's most exciting and best-known motor races.

## CHAMPIONS
(as at September 22nd, 1972)

| | |
|---|---|
| Buenos Aires Grand Prix | Jackie Stewart (Tyrrell-Ford) |
| South African Grand Prix | Denny Hulme (McLaren) |
| Spanish Grand Prix | Emerson Fittipaldi (John Player Special) |
| Monaco Grand Prix | Jean-Pierre Beltoise (Marlborough BRM) |
| Belgian Grand Prix | Emerson Fittipaldi (John Player Special) |
| French Grand Prix | Jackie Stewart (Tyrrell-Ford) |
| British Grand Prix | Emerson Fittipaldi (John Player Special) |
| German Grand Prix | Jackie Ickx (Ferrari) |
| Austrian Grand Prix | Emerson Fittipaldi (John Player Special) |
| Italian Grand Prix | Emerson Fittipaldi (John Player Special) |
| Canadian Grand Prix | Jackie Stewart (Tyrrell-Ford) |
| Monte Carlo Rally | Sandro Munari & Mario Mannucci (Lancia) |
| 24-Hour – Le Mans | Graham Hill & Henri Pescarolo (Matra-Simca 6-60) |

# Rugby

The Rugby Football Union was formed in 1871. But the game of Rugby Football is thought to date from 1823 when a player at Rugby School took the ball in his arms and ran with it. From this breakage of the football rules a new game gradually evolved.

As a result of an argument about whether players should be compensated for loss of earnings sustained as a result of playing the game, twenty-two clubs from Yorkshire, Lancashire and Cheshire left the Rugby Union in

1895 and founded what became known as the Rugby League. The major differences between Rugby League and Rugby Union today are that Rugby League is played on a professional or an amateur basis with 13 players and Rugby Union is played on an amateur basis with 15 players.

The Rugby League Challenge Cup competition was inaugurated in 1897, the winners being Batley who defeated St Helens.

## CHALLENGE CUP COMPETITION

| | | | | | |
|---|---|---|---|---|---|
| 1945 | Huddersfield | 1953 | Huddersfield | 1964 | Widnes |
| 1946 | Wakefield Trinity | 1954 | Warrington | 1965 | Wigan |
| 1947 | Bradford Northern | 1955 | Barrow | 1966 | St Helens |
| | | 1956 | St Helens | 1967 | Featherstone Rovers |
| 1948 | Wigan | 1957 | Leeds | | |
| 1949 | Bradford Northern | 1958 | Wigan | 1968 | Leeds |
| | | 1959 | Wigan | 1969 | Castleford |
| 1950 | Warrington | 1960 | Wakefield Trinity | 1970 | Castleford |
| 1951 | Wigan | 1961 | St Helens | 1971 | Leigh |
| 1952 | Workington Town | 1962 | Wakefield Trinity | 1972 | St Helens |
| | | 1963 | Wakefield Trinity | | |

# Rugby Union

## INTERNATIONAL CHAMPIONSHIP

An annual competition between England, Scotland, Wales and France.

| | | | |
|---|---|---|---|
| 1947 | Wales and England, tie | 1960 | England and France, tie |
| 1948 | Ireland | 1961 | France |
| 1949 | Ireland | 1962 | France |
| 1950 | Wales | 1963 | England |
| 1951 | Ireland | 1964 | Scotland and Wales, tie |
| 1952 | Wales | 1965 | Wales |
| 1953 | England | 1966 | Wales |
| 1954 | England, France and Wales tie | 1967 | France |
| | | 1968 | France |
| 1955 | Wales and France, tie | 1969 | Wales |
| 1956 | Wales | 1970 | France and Wales, tie |
| 1957 | England | 1971 | Wales |
| 1958 | England | 1972 | (No result) |
| 1959 | France | | |

## COUNTY CHAMPIONSHIP

| | | | |
|---|---|---|---|
| **1950** | Cheshire | **1962** | Warwickshire |
| **1951** | East Midlands | **1963** | Warwickshire |
| **1952** | Middlesex | **1964** | Warwickshire |
| **1953** | Yorkshire | **1965** | Warwickshire |
| **1954** | Middlesex | **1966** | Middlesex |
| **1955** | Lancashire | **1967** | Surrey and Durham |
| **1956** | Middlesex | **1968** | Middlesex |
| **1957** | Devon | **1969** | Lancashire |
| **1958** | Warwickshire | **1970** | Staffordshire |
| **1959** | Warwickshire | **1971** | Surrey |
| **1960** | Warwickshire | **1972** | Gloucestershire |
| **1961** | Cheshire | | |

# Swimming

## WORLD AND BRITISH NATIVE LONG COURSE RECORDS
(as at December, 1972)

### MEN

| | *World* | min. s. | *British Native* | min. s. |
|---|---|---|---|---|
| **Freestyle** | | | | |
| 100 m. | M. Spitz (USA) | 51·22 | R. B. McGregor | 53·4 |
| 200 m. | M. Spitz (USA) | 1:52·78 | B. Brinkley | 1:56·99 |
| 400 m. | K. Krumpholz (USA) | 4:00·1 | B. Brinkley | 4:06·69 |
| 800 m. | G. Windeatt (Aus.) | 8:28·6 | B. Brinkley | 8:42·6 |
| 1,500 m. | M. Burton (USA) | 15:52·58 | B. Brinkley | 16:39·8 |
| **Breaststroke** | | | | |
| 100 m. | N. Taguchi (Japan) | 1:04·94 | D. Wilkie | 1:06·35 |
| 200 m. | J. Henken (USA) | 2:21·55 | D. Wilkie | 2:23·67 |
| **Butterflystroke** | | | | |
| 100 m. | M. Spitz (USA) | 54·27 | J. Mills | 58·13 |
| 200 m. | H. Fassnacht (GFR) | 2:00·70 | B. Brinkley | 2:05·6 |
| **Backstroke** | | | | |
| 100 m. | R. Matthes (DDR) | 56·3 | C. Cunningham | 1:00·3 |
| 200 m. | R. Matthes (DDR) | 2:02·82 | C. Cunningham | 2:09·5 |
| **Individual Medley** | | | | |
| 200 m. | G. Larsson (Swe) | 2:07·17 | R. J. Terrell | 2:11·9 |
| 400 m. | G. Hall (USA) | 4:31·0 | R. J. Terrell | 4:42·7 |

**Freestyle Relay**

4×100 m.  USA (D. Edgar, J.
            Murphy, J. Heindenrich,
            M. Spitz)            3:26·42   No record

4×200 m.  USA (M. Spitz, S.
            Genter, F. Tyler, J.
            Kinsella)            7:35·78   No record

**Medley Relay**

4×100 m.  USA (M. Stamm, T.
            Bruce, M. Spitz, J.
            Heidenrich)          3:48·16   No record

# WORLD AND BRITISH NATIVE LONG COURSE RECORDS
(as at December, 1972)

## WOMEN

| | *World* | | *British Native* | |
|---|---|---|---|---|
| **Freestyle** | | min. s. | | min. s. |
| 100 m. | S. Gould (Aus.) | 58·05 | A. E. Jackson | 1:00·5 |
| 200 m. | S. Gould (Aus.) | 2:03·6 | L. Allardice | 2:12·2 |
| 400 m. | S. Gould (Aus.) | 4:19·04 | J. Green | 4:35·4 |
| 800 m. | S. Gould (Aus.) | 8:53·68 | J. Green | 9:31·3 |
| 1,500 m. | S. Gould (Aus.) | 17:00·6 | (Standard time) | 19:40·0 |
| **Breaststroke** | | | | |
| 100 m. | C. Carr (USA) | 1:13·58 | D. Harrison | 1:16·53 |
| 200 m. | C. Ball (USA) | 2:38·5 | D. Harrison | 2:45·0 |
| **Butterflystroke** | | | | |
| 100 m. | M. Aoki (Japan) | 1:03·34 | J. Jeavons | 1:06·6 |
| 200 m. | K. Moe (USA) | 2:15·57 | J. Jeavons | 2:23·6 |
| **Backstroke** | | | | |
| 100 m. | K. Muir (S. Africa) | 1:05·6 | L. K. Ludgrove | 1:08·7 |
| 200 m. | M. Belote (USA) | 2:19·19 | W. Burrell | 2:26·2 |
| **Individual Medley** | | | | |
| 200 m. | S. Gould (Aus.) | 2:23·07 | S. H. Ratcliffe | 2:29·5 |
| 400 m. | G. Neall (Aus.) | 5:02·97 | S. H. Ratcliffe | 5:15·4 |

**Freestyle Relay**

4×100 m.  USA (S. Neilson,
            J. Kemp, J. Barkman,
            S. Babashoff)        3:55·19   No record

**Medley Relay**

4×100 m.  USA (M. Belote,
            C. Carr, D. Dearduff,
            S. Neilson)          4:20·75   No record

# 13 MEDICINE

## The Hippocratic Oath

Hippocrates, the 'father of medicine', was born on the island of Cos off the coast of Asia Minor in about 460 BC. Little is known of his life except that he taught and practised medicine in Cos and other parts of Greece and died at a great age.

Stethoscopes and thermometers were not then known, and Hippocrates used his own powers of observation and logical reasoning to diagnose disease. His abilities as a physician were venerated by medical men in the ages which followed. The oath of Hippocrates, an appeal for correct conduct, was perhaps the greatest legacy he left to the medical profession. It has been adopted by medical men as an ethical code or ideal – it is not a law. It is still used during the graduation ceremony at certain universities and schools of medicine. It runs as follows:

'I will look upon him who shall have taught me this Art even as one of my parents. I will share my substance with him, and I will supply his necessities, if he be in need. I will regard his offspring even as my own brethren, and I will teach them this Art, if they would learn it, without fee or covenant. I will impart this Art by precept, by lecture and by every mode of teaching, not only to my own sons but to the sons of him who has taught me, and to disciples bound by covenant and oath, according to the Law of Medicine.

'The regimen I adopt shall be for the benefit of my patients according to my ability and judgement, and not for their hurt or for any wrong. I will give no deadly drug to any, though it be asked of me, nor will I counsel such, and especially I will not aid a woman to procure abortion. Whatsoever house I enter, there will I go for the benefit of the sick, refraining from all wrong doing or corruption, and especially from any act of seduction, of male or female, of bond or free. Whatsoever things I see or hear concerning the life of men, in my attendance on the sick or even apart therefrom, which ought not to be noised abroad, I will keep silence thereon, counting such things to be as sacred secrets.'

# Medical Note

Normal Pulse – 72 per minute
Normal Breathing – 15–18 per minute
Normal body Temperature – 98·4 deg.

## BRIEF NURSING GLOSSARY

**Abrasion** – superficial injury: scraping of the skin

**Ampoule** – small sealed glass phial containing a drug

**Antibiotic** – a substance, derived from fungi or moulds, used to treat infection

**Antiseptic** – a substance which inhibits the growth of bacteria

**Bacteria** – minute living creatures. Many are beneficial, but many cause disease

**Calorie** – amount of heat required to raise 1 kg of water through 1° C. Used as a unit to estimate the value of food

**Chiropody** – treatment of foot conditions

**Deodorant** – a substance which masks or destroys an unpleasant smell

**Diagnosis** – identification of the disease from which the patient is suffering

**Dyspnoea** – difficult breathing

**Haemorrhage** – loss of blood

**Immunity** – resistance to infection

**Malaise** – feeling of illness or discomfort

**Narcotic** – a drug which produces deep sleep

**Occupational Therapy** – occupations for treatment in either physical or mental illness

**Physiotherapy** – treatment with physical measures, such as heat, light, massage and exercise

**Paediatrics** – branch of medicine dealing with childen

**Radiograph** – an X-ray picture

**Sphygmomanometer** – apparatus for measuring blood pressure

**X-rays** – short rays of the electro magnietic spectrum, used for diagnosis or treatment

# 14 INVENTION AND DISCOVERY

## Discoveries and Innovations in Chemistry, Physics, Biology and Medicine

| Invention/Discovery | Name | Nationality | Date |
|---|---|---|---|
| Adrenalin | Takamine | Japanese | 1901 |
| Antiseptic surgery | Lister | English | 1867 |
| Aspirin | Dreser | German | 1889 |
| Atomic Theory | Dalton | English | 1803 |
| Bleaching Powder | Tennant | English | 1798 |
| Chloroform | Guthrie, S. | American | 1831 |
| Cocaine | Niemann | German | 1860 |
| Cosmic Rays | Gockel | Swiss | 1910 |
| Cyanide | Caro, Frank | German | 1905 |
| Evolution (Natural Selection) | Darwin | English | 1858 |
| Human Heart Transplant | Barnard | S. African | 1967 |
| Insulin | Bantry, Best, MacLeod | Canadian | 1922 |
| Neutron | Chadwick | English | 1932 |
| Oxygen | Priestley | English | 1774 |
| Penicillin | Fleming, Alexander | English | 1929 |
| Radioactivity | Becquerel | French | 1896 |
| Radium | Curie, Pierre | French | 1896 |
| Streptomycin | Waksman | American | 1945 |
| Sulphuric Acid | Phillips | English | 1831 |
| Vitamin A | McCollum, Davis | American | 1913 |
| Vitamin B | McCollum | American | 1916 |

| Invention/Discovery | Name | Nationality | |
|---|---|---|---|
| Vitamin C | Holst, Froelich | Norwegian | 1912 |
| Vitamin D | McCollum | American | 1922 |
| Uranium fission, (atomic reactor) | Enrico Fermi } Leo Szilard } | Italian American | 1942 |

# Great Inventions and Scientific Discoveries

| Invention/Discovery | Name | Date |
|---|---|---|
| Adding Machine | Blaise Pascal (France) | 1642 |
| Air Conditioning | Willis H. Carrier (USA) | 1911 |
| Balloon | Jacques and Joseph Montgolfier (France) | 1783 |
| Barometer | Evangelista Torricelli (Italy) | 1643 |
| Bicycle | Kirkpatrick Macmillan (Scotland) | 1839 |
| Bifocal lens | Benjamin Franklin (USA) | 1780 |
| Car (Internal combustion) | Jean Joseph Etienne Lenoir (France) | patented 1860 |
| Car (Petrol driven) | Karl-Friedrich Benz (Ger.) | patented 1886 |
| Cash Register | James Ritty (USA) | 1879 |
| Cathode Ray Tube | Karl Ferdinand Braun (Ger.) | 1897 (first commercial use) |
| Cement | L. J. Vicat (France) | 1824 (invented cement made from chalk and clay) |
| Clock (Earliest mechanical) | I'Hsing and Liang Ling-tsan (China) | Completed AD 725 |
| Clock (Pendulum) | Christian Huygens (Holland) | 1657 |
| Dynamite | Alfred Nobel (Sweden) | Invented 1867 |
| Dynamo | Antonio Picinotti (Italy) | 1860 |
| Electric lamp | Thomas Alva Edison (USA) | 1879 |
| Electronic Computer | J. G. Brainerd, J. P. Eckert, J. W. Manchly (USA) | 1942 |
| Gas Turbine Engine | John Barber (England) | 1791 |

| Invention/Discovery | Name | Date |
|---|---|---|
| Gear (Differential) | Onésiphore Pecquer (France) | Invented 1828 |
| Gramophone (Phonograph) | Thomas Alva Edison (USA) | Patented 1878 |
| Gyro compass | Elmer Sperry (USA) | 1911 |
| Hovercraft | Sir Christopher Cockerell (Britain) | Patented 1955 |
| Incubator | Cornelius Drebbel (Holland) | 1666 (Patented by John Champion of London 1770) |
| Jet engine | Sir Frank Whittle (England) | 1929 (An engine similar to Whittle's was patented by a Frenchman, Guillaume in 1900. Earliest test-bed run, 1937) |
| Lifeboat | Henry Greathead (England) | Invented 1789 (Patent granted to Lukin, 1785) |
| Lightning conductor | Benjamin Franklin (USA) | Invented 1752 |
| Long-playing Record | Dr Peter Goldmark (USA) | First introduced 1948 |
| Magnetic Recording | Vlademar Poulsen (Denmark) | Patent filed 1898 |
| Margarine | Hippolyte Mège-Mouries (France) | 1863 |
| Match (Safety) | J. E. Lundstrom (Sweden) | 1855 |
| Microphone | Alexander Graham Bell (USA) | 1876 |
| Microscope | Zacharias Janssen (Netherlands) | 1590 |
| Nylon | Dr Wallace H. Carothers (USA) | 1937 |
| Parking Meter | Carl C. Magee (USA) | Installed in Oklahoma, USA, 1935 |
| Passenger lift | Elisha G. Otis (USA) | 1852 |
| Piano | Bartolommeo Cristofori (Italy) | Earliest in existence, 1720 |

| Invention/Discovery | Name | Date |
|---|---|---|
| Radar | Robert Watson-Watt (Britain) | 1935 |
| Radio | Guglielmo Marconi (Italy/Ireland) | 1896 (First patent for a system of communication by means of electromagnetic waves) |
| Rayon | Sir Joseph Swan (British) | 1883 |
| Rubber (latex foam) | E. A. Murphy (British) | 1928 |
| Rubber (vulcanized) | Charles Goodyear (USA) | 1841 |
| Safety-pin | William Hunt (USA) | 1849 |
| Safety razor | William Samuel Henson (England) | 1847 |
| Telephone | { J. Philip Reis (Germany) | 1861 |
| | Alexander Graham Bell (USA) | 1876 |
| Telescope (Refracting) | Johannes Lippershey (Netherlands) | 1608 |
| Telegraph | William Coke, Charles Wheatstone (British) | 1837 |
| Terylene | J. R. Whinfield, J. T. Dickson (England) | 1941 |
| Thermometer | Galileo Galilei (Italy) | 1593 |
| Transistor | Shockley, Brittain and Bardeen (USA) | 1947 |
| Typewriter | Austin Burt (USA) | Invented 1829 (First patented by Henry Mill, 1744) |
| Zip fastener | Whitcomb L. Judson (USA) | Patent issued 1891 |

THE EARLIEST CROSSWORD PUZZLE was invented by Liverpool-born Arthur Wynne, and published in the 'New York World' on December 21st, 1913.

THE LARGEST CROSSWORD PUZZLE – with over 3,000 clues down and over 3,000 clues across was compiled, in his spare time, by Robert M. Stilgenbauer. It took him 7½ years.

## Chemical Elements

All known matter in the Solar System is made up of chemical elements. An element in chemistry is any substance that cannot be separated by chemical means into simpler substances. Ninety-four naturally-occurring elements have been detected so far. They are listed in the following table.

## Table of Chemical Elements

| Element | Chemical Symbol | Atomic Number | Atomic Weight | Element | Chemical Symbol | Atomic Number | Atomic Weight |
|---|---|---|---|---|---|---|---|
| Actinium | Ac | 89 | 227 | Cadmium | Cd | 48 | 112·4 |
| Aluminium | Al | 13 | 27 | Caesium | Cs | 55 | 132·9 |
| Americium | Am | 95 | 243 | Calcium | Ca | 20 | 40·1 |
| Antimony | Sb | 51 | 121·8 | Californium | Cf | 98 | 251 |
| Argon | Ar | 18 | 39·9 | Carbon | C | 6 | 12 |
| Arsenic | As | 33 | 74·9 | Cerium | Ce | 58 | 140·1 |
| Astatine | At | 85 | 210 | Chlorine | Cl | 17 | 35·5 |
| Barium | Ba | 56 | 137·3 | Chromium | Cr | 24 | 52 |
| Berkelium | Bk | 97 | 249 | Cobalt | Co | 27 | 58·9 |
| Beryllium | Be | 4 | 9 | Copper | Cu | 29 | 63·5 |
| Bismuth | Bi | 83 | 209 | Curium | Cm | 96 | 247 |
| Boron | B | 5 | 10·8 | Dysprosium | Dy | 66 | 162·5 |
| Bromine | Br | 35 | 79·9 | Einsteinium | Es | 99 | 254 |

| Element | Chemical Symbol | Atomic Number | Atomic Weight | Element | Chemical Symbol | Atomic Number | Atomic Weight |
|---|---|---|---|---|---|---|---|
| Erbium | Er | 68 | 167·3 | Phosphorus | P | 15 | 31 |
| Europium | Eu | 63 | 152 | Platinum | Pt | 78 | 195·1 |
| Fermium | Fm | 100 | 253 | Plutonium | Pu | 94 | 242 |
| Fluorine | F | 9 | 19 | Polonium | Po | 84 | 210 |
| Francium | Fr | 87 | 223 | Potassium | K | 19 | 39·1 |
| Gadolinium | Gd | 64 | 157·3 | Praseodymium | Pr | 59 | 140·9 |
| Gallium | Ga | 31 | 69·7 | Promethium | Pm | 61 | 147 |
| Germanium | Ge | 32 | 72·6 | Protactinium | Pa | 91 | 231 |
| Gold | Au | 79 | 197 | Radium | Ra | 88 | 226 |
| Hafnium | Hf | 72 | 178·5 | Radon | Rn | 86 | 222 |
| Helium | He | 2 | 4 | Rhenium | Re | 75 | 186·2 |
| Holmium | Ho | 67 | 164·9 | Rhodium | Rh | 45 | 102·9 |
| Hydrogen | H | 1 | 1 | Rubidium | Rb | 37 | 85·5 |
| Indium | In | 49 | 114·8 | Ruthenium | Ru | 44 | 101·1 |
| Iodine | I | 53 | 126·9 | Samarium | Sm | 62 | 150·4 |
| Iridium | Ir | 77 | 192·2 | Scandium | Sc | 21 | 45 |
| Iron | Fe | 26 | 55·8 | Selenium | Se | 34 | 79 |
| Krypton | Kr | 36 | 83·8 | Silicon | Si | 14 | 28·1 |
| Kurchatovium | Ku | 104 | 260 | Silver | Ag | 47 | 107·9 |
| Lanthanum | La | 57 | 138·9 | Sodium | Na | 11 | 23 |
| Lawrencium | Lw | 103 | 257 | Strontium | Sr | 38 | 87·6 |
| Lead | Pb | 82 | 207·2 | Sulphur | S | 16 | 32·1 |
| Lithium | Li | 3 | 6·9 | Tantalum | Ta | 73 | 180·9 |
| Lutetium | Lu | 71 | 175 | Technetium | Tc | 43 | 99 |
| Magnesium | Mg | 12 | 24·3 | Tellurium | Te | 52 | 127·6 |
| Manganese | Mn | 25 | 54·9 | Terbium | Tb | 65 | 158·9 |
| Mendelevium | Md | 101 | 256 | Thallium | Tl | 81 | 204·4 |
| Mercury | Hg | 80 | 200·6 | Thorium | Th | 90 | 232 |
| Molybdenum | Mo | 42 | 95·9 | Thulium | Tm | 69 | 168·9 |
| Neodymium | Nd | 60 | 144·2 | Tin | Sn | 50 | 118·7 |
| Neon | Ne | 10 | 20·2 | Titanium | Ti | 22 | 47·9 |
| Neptunium | Np | 93 | 237 | Tungsten | W | 74 | 183·9 |
| Nickel | Ni | 28 | 58·7 | Uranium | U | 92 | 238 |
| Niobium | Nb | 41 | 92·9 | Vanadium | V | 23 | 50·9 |
| Nitrogen | N | 7 | 14 | Xenon | Xe | 54 | 131·3 |
| Nobelium | No | 102 | 254 | Ytterbium | Yb | 70 | 173 |
| Osmium | Os | 76 | 190·2 | Yttrium | Y | 39 | 88·9 |
| Oxygen | O | 8 | 16 | Zinc | Zn | 30 | 65·4 |
| Palladium | Pd | 46 | 106·4 | Zirconium | Zr | 40 | 91·2 |

# Relative Densities of Common Substances

| Gases (at Normal Temperature & Pressure) | |
|---|---|
| Air | 0·00129 |
| Argon | 0·00178 |
| Carbon dioxide | 0·00198 |
| Helium | 0·000179 |
| Hydrogen | 0·00009 |
| Methane | 0·000717 |
| Oxygen | 0·00143 |

| Liquids (at 15°C) | |
|---|---|
| Acetone | 0·79 |
| Alcohol | 0·79 |
| Ether | 0·74 |
| Glycerine | 1·26 |
| Oil (lubricating) | 0·9–0·92 |
| Turpentine | 0·87 |
| Blood | 1·04–1·067 |
| (Water at 4°C) | 1·00 |

| Metals | |
|---|---|
| Steel | 7·6–7·8 |
| Brass | 8·4–8·7 |
| Aluminium | 2·70 |
| Copper | 8·89 |
| Lead | 11·34 |
| Titanium | 4·5 |
| Mercury | 13·6 |

| Miscellaneous Solids | |
|---|---|
| Celluloid | 1·4 |
| Glass | 2·4–2·8 |
| Ice | 0·92 |
| Brick | 2·1 |
| Diamond | 3·5 |
| Rubber | 0·97–0·99 |
| Oak | 0·74 |
| Cork | 0·24 |

# Specific Heats of Common Substances

| | | | |
|---|---|---|---|
| Aluminium | 0·202 | Alcohol | 0·580 |
| Brass | 0·092 | Chloroform | 0·234 |
| Copper | 0·093 | Air | 0·241* |
| Iron | 0·113 | Carbon Dioxide | 0·202* |
| Rubber | 0·400 | Oxygen | 0·218* |
| Wood | 0·400 | Water | 1·000 |
| | | (*at constant pressure) | |

# Air

Normal dry air has the following composition by volume:

|  | % |  | % |
|---|---|---|---|
| Nitrogen | 78·08 | Helium | 0·0005 |
| Oxygen | 20·94 | Krypton | 0·0001 |
| Argon | 0·9325 | Xenon | 0·000009 |
| Carbon dioxide | 0·03 | Radon | $6 \times 10\%^{-18}$ |
| Neon | 0·0018 |  |  |

# Chemical and Common Names of Some Familiar Substances

| | |
|---|---|
| Alum | Potassium aluminium sulphate ($K_2SO_4$, $Al_2(SO_4)_3$, $24H_2O$). |
| Aqua fortis | Concentrated nitric acid ($HNO_3$). |
| Aqua regia | Concentrated nitric and hydrochloric acids in ratio of one part $HNO_3$ to four parts HCl. |
| Boracic acid | Boric acid ($H_3BO_3$). |
| Borax | Sodium pyroborate ($Na_2B_4O_7$). |
| Bromide | Potassium bromide (KBr). |
| Carbolic acid | Phenol ($C_6H_5OH$). |
| Carbonic acid gas | Carbon dioxide ($CO_2$). |
| Caustic soda | Sodium hydroxide (NaOH). |
| Chalk | Calcium carbonate ($CaCO_3$). |
| Common salt | Sodium chloride (NaCl). |
| Epsom salt | Crystalline magnesium sulphate ($MgSO_4$, $7H_2O$). |
| Hypo | Sodium thiosulphate ($Na_2S_2O_3$). |
| Lime | Calcium oxide (CaO). |
| Magnesia | Magnesium oxide (MgO). |
| Muriate of potash | Potassium chloride (KCl). |
| Nitre | Potassium nitrate ($KNO_3$). |
| Oil of vitriol | Concentrated sulphuric acid ($H_2SO_4$). |
| Plaster of Paris | Form of calcium sulphate having the formula $CaSO_4, \frac{1}{2}H_2O$. |

| Quicklime | Calcium oxide (CaO). |
| Potash | Potassium carbonate ($K_2CO_3$). |
| Red Lead | Red lead oxide ($Pb_3O_4$). |
| Saltpetre | Potassium nitrate ($KNO_3$). |
| Sal volatile | Ammonium carbonate (($NH_4)_2CO_3$). |
| Salts of lemon | Potassium hydrogen oxalate ($KH_3(OOC)_4, 2H_2O$). |
| Slaked lime | Calcium hydroxide ($Ca(OH)_2$). |
| Spirits of salt | Solution of hydrochloric acid (HCl). |
| Vinegar | Solution of acetic acid ($CH_3COOH$). |
| Vitriol (Blue) | Crystalline copper sulphate ($CuSO_4, 5H_2O$). |
| (Green) | Crystalline ferrous sulphate ($FeSO_4, 7H_2O$). |
| Washing Soda | Crystalline sodium carbonate ($Na_2CO_3lOH_2O$). |

# Some Abbreviations in Common Use in Chemistry and Physics

| | | | |
|---|---|---|---|
| a. | Acid | eth. | Ether |
| a.c. | Alternating current | exp. | Explodes |
| al. | Alcohol | fl. | Fluid |
| aq. | Aqua; water | glyc. | Glycerine |
| atm. *or* atmos. | Atmosphere (Atmospheric) | hor. | Horizontal |
| | | i. | Insoluble |
| av. *or* avoir. | Avoirdupois | km. | Kilometre |
| bar. | Barometer | kw. | Kilowatt |
| b.p. | Boiling point | lat. | Latitude |
| cc *or* c.c. | Cubic centimetre | mg. | Milligram |
| chl. | Chloroform | mic. | Microscopic |
| cm. | Centimetre | mm. | Millimetre |
| cu. ft. | Cubic foot | m.p. | Melting point |
| cwt. | Hundredweight | oz. | Ounce |
| d.c. | Direct current | pr. | Prisms |
| diam. | Diameter | Q. | Quantity |
| dil. | Dilute | r.p.m. | Revolutions per minute |
| dissd. | Dissolved | | |
| dr. | Dram | sc. | Scales |
| dwt. | Pennyweight | sol. | Solution; Soluble |

| | | | |
|---|---|---|---|
| sp. gr. | Specific gravity | w. | Water |
| sq. | Square | wt. | Weight |
| t. | Troy | yr. | Year |
| temp. | Temperature | | |
| turp. | Turpentine | | |

# Mathematical Formula

To find the area of a:

CIRCLE – Multiply the square of the diameter by ·7854
RECTANGLE – Multiply the length of the base by the height
SQUARE – Square the length of one side
TRIANGLE – Multiply the base by the height and divide by 2.

# Mathematical Signs

| | | | |
|---|---|---|---|
| $=$ | Is equal to | $\not>$ | Not greater than |
| $\neq$ | Is not equal to | $<$ | Less than |
| $\fallingdotseq$ | Is approx. equal to | $\not<$ | Not less than |
| $\equiv$ | Is identical to | $\Sigma$ | The sum of |
| $\sim$ | The difference between | $\delta$ | A small difference |
| $\propto$ | Varies as | $\angle$ | Angle |
| $>$ | Greater than | $\infty$ | Infinity |

60 seconds ($''$) = 1 minute ($'$)          90 degrees = 1 right angle
60 minutes = 1 degree ($°$)          4 right angles = 1 circle (360°)

# British Measures and Equivalents

**Length**

| | |
|---|---|
| 1 inch | 2·54 cm. |
| 1 foot = 12 inches | 0·3048 m. |
| 1 yard = 3 feet | 0·9144 m. |
| 1 chain = 4 rods = 22 yards | 20·1168 m. |
| 1 mile = 8 furlongs = 80 chains | 1·6093 km. |
| 1 nautical mile = 6,080 feet | 1·852 km. |

**Surface or Area**

| | |
|---|---|
| 1 sq. inch | 6·4516 sq. cm. |
| 1 sq. foot = 144 sq. inch | 9·2903 sq. dm. |
| 1 sq. yard = 9 sq. feet | 0·836 sq. m. |
| 1 acre = 4 roods = 4,840 sq. yards | 4,046·556 sq. m. |
| 1 sq. mile = 640 acres | 258·99 hectares |

**Capacity**

| | |
|---|---|
| 1 cu. inch | 16·387 cu. cm. |
| 1 cu. foot = 1,728 cu. inch | 28·317 cu. dm. |
| 1 cu. yard = 27 cu. feet | 0·7646 cu. m. |
| 1 pint = 4 gills | 0·568 litres |
| 1 gallon = 4 quarts = 8 pints | 4·546 litres |
| 1 bushel = 4 pecks = 8 gallons | 36·368 litres |

**Weight**

| | |
|---|---|
| 1 ounce = 16 drams = 437·5 grains | 28·35 gm. |
| 1 pound = 16 ounces | 0·4536 kg. |
| 1 stone = 14 pounds | 6·35 kg. |
| 1 hundredweight = 4 quarters = 8 stones | 0·5080 quintal |
| 1 ton = 20 hundredweight | 1·016 tonnes |

# Metric Measures and Equivalents

**Length**

| | |
|---|---|
| 1 centimetre (cm.) = 10 millimetres (mm.) | 0·3937 in. |
| 1 metre (m.) = 100 centimetres | 1·094 yd. |
| 1 kilometre (km.) = 1,000 metres | 0·62137 mile |

(A kilometre is approximately *five-eighths* of a mile, so that 8 kilometres may be regarded as 5 miles.)

**Surface or Area**

| | |
|---|---|
| 1 sq. centimetre = 100 sq. mm. | 0·155 sq. in. |
| 1 sq. metre = 10,000 sq. cm. | 1,196 sq. yd. |
| 1 are = 100 sq. m. | 119·6 sq. yd. |
| 1 hectare = 100 ares | 2·4711 acres |
| 1 sq. kilometre = 100 hectares | 0·386103 sq. mile |

## Capacity

| | |
|---|---|
| 1 cu. centimetre | 0·061 cu. in. |
| 1 cu. metre = 999·972 litres | 1·30795 cu. yd. |
| 1 litre = 1·000028 cu. dm. | 1·7598 pint |

## Weight

| | |
|---|---|
| 1 milligramme (mg.) | 0·015 grain |
| 1 gramme (g.) = 1,000 milligrammes | 15·432 grains |
| 1 kilogramme (kg.) = 1,000 grams | 2·2046 lb. |
| 1 quintal = 100 kilograms | 1·968 cwt. |
| 1 tonne = 10 quintals | 0·9842 ton |

## World Currencies

| Country | Monetary Unit | Denominations in Circulation (Notes) | (Coins) |
|---|---|---|---|
| Albania | Lek of 100 Qintar | Leks 100, 50, 25, 10, 5, 3, 1 | Lek 1; Qintars 50, 20, 10, 5 |
| Algeria | Dinar of 100 Centimes | Dinars 100, 50, 10, 5 | Dinars 1; Centimes 50, 20, 10, 5, 2, 1 |
| Argentina | Peso of 100 Centavos or 100 Old Pesos | Pesos 1,000, 500, 100, 50, 10, 5, 1 | Old Pesos 25, 10, 5, 1; Centavos 50, 20, 10, 5, 1 |
| Australia | Dollar of 100 Cents | $A 20, 10, 5, 2, 1 | Cents 50, 20, 10, 5, 2, 1 |
| Austria | Schilling of 100 Groschen | Schillings 1,000, 500, 100, 50, 20 | Schillings 50, 25, 10, 5, 1; Groschen 50, 10, 5, 2, 1 |
| Belgium | Belgian Franc of 100 Centimes | Frs. 5,000, 1,000, 500, 100, 50, 20 | Frs. 100, 50, 10, 5, 1; Centimes 50, 25 |
| Brazil | Cruzeiro of 100 Centavos | Cruzeiros 100, 50, 10, 5, 1 | Cruzeiro 1; Centavos 50, 20, 10, 5, 2, 1 |
| Bulgaria | Lev of 100 Stotinki | Léva 20, 10, 5, 2, 1 | Léva 2, 1; Stotinki 50, 20, 10, 5, 2, 1 |

| Country | Monetary Unit | Denominations in Circulation | |
|---|---|---|---|
| | | (Notes) | (Coins) |
| Burma | Kyat of 100 Pyas | Kyats 20, 10, 5, 1 | Kyat 1; Pyas 50, 25, 10, 5, 1 |
| Canada | Dollar of 100 Cents | Dollars 1,000 100, 50, 20, 10, 5, 2, 1 | Dollars 1; Cents 50, 25, 10, 5, 1 |
| Chile | Escudo of 100 Cóndores or 100 Centésimos (= 1,000 Pesos or 1,000 Milésimos) | Escudos 100, 50, 10, 5, 1, 0·50 | Escudos 0·10, 0·05, 0·02 |
| China | Renminbi or Yuan of 10 Jiao or 100 Fen | Yuan 10, 5, 2, 1; Jiao 5, 2, 1 | Fen 5, 2, 1 |
| Cuba | Peso of 100 Centavos | Pesos 100, 50, 20, 10, 5, 1 | Centavos 40, 20, 5, 2, 1 |
| Cyprus | Cyprus Pound of 1,000 Mils | £5, £1; Mils 500, 250 | Mils 500, 100, 50, 25, 5, 3, 1 |
| Czechoslo- vakia | Koruna (Crown) of 100 Halérů (Heller) | Korunas 100, 50, 25, 10, 5, 3 | Korunas 5, 3, 1; Heller 50, 25, 10, 5, 3, 1 |
| Denmark | Krone of 100 Ore | Kroner 500, 100, 50, 10 | Kroner 5, 1; Ore 25, 10, 5, 2, 1 |
| Ethiopia | Ethiopian Dollar of 100 Cents | Dollars 500, 100, 50, 20, 10, 5, 1 | Cents 50, 25, 10 5, 1 |
| Finland | Markka of 100 Penniä | Markkas 100, 50, 10, 5, 1 | Markkas 10, 5, 1; Penniä 50, 20, 10, 5, 1 |
| Formosa | New Taiwan Dollar | NT$ 100, 50, 10, 5, 1; Cents 50, 10, 5, 1 | $5, $1; Cents 50, 20, 10 |
| France | Franc of 100 Centimes (1 Franc = 100 old Francs) | Francs 500, 100, 50, 10, 5 | Francs 10, 5, 1, ½; Old Francs 2, 1; Centimes 20, 10, 5, 1 |
| Gambia | Dalasi of 100 Bututs | Dalasis 25, 5, 1 | Dalasi 1; Bututs 50, 25, 10, 5, 1 |

| Country | Monetary Unit | Denominations in Circulation (Notes) | (Coins) |
|---------|---------------|--------------------------------------|---------|
| Germany (East) | Mark der Deutschen Demokratischen Republik (M.) of 100 Pfennig | M. 100, 50, 20, 10, 5 | M. 20, 10, 5, 2, 1; Pfennig 50, 20, 10, 5, 1 |
| Germany (Federal Republic of) | Deutsche Mark of 100 Pfennig | D.M. 1,000, 500, 100, 50, 20, 10, 5 | D.M. 10, 5, 2, 1; Pfennig 50, 10, 5, 2, 1 |
| Greece | Drachma of 100 Lepta | Drachmae 1,000, 500, 100, 50 | Drachmae 20, 10 5, 2, 1; Lepta 50, 20, 10, 5 |
| Guyana | Guyana Dollar of 100 Cents | Dollars 20, 10, 5, 1 | Cents 100, 50, 25, 10, 5, 1 |
| Hungary | Forint of 100 Fillér | Forints 100, 50, 20, 10 | Forints 25, 20, 10, 5, 2, 1; Fillér 50, 20, 10, 5, 2 |
| Iceland | Króna of 100 Aurar | Króna 5,000, 1,000, 500, 100, 25 | Króna 50, 10, 5, 1; Aurar 50, 10 |
| India | Rupee of 100 Paise | Rupees 10,000, 5,000, 1,000, 100, 10, 5, 2, 1 | Rupees 1, $\frac{1}{2}$, $\frac{1}{4}$; Paise 50, 25, 20, 10, 5, 3, 2, 1 |
| Indonesia | Rupiah of 100 Sen | Rupiahs 10,000, 5,000, 1,000, 500, 100, 50, 25, 10, 5, 2$\frac{1}{2}$, 1; Sen 50, 25, 10, 5, 1 | Rupiahs 10, 5, 2, 1 |
| Iran | Rial of 100 Dinars | Rials 5,000, 1,000, 500, 200, 100, 50, 20, 10, 5 | Rials 10, 5, 2, 1; Dinars 50, 25, 10, 5 |
| Iraq | Iraqi Dinar of 1,000 Fils | Dinars 10, 5, 1, $\frac{1}{2}$, $\frac{1}{4}$ | Dinars 5, 1; Fils 500, 250, 100, 50, 25, 10, 5, 1 |

| Country | Monetary Unit | Denominations in Circulation (Notes) | (Coins) |
| --- | --- | --- | --- |
| Israel | Israel Pound of 100 Agorot (formerly 1,000 Prutot) | Pounds 100, 50, 10, 5, 1, $\frac{1}{2}$; Prutot 500, 250, 100, 50 | Pounds 1, $\frac{1}{2}$; Agorot 25, 10, 5, 1; Prutot 250, 100, 50, 25, 10, 5, 1 |
| Italy | Lira of 100 Centesimi | Lire 100,000, 50,000, 10,000 5,000, 1,000, 500 | Lire 1,000, 500, 100, 50, 20, 10, 5, 2, 1 |
| Jamaica | Jamaican Dollar of 100 Cents | $10, 2, 1; Cents 50 | Cents 25, 20, 10, 5, 1 |
| Japan | Yen | Yen 10,000, 5,000, 1,000, 500, 100 | Yen 1,000, 100, 50, 10, 5, 1 |
| Kenya | Kenya Shilling of 100 Cents | Shillings 100, 50, 20, 10, 5 | Shillings 2, 1; Cents 50, 25, 10, 5 |
| Kuwait | Kuwaiti Dinar of 1,000 Fils | Dinars 10, 5, 1, $\frac{1}{2}$, $\frac{1}{4}$ | Fils 100, 50, 20, 10, 5, 1 |
| Laos | Kip of 100 Ats | Kips 1,000, 500, 200, 100, 50, 20, 10, 5, 1 | — |
| Lebanon | Lebanese Pound of 100 Piastres | Pounds 100, 50, 25, 10, 5, 1 | Piastres 50, 25, 10, 5, 2$\frac{1}{2}$, 1 |
| Luxemburg | Franc of 100 Centimes | Francs 100, 50, 20, 10 | Francs 250, 100, 5, 1; Centimes 25 |
| Madagascar | Franc Malgache (F.M.G.) | Frs. 5,000, 1,000, 500, 100, 50 | Frs. 20, 10, 5, 2, 1 |
| Malaysia | Malaysian Dollar (Ringit) of 100 cents (Sen) | Dollars 1,000, 100, 50, 10, 5, 1 | Dollar 1; Cents 50, 20, 10, 5, 1 |
| Mexico | Peso of 100 Centavos | Pesos 10,000, 1,000, 500, 100, 50, 20, 10, 5, 1 | Pesos 25, 10, 5, 1; Centavos 50, 25, 20, 10, 5, 1 |
| Mongolian People's Republic | Tugrik of 100 Mongo | Tugriks 100, 50, 25, 10, 3, 1 | Mongo 20, 15, 10, 2, 1 |

| Country | Monetary Unit | Denominations in Circulation (Notes) | (Coins) |
|---------|---------------|---------------------------------------|---------|
| Morocco | Dirham of 100 Francs | Dirham 100, 50, 10, 5; Francs 10,000 | Dirham 5, 1; Francs 500, 200, 100, 50, 20, 10, 5, 2, 1 |
| Mozambique | Escudo of 100 Centavos | Escudos 1,000, 500, 100, 50 | Escudos 20, 10, 5, $2\frac{1}{2}$, 1; Centavos 50, 20, 10 |
| Nepal | Rupee of 100 Paisa | Rupees 1,000, 100, 10, 5, 1 | Rupee 1; Paisa 50, 25, 10, 5, 2, 1 |
| Netherlands (The) | Florin (Guilder) of 100 Cents | Florins 1,000, 100, 25, 10, 5, $2\frac{1}{2}$, 1 | Florins 10, $2\frac{1}{2}$, 1; Cents 25, 10, 5, 1 |
| Netherlands Antilles (The) | N.A. Guilder of 100 Cents | Guilders 500, 250, 100, 50, 25, 10, 5, $2\frac{1}{2}$, 1 | Guilders $2\frac{1}{2}$, 1, $\frac{1}{4}$, $\frac{1}{10}$; Cents 5, $2\frac{1}{2}$, 1 |
| New Zealand | New Zealand Dollar of 100 Cents | N.Z.$ 100, 20, 10, 5, 2, 1 | Cents 50, 20, 10, 5, 2, 1 |
| Norway | Krone of 100 Ore | Kroner 1,000, 500, 100, 50, 5 | Kroner 5, 1; Ore 50, 25, 10, 5, 2, 1 |
| Paraguay | Guarani of 100 Centimes | Guaranies 10,000, 5,000, 1,000, 500, 100, 50, 10, 5, 1 | — |
| Peru | Gold Sol of 100 Centavos | Soles 1,000, 500, 200, 100, 50, 10, 5 | Soles 10, 5, 1; Centavos 50, 25, 20, 10, 5, 2, 1 |
| Philippines | Philippine Peso of 100 Centavos | Pesos 100, 50, 20, 10, 5, 2, 1 | Peso 1; Centavos 50, 25, 20, 10, 5, 1 |
| Poland | Zloty of 100 Groszy | Zlotys 1,000, 500, 100, 50, 20 | Zlotys 100, 10, 5, 2, 1; Groszy 50, 20, 10, 5, 1 |
| Portugal | Escudo of 100 Centavos | Escudos 1,000, 500, 100, 50, 20 | Escudos 20, 10, 5, $2\frac{1}{2}$, 1, $\frac{1}{2}$; Centavos 20, 10 |

| Country | Monetary Unit | Denominations in Circulation | |
|---------|---------------|------------------------------|---|
| | | (Notes) | (Coins) |
| Rumania | Leu of 100 Bani | Lei 100, 50, 25, 10, 5, 3, 1 | Lei 3, 1; Bani 25, 15, 10, 5, 3, 1 |
| Saudi Arabia | Riyal of 20 Qursh or 100 Halalas | Riyals 100, 50, 10, 5, 1 | Qursh 4, 2, 1; Halala 1 |
| Seychelles | Rupee of 100 Cents | Rs. 100, 50, 20, 10, 5 | Rupee 5, 1; Cents 50, 25, 10, 5, 2, 1 |
| Sierra Leone | Leone of 100 Cents | Leone 5, 2, 1 | Cents 20, 10, 5, 1, $\frac{1}{2}$ |
| Singapore | S. Dollar of 100 Cents | $1,000, 100, 50, 10, 5, 1 | $1; Cents 50, 20, 10, 5, 1 |
| South Africa (Republic of) | Rand of 100 Cents | Rands 20, 10, 5, 2, 1; £SA 100, 20, 10, 5, 1; 10s. | Rand 1; Cents 50, 20, 10, 5, 2, 1, $\frac{1}{2}$ |
| Spain | Peseta of 100 Céntimos | Pesetas 1,000, 500, 100, 50, 25, 5, 1 | Pesetas 100, 50, 25, 5, 2$\frac{1}{2}$, 1; Céntimos 50, 10 |
| Sudan | Sudanese Pound of 100 Piastres or 1,000 Milliemes | £S 10, 5, 1; Piastres 50, 25 | Piastres 10, 5, 2; Milliemes 10, 5, 2, 1 |
| Sweden | Krona of 100 Ore | Kronor 10,000, 1,000, 100, 50, 10, 5 | Kronor 5, 2, 1; Ore 50, 25, 10, 5, 2, 1 |
| Switzerland | Franc of 100 Centimes | Francs 1,000, 500, 100, 50, 20, 10, 5 | Francs 5, 2, 1; Centimes 50, 20, 10, 5, 2, 1 |
| Thailand | Baht of 100 Stangs | Bahts 100, 20, 10, 5, 1; Stangs 50 | Baht 1; Stangs 50, 25, 20, 10, 5, 1, $\frac{1}{2}$ |
| Tonga | Pa'Anga (T$) of 100 Seniti | Pa'Anga 10, 5, 2, 1, $\frac{1}{2}$ | Pa'Anga 2, 1; Seniti 50, 20, 10, 5, 2, 1 |
| Trinidad & Tobago | Trinidad & Tobago Dollar of 100 Cents | Dollars 20, 10, 5, 1 | Dollar 1; Cents 50, 25, 10, 5, 1 |
| Tunisia | Tunisian Dinar of 1,000 Millimes | Dinars 10, 5, 1, $\frac{1}{2}$ | Dinar $\frac{1}{2}$; Millimes 100, 50, 20, 10, 5, 2, 1 |

| Country | Monetary Unit | Denominations in Circulation (Notes) | (Coins) |
|---|---|---|---|
| Turkey | Turkish Lira of 100 Kurus | TL 1,000, 500, 100, 50, 20, 10, 5 | TL 10, $2\frac{1}{2}$, 1; Kurus 50, 25, 10, 5, 1 |
| Uganda | U. Shilling of 100 Cents | Shillings 100, 20, 10, 5 | Shillings 5, 2, 1; Cents 50, 20, 10, 5 |
| United Arab Republic | Egyptian Pound of 100 Piastres of 1,000 Milliemes | £E 10, 5, 1, $\frac{1}{2}$, $\frac{1}{4}$; Piastres 10, 5 | Piastres 10, 5; Milliemes 20, 10, 5, 2, 1 |
| United Kingdom | Pound of 100 new pence | £20, £10, £5, £1 | Pence 50, 10, 5, 2, 1, $\frac{1}{2}$ |
| United States of America | Dollar of 100 Cents | $100, 50, 20, 10, 5, 1 | $1; Cents 50, 25, 10, 5, 1 |
| Uruguay | Peso of 100 Centésimos | Pesos 10,000, 5,000, 1,000, 500, 100, 50, 10, 5, 1 | Pesos 10, 5, 1 |
| USSR | Rouble of 100 Copecks | Roubles 100, 50, 25, 10, 5, 3, 1 | Rouble 1; Copecks 50, 20, 15, 10, 5, 3, 2, 1 |
| Venezuela | Bolivar | Bolivares 500, 100, 50, 20, 10, 5 | Bolivares 100, 20, 10, 5, 2, 1, $\frac{1}{2}$, $\frac{1}{4}$, $\frac{1}{8}$, $\frac{1}{20}$ |
| Vietnam (North) | Dong of 100 Hào or 100 Xu | Dong 10, 5, 2, 1; Hào 5, 2, 1; Xu 2 | Xu 5, 2, 1 |
| Vietnam (South) | Dong of 100 Cents | Dong 500, 200, 100, 50, 20, 10, 5, 2, 1 | Dong 20, 10, 5, 1; Cents 50, 20, 10 |
| West Indies (The) | East Caribbean Dollar of 100 Cents | $100, 20, 5, 1 | Cents 50, 25, 10, 5, 2, 1 |
| Yemen (Arab Republic) | Riyal of 40 Bugshas | Riyals 50, 20, 10, 5, 1; Bugshas 20, 10 | Bugshas 2, 1, $\frac{1}{2}$ |

| Country | Monetary Unit | Denominations in Circulation (Notes) | (Coins) |
|---------|---------------|--------------------------------------|---------|
| **Yemen (People's Democratic Republic)** | Southern Yemen Dinar (£SY) of 1,000 Fils | £SY 10, 5, 1, Fils 500, 250 | Fils 50, 25, 5, 1 |
| **Yugoslavia** | Dinar of 100 Old Dinars or 100 Paras | Dinars 100, 50, 10, 5 | Old Dinars 50, 20, 10; Dinar 5, 2, 1; Paras 50, 20, 10, 5 |
| **Zambia** | Kwacha of 100 Ngwee | Kwacha 20, 10, 2, 1; Ngwee 50 | Ngwee 20, 10, 5, 2, 1 |

# British Monetary Units in 1922

The authorized coinage of the United Kingdom in 1922 consisted of the following pieces:

| Denomination | Standard Weight | Remedy of Weight** |
|--------------|-----------------|---------------------|
| **Gold** | | |
| *Five Pound £5 | 616·37239 | 1·00 |
| *Two Pound £2 | 246·54895 | 0·40 |
| Sovereign £1 | 123·27447 | 0·20 |
| Half-Sovereign 10s. | 61·63723 | 0·15 |
| **Silver** | | |
| Crown 5s | 436·36363 | 2·000 |
| Double Florin 4s | 349·09090 | 1·678 |
| Half-Crown 2s 6d | 218·18181 | 1·264 |
| Florin 2s | 174·54545 | 0·997 |
| Shilling 1s | 87·27272 | 0·578 |
| Sixpence 6d | 43·63636 | 0·346 |
| *Groat or 4d | 29·09090 | 0·262 |
| Threepence 3d | 21·81818 | 0·212 |
| *Twopence 2d | 14·54545 | 0·144 |
| *Penny 1d | 7·27272 | 0·087 |

| Denomination | Standard Weight | Remedy of Weight |
|---|---|---|
| **Bronze** | | |
| Penny 1d | 145·83333 | 2·916 |
| Halfpenny ½d | 87·50000 | 1·750 |
| Farthing ¼d | 43·75000 | 0·875 |

*Issued on special occasions only.
**The 'Remedy' is the amount of variation from standard permitted in fineness and in weight of coins when first issued from the Mint.

# British Monetary Units in 1972

COIN

**Bronze Coins**
½ New Penny
1 New Penny
2 New Pence

**Cupro-Nickel (Silver)**

| | |
|---|---|
| Sixpence 6d | 2½p |
| Shilling 1s | } 5p |
| 5 New Pence | |
| Florin 2s | } 10p |
| 10 New Pence | |
| Crown* 5s | 25p |
| 50 New Pence | 50p |

**Silver Coins**

The Maundy Money: gifts of special money distributed by the Sovereign annually to the number of aged poor people corresponding to the Sovereign's age.

| | |
|---|---|
| Fourpence | 4p |
| Threepence | 3p |
| Twopence | 2p |
| Penny | 1p |

**Gold Coins****

| | |
|---|---|
| Five Pound | £5 |
| Two Pound | £2 |
| Sovereign | £1 |
| Half-Sovereign | 10s |

*Legal tender but not in general circulation as collector's value greater than face value. Issued on special occasions mainly connected with the Royal Family.
**Discontinued.

BANK NOTES
Bank of England notes are issued in denominations of £1, £5, £10 and £20.

SIZES AND WEIGHTS OF DECIMAL COINS

| Denomination | Metal | Standard Weight (Grams) | Standard Diameter (Centimetres) |
|---|---|---|---|
| New Halfpenny | Bronze | 1·78200 | 1·7145 |
| New Penny | Bronze | 3·56400 | 2·0320 |
| 2 New Pence | Bronze | 7·12800 | 2·5910 |
| 5 New Pence | Cupro-nickel | 5·65518 | 2·3595 |
| 10 New Pence | Cupro-nickel | 11·31036 | 2·8500 |
| 50 New Pence | Cupro-nickel | 13·5 | 3 |

# Premium Savings Bonds

Premium Savings Bonds were proposed by the Chancellor of the Exchequer, Mr Harold Macmillan, in his Budget of April 1956. They are a Government Security.

Series A bonds were sold from November 1st, 1956, to July 31st, 1960. A fresh issue (Series B), offering improved terms, was put on sale on August 1st, 1960.

Premium Savings Bonds do not bear interest for their individual owners. Instead, a sum equivalent to interest is pooled to form a fund, and is distributed by weekly and monthly prize draws. A bond first becomes eligible for a draw after it has been held for three complete calendar months; it remains eligible until the end of the month in which it is repaid or until the end of the twelfth month following the month in which the holder dies.

Bonds are issued in 19 different values ranging from £2 to £500. Each £1 invested buys one bond unit and gives one chance in each of the prize draws for which the unit is eligible. The maximum permitted individual holding is 2,000 £1 units (of series A and B together).

Winning numbers are selected by electronic random number indicator equipment, popularly known as ERNIE.

Ernie is electronic, but it may be helpful to think of it as if it were a box with nine wheels in it spinning behind small windows – one for each of the figures or letters in the bond unit numbers. The numbers generated by Ernie actually depend on the chance movement of atomic particles in electrified neon gas. The device used is a neon diode – a tube fitted with two metal plates and filled with neon gas. When electric current is passed through such a tube the neon glows and its particles rush about and collide erratically with one another. Consequently, the number of particles reaching the metal plates changes unpredictably from moment to moment, depending upon the unknown and uncontrolled hazards the particles meet on their journey. Each particle carries a small contribution to the total electric current and the minute fluctuations in current can be measured by an electronic counter.

To doubly ensure randomness two neon tubes are used, and the counter records the difference between the two numbers generated to produce one of the nine characters of the bond number.

The whole bond number is generated by nine pairings of neon tubes and counters; the letters of the bond number are generated in the same way as the figures, the counters counting A B C . . . instead of 123.

Ernie thus generates separately, but at the same time, each of the nine letters or figures which make a complete bond unit number. It then puts these separate characters together to make a complete number.

The monthly prize fund is allocated in prizes as follows:

1. For the weekly draws an amount is set aside to allow for single prizes each week, the number of such prizes being equal to the number of Saturdays in the month;
2. For the monthly draw the remaining prize fund is allocated as follows:

   i. A single prize of £50,000.
   ii. Of the remainder, each complete £100,000 is divided into:

   | | |
   |---|---|
   | 1 prize of £5,000 | 25 prizes of £100 |
   | 10 prizes of £1,000 | 500 prizes of £50 |
   | 10 prizes of £500 | 2,000 prizes of £25 |
   | 10 prizes of £250 | |

   iii. Of the remainder, each complete £10,000 is divided into:

   | | |
   |---|---|
   | 1 prize of £1,000 | 5 prizes of £100 |
   | 1 prize of £500 | 50 prizes of £50 |
   | 2 prizes of £250 | 200 prizes of £25 |

By the end of August 1972 the number of bondholders was estimated to be over 20 million and the net amount standing to their credit was approximately £900 million. Since the inception of the scheme 9 million prizes valued at just over £325 million have been paid out.

# 17 PRIME MINISTERS AND PRESIDENTS

---

## British Prime Ministers

---

| *Name* | *Party* | *Date* |
|--------|---------|--------|
| **Sir Robert Walpole** | Whig | April 3rd, 1721 |
| **Earl of Wilmington** | Whig | February 16th, 1742 |
| **Henry Pelham** | Whig | August 25th, 1743 |
| **Duke of Newcastle** | Whig | May 18th, 1754 |
| **Duke of Devonshire** | Whig | November 16th, 1756 |
| **Duke of Newcastle** | Whig | July 2nd, 1757 |
| **Earl of Bute** | Tory | May 28th, 1762 |
| **George Grenville** | Whig | April 15th, 1763 |
| **Marquess of Rockingham** | Whig | July 10th, 1765 |
| **Earl of Chatham** | Whig | August 2nd, 1766 |
| **Duke of Grafton** | Whig | December 1767 |
| **Lord North** | Tory | February 6th, 1770 |
| **Marquess of Rockingham** | Whig | March 27th, 1782 |
| **Earl of Shelburne** | Whig | July 13th, 1782 |
| **Duke of Portland** | Coalition | April 4th, 1783 |
| **William Pitt** | Tory | December 7th, 1783 |
| **Henry Addington** | Tory | March 21st, 1801 |
| **William Pitt** | Tory | May 16th, 1804 |
| **Lord Grenville** | Whig | February 10th, 1806 |
| **Duke of Portland** | Tory | March 31st, 1807 |
| **Spencer Perceval** | Tory | December 6th, 1809 |
| **Earl of Liverpool** | Tory | June 16th, 1812 |

| Name | Party | Date |
|------|-------|------|
| George Canning | Tory | April 30th, 1827 |
| Viscount Goderich | Tory | September 8th, 1827 |
| Duke of Wellington | Tory | January 26th, 1828 |
| Earl Grey | Whig | November 24th, 1830 |
| Viscount Melbourne | Whig | July 13th, 1834 |
| Sir Robert Peel | Tory | December 26th, 1834 |
| Viscount Melbourne | Whig | March 18th, 1835 |
| Sir Robert Peel | Tory | September 6th, 1841 |
| Lord John Russell | Whig | July 6th, 1846 |
| Earl of Derby | Tory | February 28th, 1852 |
| Earl of Aberdeen | Peelite | December 28th, 1852 |
| Viscount Palmerston | Liberal | February 10th, 1855 |
| Earl of Derby | Conservative | February 25th, 1858 |
| Viscount Palmerston | Liberal | June 18th, 1859 |
| Earl Russell | Liberal | November 6th, 1865 |
| Earl of Derby | Conservative | July 6th, 1866 |
| Benjamin Disraeli | Conservative | February 27th, 1868 |
| W. E. Gladstone | Liberal | December 9th, 1868 |
| Benjamin Disraeli | Conservative | February 21st, 1874 |
| W. E. Gladstone | Liberal | April 28th, 1880 |
| Marquess of Salisbury | Conservative | June 24th, 1885 |
| W. E. Gladstone | Liberal | February 6th, 1886 |
| Marquess of Salisbury | Conservative | August 3rd, 1886 |
| W. E. Gladstone | Liberal | August 18th, 1892 |
| Earl of Rosebery | Liberal | March 3rd, 1894 |
| Marquess of Salisbury | Conservative | July 2nd, 1895 |
| A. J. Balfour | Conservative | July 12th, 1902 |
| Sir H. Campbell-Bannerman | Liberal | December 5th, 1905 |
| H. H. Asquith | Liberal | April 8th, 1908 |
| H. H. Asquith | Coalition | May 26th, 1915 |
| D. Lloyd-George | Coalition | December 7th, 1916 |
| A. Bonar Law | Conservative | October 23rd, 1922 |
| Stanley Baldwin | Conservative | May 22nd, 1923 |
| J. Ramsay MacDonald | Labour | January 22nd, 1924 |
| Stanley Baldwin | Conservative | November 4th, 1924 |
| J. Ramsay MacDonald | Labour | June 8th, 1929 |
| J. Ramsay MacDonald | Coalition | August 25th, 1931 |
| Stanley Baldwin | Coalition | June 7th, 1935 |
| Neville Chamberlain | Coalition | May 28th, 1937 |
| Winston S. Churchill | Coalition | May 11th, 1940 |

| Name | Party | Date |
|------|-------|------|
| Winston S. Churchill | Conservative | May 23rd, 1945 |
| Clement R. Attlee | Labour | July 26th, 1945 |
| Sir Winston S. Churchill | Conservative | October 26th, 1951 |
| Sir Anthony Eden | Conservative | April 6th, 1955 |
| Harold Macmillan | Conservative | January 13th, 1957 |
| Sir Alec Douglas-Home | Conservative | October 19th, 1963 |
| J. H. Wilson | Labour | October 16th, 1964 |
| E. R. G. Heath | Conservative | June 19th, 1970 |

# Presidents of the United States of America

| Name | Party | Date |
|------|-------|------|
| 1. George Washington | Federalist | 1789–97 |
| 2. John Adams | Federalist | 1797–1801 |
| 3. Thomas Jefferson | Republican | 1801–9 |
| 4. James Madison | Republican | 1809–17 |
| 5. James Monroe | Republican | 1817–25 |
| 6. John Quincy Adams | Republican | 1825–29 |
| 7. Andrew Jackson | Democrat | 1829–37 |
| 8. Martin Van Buren | Democrat | 1837–41 |
| 9. William H. Harrison | Whig | 1841 |
| 10. John Tyler | Whig | 1841–45 |
| 11. James Knox Polk | Democrat | 1845–49 |
| 12. Zachary Taylor | Whig | 1849–50 |
| 13. Millard Fillmore | Whig | 1850–53 |
| 14. Franklin Pierce | Democrat | 1853–57 |
| 15. James Buchanan | Democrat | 1857–61 |
| 16. Abraham Lincoln | Republican | 1861–65 |
| 17. Andrew Johnson | Republican | 1865–69 |
| 18. Ulysses S. Grant | Republican | 1869–77 |
| 19. Rutherford B. Hayes | Republican | 1877–81 |
| 20. James A. Garfield | Republican | 1881 |
| 21. Chester A. Arthur | Republican | 1881–85 |
| 22. Grover Cleveland | Democrat | 1885–89 |
| 23. Benjamin Harrison | Republican | 1889–93 |
| 24. Grover Cleveland | Democrat | 1893–97 |
| 25. William McKinley | Republican | 1897–1901 |
| 26. Theodore Roosevelt | Republican | 1901–9 |

| Name | Party | Date |
|------|-------|------|
| 27. William H. Taft | Republican | 1909–13 |
| 28. Woodrow Wilson | Democrat | 1913–21 |
| 29. Warren G. Harding | Republican | 1921–23 |
| 30. Calvin Coolidge | Republican | 1923–29 |
| 31. Herbert Hoover | Republican | 1929–33 |
| 32. Franklin D. Roosevelt | Democrat | 1933–45 |
| 33. Harry S. Truman | Democrat | 1945–53 |
| 34. Dwight D. Eisenhower | Republican | 1953–61 |
| 35. John F. Kennedy | Democrat | 1961–63 |
| 36. Lyndon B. Johnson | Democrat | 1963–69 |
| 37. Richard M. Nixon | Republican | 1969– |

# The Caesars

| | |
|---|---|
| Julius Caesar (Dictator) | 49–44 BC |
| Augustus | 29 BC–AD 14 |
| Tiberius | AD 14–37 |
| Caligula | AD 37–41 |
| Claudius | AD 41–54 |
| Nero | AD 54–68 |
| Galba | AD 68–69 |
| Otho | AD 69 |
| Vitellius | AD 69 |
| Vespasian | AD 69–79 |
| Titus | AD 79–81 |
| Domitian | AD 81–96 |

(Only the first six were of the family of Julius.)

## English Kings and Queens

| Sovereign | Date of Accession | Date of Death |
|---|---|---|
| SAXON | | |
| Egbert | 827 | 839 |
| Ethelwulf | 839 | 858 |
| Ethelbald | 858 | 860 |
| Ethelbert | 858 | 866 |
| Ethelred | 866 | 871 |
| Alfred the Great | 871 | 901 |
| Edward the Elder | 901 | 925 |
| Athelstan | 925 | 940 |
| Edmund | 940 | 946 |
| Edred | 946 | 955 |
| Edwy | 955 | 959 |
| Edgar | 959 | 975 |
| Edward the Martyr | 975 | 978 |
| Ethelred II | 978 | 1016 |
| Edmund Ironside | 1016 | 1016 |
| DANISH | | |
| Canute the Dane | 1017 | 1035 |
| Harold I | 1035 | 1040 |
| Hardicanute | 1040 | 1042 |
| SAXON | | |
| Edward the Confessor | 1042 | 1066 |
| Harold II | 1066 | 1066 |

| Sovereign | Date of Accession | Date of Death |
|-----------|-------------------|---------------|
| **THE HOUSE OF NORMANDY** | | |
| William I | 1066 | 1087 |
| William II | 1087 | 1100 |
| Henry I | 1100 | 1135 |
| Stephen | 1135 | 1154 |
| | | |
| **THE HOUSE OF PLANTAGENET** | | |
| Henry II | 1154 | 1189 |
| Richard I | 1189 | 1199 |
| John | 1199 | 1216 |
| Henry III | 1216 | 1272 |
| Edward I | 1272 | 1307 |
| Edward II | 1307 | 1327 |
| Edward III | 1327 | 1377 |
| Richard II | 1377 | 1400 |
| | | (Deposed 1399) |
| | | |
| **THE HOUSE OF LANCASTER** | | |
| Henry IV | 1399 | 1413 |
| Henry V | 1413 | 1422 |
| Henry VI | 1422 | 1471 |
| | | (Deposed 1461) |
| | | |
| **THE HOUSE OF YORK** | | |
| Edward IV | 1461 | 1483 |
| Edward V | 1483 | 1483 |
| Richard III | 1483 | 1485 |
| | | |
| **THE HOUSE OF TUDOR** | | |
| Henry VII | 1485 | 1509 |
| Henry VIII | 1509 | 1547 |
| Edward VI | 1547 | 1553 |
| Jane* | 1553 | 1554 |
| Mary I | 1553 | 1558 |
| Elizabeth I | 1558 | 1603 |

*Lady Jane Grey

# British Kings and Queens

| Sovereign | Date of Accession | Date of Death |
|---|---|---|
| THE HOUSE OF STUART | | |
| James I (VI of Scotland) | 1603 | 1625 |
| Charles I | 1625 (Beheaded) | 1649 |
| Charles II | 1649 | 1685 |

COMMONWEALTH DECLARED MAY 19TH, 1649
OLIVER CROMWELL, LORD PROTECTOR, 1653–8
RICHARD CROMWELL, LORD PROTECTOR, 1658–9

| Sovereign | Date of Accession | Date of Death |
|---|---|---|
| THE HOUSE OF STUART | | |
| James II (VII of Scotland) | 1685 (Deposed 1688) | |
| William III and ⎫ | 1689 | 1702 |
| Mary II ⎭ | 1689 | 1694 |
| Anne | 1702 | 1714 |
| THE HOUSE OF HANOVER | | |
| George I | 1714 | 1727 |
| George II | 1727 | 1760 |
| George III | 1760 | 1820 |
| George IV | 1820 | 1830 |
| William IV | 1830 | 1837 |
| Victoria | 1837 | 1901 |
| THE HOUSE OF SAXE-COBURG | | |
| Edward VII | 1901 | 1910 |
| THE HOUSE OF WINDSOR | | |
| George V | 1910 | 1936 |
| Edward VIII | 1936 (Abdicated 1936) | 1972 |
| George VI | 1936 | 1952 |
| Elizabeth II | 1952 | — |

# Scottish Kings and Queens

| Sovereign | Date of Accession | Date of Death |
|---|---|---|
| Malcolm III (Canmore) | 1057 | 1093 |
| Donald Ban | 1093 | — |
| Duncan II | 1094 | 1094 |
| Donald Ban (Restored) | 1094 | 1097 |
| Edgar | 1097 | 1107 |
| Alexander I | 1107 | 1124 |
| David I | 1124 | 1153 |
| Malcolm IV (The Maiden) | 1153 | 1165 |
| William I (The Lion) | 1165 | 1214 |
| Alexander II | 1214 | 1249 |
| Alexander III | 1249 | 1286 |
| Margaret, Maid of Norway | 1286 | 1290 |
| John Baliol | 1292 | 1296 |
| Robert I (Bruce) | 1306 | 1329 |
| David II | 1329 | 1371 |
| Robert II (Stewart) | 1371 | 1390 |
| Robert III | 1390 | 1406 |
| James I | 1406 | 1437 |
| James II | 1437 | 1460 |
| James III | 1460 | 1488 |
| James IV | 1488 | 1513 |
| James V | 1513 | 1542 |
| Mary | 1542 | 1587 |
| James VI (Ascended the Throne of England, 1603) | 1567 | 1625 |

# 19 ORDERS OF CHIVALRY

---

## The British Orders of Chivalry

---

(In order of importance)

THE MOST NOBLE ORDER OF THE GARTER (1348) – KG.
Generally confined to Royalty and Peers.

THE MOST ANCIENT AND MOST NOBLE ORDER OF THE THISTLE
    (1687) – KT.
Confined to Royalty and Scottish nobles.

THE MOST ILLUSTRIOUS ORDER OF ST PATRICK (1783) – KP.
Consists only of Her Majesty the Queen, and the Dukes of Gloucester
and Windsor.

THE MOST HONOURABLE ORDER OF THE BATH (1725)
The most important order of chivalry conferred on commoners. It has
both civil and military divisions in three grades: 1st class, Knight Grand
Cross (GCB); 2nd class, Knight Commander (KCB); 3rd class,
Companion (CB).

THE ORDER OF MERIT (1902) – OM.
Limited to 24 members. It has two divisions – civil and military.

THE MOST EXALTED ORDER OF THE STAR OF INDIA (1861)
This Order has three classes – Knight Grand Commander (GCSI);
Knight Commander (KCSI); and Companion (CSI). It has not been
conferred since 1947 and is obsolescent.

THE MOST DISTINGUISHED ORDER OF ST MICHAEL AND ST
GEORGE (1818)
The usual reward for distinguished service in the British Empire and
Commonwealth. The grades are Knight Grand Cross (GCMG); Knight
Commander (KCMG) and Companion (CMG).

THE MOST EMINENT ORDER OF THE INDIAN EMPIRE (1877)
Has not been conferred since 1947 when India achieved independence.
There are three grades – Knight Grand Commander (GCIE); Knight
Commander (KCIE), and Companion (CIE).

THE ROYAL VICTORIAN ORDER (1896)
Awarded for service to the Royal Family. There are five classes – Knights
Grand Cross (GCVO), Knights Commander (KCVO), Commanders
(CVO), and Members (MVO). Women are admitted and a Dame
Commander uses the letters DCVO after her name.

THE MOST EXCELLENT ORDER OF THE BRITISH EMPIRE (1917)
There are five classes of member – Knights Grand Cross (GBE),
Knights Commander (KBE), Commanders (CBE), Officers (OBE)
and Members (MBE). A Dame Commander uses the letters DBE after
her name.

ORDER OF THE COMPANIONS OF HONOUR (1917) – CH.
Limited to sixty-five recipients.

THE KNIGHTS BACHELOR do not constitute a Royal Order – they
comprise the surviving representation of the ancient State Orders of
Knighthood.

# Principal British Decorations and Medals

(In order of precedence)

The Victoria Cross (1856) – VC – 'For Valour'
The George Cross (1940) – GC – 'For Gallantry'
British Orders of Knighthood
Royal Red Cross (1883) – RRC – For Ladies
Distinguished Service Cross (1914) – DSC
Military Cross (December 1914) – MC
Distinguished Flying Cross (1918) – DFC
Air Force Cross (1918) – AFC
Albert Medal (1866) – AM – 'For Gallantry in Saving Life at Sea' or
'on Land'

Medal for Distinguished Conduct in the Field (1854) – DCM
Conspicuous Gallantry Medal (1874) – CGM
The George Medal (1940) – GM
Distinguished Service Medal (1914) – DSM
Military Medal (1916) – MM
Distinguished Flying Medal (1918) – DFM
British Empire Medal (formerly the Medal of the Order of the British
Empire, for Meritorious Service) – BEM

G

## British Flags

The word flag is of Germanic origin and was used in the 15th and 16th centuries to mean a piece of cloth or other material displaying the insignia of a community or armed force, an individual or an office. Flags were signs of leadership and were used originally mainly in warfare. They served to identify friend and foe, and were useful as rallying points. Flags of various forms are known as colours, standards, banners, ensigns, pennons, guidons and burgees.

THE UNION JACK, the national flag of the United Kingdom, was adopted after the Union of England and Scotland in 1606. The name is derived from the use of the Union Flag on the jack staff of naval vessels. It consists of the cross of St George, the patron saint of England (a red cross on a white field), the cross of St Andrew, patron saint of Scotland (a diagonal cross or saltire, white on a blue field), and a cross similar to that of St Patrick, patron saint of Ireland (a red saltire on a white field). The cross of St Patrick was added in 1801.

The Union Flag is hoisted on Government and Public buildings and, in London, on the occasion of the opening and closing of Parliament by the Queen, and from 8 A M to sunset on certain days as follows:

**February 6th (1952)** – Her Majesty's Accession
**February 19th (1960)** – Birthday of Prince Andrew
**March 1st** – St David's Day (in Wales only)
**March 10th (1964)** – Birthday of Prince Edward
**March 31st (1900)** – Birthday of the Duke of Gloucester
**April 21st (1926)** – Birthday of Her Majesty the Queen
**April 23rd** – St George's Day (in England only)
**June 2nd (1953)** – Coronation Day

**June 10th (1921)** – Birthday of the Duke of Edinburgh
**August 4th (1900)** – Birthday of Her Majesty Queen Elizabeth the Queen
Mother
**August 15th (1950)** – Birthday of Princess Anne
**August 21st (1930)** – Birthday of Princess Margaret
**November 14th (1948)** – Birthday of the Prince of Wales
**November 20th (1947)** – Her Majesty's Wedding Day
**November 30th** – St Andrew's Day (in Scotland only)
(also on the Queen's Official Birthday, June 2nd, 1973, and Remembrance
Sunday November 11th, 1973)

THE ROYAL ARMS – displayed in banner form is mistakenly referred to
as the Royal Standard. It is, in fact, a banner and is used as such – only
being flown to indicate the presence of the Sovereign.

There are several versions of the Royal Arms – the Arms of the King of
the Scots (still in use in Scotland); the Arms of Great Britain (as used
officially in Scotland); and the Arms of Great Britain (as used officially in
England). The present version of the form of the Royal Arms as used in
England came into use in the reign of Queen Victoria. It is divided into four
quarters. The 1st and 4th quarters contain the 3 lions *passant* of England;
the 2nd quarter the lion *rampant* of Scotland and the 3rd quarter the harp
of Ireland.

THE WHITE ENSIGN is the flag of the Royal Navy. A white flag bears the
cross of St George with a small Union Jack in the top corner next to the
flagstaff.

THE RED ENSIGN ('the Red Duster') is flown by all British merchant
vessels not belonging to the Royal Navy. It is plain red, with a Union Jack
in the top corner next to the flagstaff.

THE BLUE ENSIGN – similar to the Red Ensign but with a blue back-
ground – the flag of the Royal Naval Reserve.

The Union Flag and the White Ensign were worn at the Battle of Tra-
falgar in 1805 when Nelson hoisted his signal 'England expects that every
man will do his duty'. In 1800 a code of flag-signals in which each of the
hoists of flags meant a word, or even a letter, had been devised. It included
a 'telegraph' flag, ten flags numbered from 1 to 9 and 0, and a substitute
flag to repeat one already included in a hoist.

Nelson's hoists, a flag signal in code that became a watchword of the
British Navy, were: the telegraph flag; 253; 269; 863; 261; 471; 958; 220,
literally 2, substitute, 0; 370; and 4, 21, 19, 24 – the word duty, which was
not in the vocabulary and had to be spelt out.

## The Law

The Law, as we know it in England today, dates back to 1066, the year of the Norman Conquest, but it really began to take shape in the reign of Henry II (1154–89).

English law comes from three separate sources:

1. **Common Law** – the oldest source of law in the English legal system. The unwritten law, based on the practice and custom of the country, which was developed and administered by judges in the old courts. The alleged custom must be 'ancient, certain, reasonable and continuous'. It was called 'common' to distinguish it from special law such as canon (or ecclesiastical) law, or local custom.
2. **Case Law** – the decision of courts on points of common law or interpretations of Acts of Parliament that have grown up over the centuries.
3. **Statute Law** – laws laid down by Act of Parliament, local by-laws, and Orders in Council (made by Ministers under authority of an Act of Parliament).

Reinforcing the common law to make up the body of English law are over 3,000 Acts of Parliament, and 300,000 reported cases. There are some 22,500 solicitors and 2,500 barristers.

Solicitors are the 'maids of all work' of the legal profession. They draw up wills and conveyances for the transfer of property. They give advice on a whole range of problems and prepare cases for the High Court as well as acting as advocates themselves in magistrates and county courts.

Barristers are the specialists of the legal profession and can only obtain clients through a solicitor. The barrister is usually described as 'counsel'.

A barrister wears wig and gown in the House of Lords, the High Court,

# STRUCTURE OF THE CIVIL AND CRIMINAL COURTS IN ENGLAND AND WALES

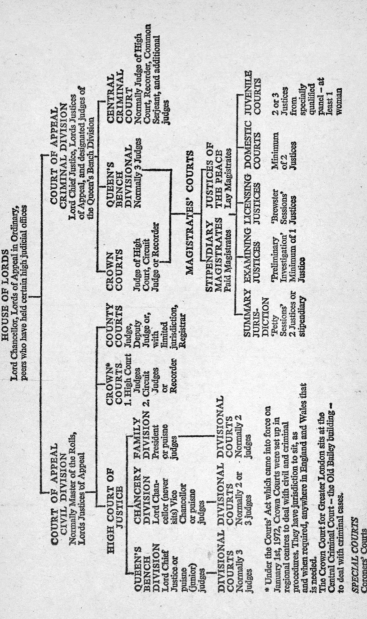

**HOUSE OF LORDS**
Lord Chancellor, Lords of Appeal in Ordinary, peers who have held certain high judicial offices

**COURT OF APPEAL, CIVIL DIVISION**
Normally Master of the Rolls, Lords Justices of Appeal

**COURT OF APPEAL, CRIMINAL DIVISION**
Lord Chief Justice, Lords Justices of Appeal, and designated judges of the Queen's Bench Division

## HIGH COURT OF JUSTICE

**QUEEN'S BENCH DIVISION**
Lord Chief Justice, or puisne (junior) judges

**CHANCERY DIVISION**
Lord Chancellor (never sits) Vice Chancellor or puisne judges

**FAMILY DIVISION**
President or puisne judges

**DIVISIONAL COURTS**
Normally 3 judges

**DIVISIONAL COURTS**
Normally 2 or 3 judges

**DIVISIONAL COURTS**
Normally 2 judges

**CROWN* COURTS**
1. High Court Judges 2. Circuit Judges or Recorder

**COUNTY COURTS**
Judge, Deputy Judge or, with limited jurisdiction, Registrar

**CROWN COURTS**
Judge of High Court, Circuit Judge or Recorder

**QUEEN'S BENCH DIVISIONAL**
Normally 3 Judges

**CENTRAL CRIMINAL COURT**
Normally Judge of High Court, Recorder, Common Serjeant, and additional judges

## MAGISTRATES' COURTS

**STIPENDIARY MAGISTRATES**
Paid Magistrates

**JUSTICES OF THE PEACE**
Lay Magistrates

**SUMMARY JURISDICTION**
'Petty Sessions' 2 Justices or stipendiary

**EXAMINING JUSTICES**
'Preliminary Investigation' Minimum of 1 Justice

**LICENSING JUSTICES**
'Brewster Sessions' 2 Justices

**DOMESTIC COURTS**
Minimum of 2 Justices

**JUVENILE COURTS**
2 or 3 Justices from specially qualified panel – at least 1 woman

* Under the Courts' Act which came into force on January 1st, 1972, Crown Courts were set up in regional centres to deal with civil and criminal procedures. They have jurisdiction to sit, as and when required, anywhere in England and Wales that is needed.
The Crown Court for Greater London sits at the Central Criminal Court – the Old Bailey building – to deal with criminal cases.

*SPECIAL COURTS*
Coroners' Courts
National Industrial Relations Court
Restrictive Practices Court

at County Courts and at Courts Martial. A solicitor wears a gown but not a wig. Neither barristers nor solicitors wear gowns in Magistrates' Courts.

There are two main divisions of the Law:

1. **Civil Law** – concerning the maintenance of private claims and the redress of private wrongs; and
2. **Criminal Law** – dealing with offences that are deemed to harm the whole community, and thus to be an offence against the Sovereign.

---

## A Table of Kindred and Affinity

---

Wherein whosoever are related are forbidden by the
Church of England to marry together

| *A man may not marry his:* | *A woman may not marry her:* |
|---|---|
| Mother | Father |
| Daughter | Son |
| Father's mother | Father's father |
| Mother's mother | Mother's father |
| Son's daughter | Son's son |
| Daughter's daughter | Daughter's son |
| Sister | Brother |
| Father's daughter | Father's son |
| Mother's daughter | Mother's son |
| Wife's mother | Husband's father |
| Wife's daughter | Husband's son |
| Father's wife | Mother's husband |
| Son's wife | Daughter's husband |
| Father's father's wife | Father's mother's husband |
| Mother's father's wife | Mother's mother's husband |
| Wife's father's mother | Husband's father's father |
| Wife's mother's mother | Husband's mother's father |
| Wife's son's daughter | Husband's son's son |
| Wife's daughter's daughter | Husband's daughter's son |
| Son's son's wife | Son's daughter's husband |
| Daughter's son's wife | Daughter's daughter's husband |
| Father's sister | Father's brother |

# Religious Populations of the World

| Religions | N. America* | S. America | Europe | Asia | Africa | Oceania† | World |
|---|---|---|---|---|---|---|---|
| Roman Catholic | 126,468,000 | 147,219,000 | 226,303,000 | 47,622,000 | 28,751,000 | 4,107,000 | 580,470,000 |
| Eastern Orthodox | 3,675,000 | 47,000 | 114,103,000 | 2,819,000 | 4,956,000 | 84,000 | 125,684,000 |
| Protestant | 84,115,000 | 3,160,000 | 101,600,000 | 11,032,000 | 8,349,000 | 9,864,000 | 218,120,000 |
| Total Christian: | 214,258,000 | 150,426,000 | 442,006,000 | 61,473,000 | 42,0560,000 | 14,055,000 | 924,274,000 |
| Jewish | 6,035,000 | 705,000 | 4,025,000 | 2,460,000 | 238,000 | 74,000 | 13,537,000 |
| Muslim | 166,000 | 416,000 | 13,848,000 | 374,167,000 | 104,297,000 | 118,000 | 493,012,000 |
| Zoroastrian | — | — | 12,000 | 126,000 | — | — | 138,000 |
| Shinto | 31,000 | 116,000 | 2,000 | 69,513,000 | — | — | 69,662,000 |
| Taoist | 16,000 | 19,000 | 12,000 | 54,277,000 | — | — | 54,324,000 |
| Confucian | 96,000 | 109,000 | 55,000 | 371,261,000 | 9,000 | 57,000 | 371,587,000 |
| Buddhist | 187,000 | 157,000 | 8,000 | 176,568,000 | — | — | 176,920,000 |
| Hindu | 55,000 | 660,000 | 160,000 | 434,447,000 | 1,205,000 | 218,000 | 436,745,000 |
| TOTALS | 220,844,000 | 152,608,000 | 460,128,000 | 1,544,292,000 | 147,805,000 | 14,522,000 | 2,540,199,000 |

* Includes Central America and the West Indies
† Includes New Zealand and Australia as well as islands of the South Pacific

| *A man may not marry his*: | *A woman may not marry her:* |
|---|---|
| Mother's sister | Mother's brother |
| Brother's daughter | Brother's son |
| Sister's daughter | Sister's son |

'Why were the saints, saints? Because they were cheerful when it was difficult to be cheerful, patient when it was difficult to be patient; and because they pushed on when they wanted to stand still, and kept silent when they wanted to talk, and were agreeable when they wanted to be disagreeable. That was all. It was quite simple and always will be.'

(Anon.)

# Patron Saints of the British Isles

Each of the countries in the British Isles has its own patron saint.

**St George** is the patron saint of England, cavalrymen, chivalry and soldiers. He is believed to have been born of Christian parents at Cappadocia in the third century, and the most famous legend associated with him is the story of how he killed the dragon. He was made the patron saint of England in the reign of Edward III. His white banner with its red cross forms the basis of the Union Jack. His feast day is on April 23rd.
*Emblems:* Knight with dragon. Red cross on shield or banner.

**St Andrew,** patron saint of Scotland, Russia and golfers, was born at Bethsaida on the Lake of Galilee and lived at Capernaum. He was a fisherman, one of the Twelve Apostles and the brother of St Peter. His annual festival is observed on November 30th.
*Emblems:* Transverse cross. Fishing net.

**St David** is the patron saint of Wales. His Day is observed on March 1st, supposedly the anniversary of his death. He was the son of a prince, became a hermit and founded a monastery. He became Bishop of Menevia, and when he died the name of Menevia was changed to St David's, and it is there in Pembrokeshire that the great Welsh Cathedral of St David's still stands.
*Emblem:* Dove on shoulder.

**St Patrick** is the patron saint of Ireland. There are so many conflicting stories about Patrick of Ireland that some scholars think there may have been two Patricks. But legends gravitate towards one great commanding figure named Magnus Sucatus Patricus, who was born in England about 389. Patrick was captured by pirates when he was sixteen years old and sold as a slave in Northern Ireland. He escaped, was ordained, returned to Ireland as a missionary and converted the country to Christianity. That was in 432. It is thought he died either in 461 or 493. His feast day is celebrated on March 17th.

*Emblems:* Bishop with serpents. Shamrock.

# Patron Saints of the Arts, Trades and Professions

| | | | |
|---|---|---|---|
| **Air Hostesses** | St Bona | **Housewives** | St Martha |
| **Animals** | St Roch | **Lawyers** | St Yvo |
| **Architects** | St Thomas | **Lovers** | St Valentine |
| **Artists** | St Luke | **Musicians** | St Cecilia |
| **Bakers** | St Honorius | **Painters** | St Luke and |
| **Barbers** | St Cosmas | | St Lazarus |
| **Bee Keepers** | St Bartholomew | **Preachers** | St Paul |
| **Beggars** | St Martin | **Queens** | St Elizabeth of |
| **Bookbinders** | St John the | | Hungary |
| | Evangelist | **Scholars** | St Catherine |
| **Cab-drivers** | St Fiacre | **Shoemakers** | St Crispin |
| **Careless People** | St Anthony of | **Thieves** | St Nicholas |
| | Padua | **Toothache** | St Apollonia |
| **Cooks** | St Laurence | **Sufferers** | |
| **Fishermen** | St Peter | **Travellers** | St Christopher |
| **Fishmongers** | St Magnus | | |

# The Books of the Old Testament

| | | |
|---|---|---|
| Genesis | Joshua | 1 Kings |
| Exodus | Judges | 2 Kings |
| Leviticus | Ruth | 1 Chronicles |
| Numbers | 1 Samuel | 2 Chronicles |
| Deuteronomy | 2 Samuel | Ezra |

| | | |
|---|---|---|
| Nehemiah | Jeremiah | Jonah |
| Esther | Lamentations | Micah |
| Job | Ezekiel | Nahum |
| Psalms | Daniel | Habakkuk |
| Proverbs | Hosea | Zephaniah |
| Ecclesiastes | Joel | Haggai |
| Song of Solomon | Amos | Zechariah |
| Isaiah | Obadiah | Malachi |

# The Books of the New Testament

| | | |
|---|---|---|
| Matthew | Ephesians | Hebrews |
| Mark | Philippians | James |
| Luke | Colossians | 1 Peter |
| John | 1 Thessalonians | 2 Peter |
| The Acts | 2 Thessalonians | 1 John |
| Romans | 1 Timothy | 2 John |
| 1 Corinthians | 2 Timothy | 3 John |
| 2 Corinthians | Titus | Jude |
| Galatians | Philemon | Revelation |

# The Ten Commandments

1. You shall have no other god to set against me.
2. You shall not make a carved image for yourself nor the likeness of anything in the heavens above, or on the earth below, or in the waters under the earth. You shall not bow down to them or worship them; for I, the LORD your God, am a jealous god. I punish the children for the sins of the fathers to the third and fourth generations of those who hate me. But I keep faith with thousands, with those who love me and keep my commandments.
3. You shall not make wrong use of the name of the LORD your God; the LORD will not leave unpunished the man who misuses his name.
4. Keep the sabbath day holy as the LORD your God commanded you. You have six days to labour and do all your work. But the seventh day is a sabbath of the LORD your God; that day you shall not do any work, neither you, your son or your daughter, your slave or your slave-girl, your ox, your ass, or any of your cattle, nor the alien

within your gates, so that your slaves and slave-girls may rest as you do. Remember that you were slaves in Egypt and the LORD your God brought you out with a strong hand and an outstretched arm, and for that reason the LORD your God commanded you to keep the sabbath day.

5. Honour your father and your mother, as the LORD your God commanded you, so that you may live long, and that it may be well with you in the land which the LORD your God is giving you.

6. You shall not commit murder.

7. You shall not commit adultery.

8. You shall not steal.

9. You shall not give false evidence against your neighbour.

10. You shall not covet your neighbour's wife; you shall not set your heart on your neighbour's house, his land, his slave, his slave-girl, his ox, his ass, or on anything that belongs to him.

## British Hallmarks on Gold and Silver Wares

Hallmarks are symbols stamped on articles of gold or silver to indicate that they have been accurately tested, or assayed, and that the precious metal conforms to one of the legal standards of purity.

Hall-marking was instituted by a statute of King Edward I in 1300. In London it is the responsibility of the Worshipful Company of Goldsmiths. The London Assay Office is at Goldsmith's Hall and this is the origin of the word 'hallmark'.

A hallmark usually consists of four symbols – the Maker's Mark, the Standard Mark, the Assay Office Mark and the Date Letter.

**The Maker's Mark** was instituted in 1363 by statute of King Edward III. It originally took the form of an emblem, a bell, a bird or a *fleur-de-lys* connected with the name of the maker or the shops where he worked. Nowadays it consists of the initials of the Christian and surname of the person or firm submitting the article to the Assay Office.

It takes the form of the symbol N M in the example overleaf.

**The Standard Mark** was introduced by the Goldsmiths' Company in 1544. It denotes the minimum gold or silver content. The current legal standards and their marks are shown overleaf.

**The Assay Office Mark** shows which Assay Office tested the article. There were formerly assay offices in other towns – Chester, Exeter, Glasgow, Newcastle, Norwich and York – each with its own distinguishing mark. The existing Assay Offices are at London, Birmingham, Sheffield, and Edinburgh and their distinguishing marks are shown overleaf.

The Date Letter denotes the year in which the article was hallmarked. It differs at the various assay offices. The date letter is changed at the London office in May each year, in July at Birmingham and Sheffield, and at Edinburgh in October.

It consists of a shield enclosing a letter of the alphabet.

| MARK | STANDARD | MINIMUM PERCENTAGE | | | |
|---|---|---|---|---|---|
| | Sterling silver Marked in England | 92.5 | | London | Sterling silver & gold |
| | Sterling silver Marked in Scotland | 92.5 | | London | Britannia silver |
| | Britannia silver | 95.84 | | Birmingham | silver & gold |
| 22 | 22 carat gold Marked in England | 91.66 | | Sheffield | silver |
| 18 | 18 carat gold Marked in England | 75.0 | | Sheffield | gold |
| 14 585 | 14 carat gold | 58.5 | | Edinburgh | silver & gold |
| 9 375 | 9 carat gold | 37.5 | | | |

# 24 THE ARTS

## A. Music

## Popular Music

The 'pop' music industry has grown to enormous proportions since the end of the Second World War.

In 1954 two important events took place in the world of popular music in the United States. The first was that Bill (William John Clifton) Haley launched a group called The Comets. By January 1970 collective sales of their top-selling 'pop' record *Rock around the Clock* made on April 12th, 1954 had reached 22,000,000.

The second was that Elvis Presley made some recordings in a somewhat similar style – and without Presley there would be no 'pop' as we know it today. The age of 'Rock and Roll' had begun. Towards the end of the Fifties Traditional Jazz was popular, followed a decade later by Rhythm and Blues, and later still by Soul Music. Progressive pop arose out of the attempts in the Sixties to link popular music with, for example, the classical arrangement of music, the Indian sitar, and so on.

The first record to sell a million copies was the aria 'Vesti la giubba' ('On with the motley') from Leoncavallo's opera 'I Pagliacci', sung by Enrico Caruso, and first recorded on November 12th, 1902.

The first actual golden disc was one sprayed by RCA and presented to US trombonist and bandleader Glenn Miller for *Chattanooga Choo Choo* on February 10th, 1942.

Elvis Presley lays claim to have more golden discs than any other performer. The most accurate estimate, up to July 1971, is a total of 95 Gold Records for million-selling singles, EPs and LPs. Some records have won two Gold Discs – like the LP *Blue Hawaii* – not forgetting the fantastic *Don't Be Cruel*. In 1970 the total singles record sales alone topped the 100 million mark, world-wide.

The only *audited* measure of million-selling discs, however, is certification by the Recording Industry of America (RIAA), which began in 1958. They put the Beatles top with 21 Golden Discs for singles which sold more than 1 million copies and 17 for LPs each of which sold more than $1 million worth by September 1st, 1970, and Presley second with 10 Golden Discs and an added 9 for million dollar sales.

The Beatles world total of million-selling titles was believed to be 57 by September 1970. In their first tour of the United States they grossed $19,000,000, and for one performance in the USA in 1966 they received a fee of $189,000 (then £67,500) – the highest fee ever paid to recording artists for a single performance.

The Beatles first single, *Love Me Do*, was released on October 5th, 1962. The last record they made together as a group was *Let It Be* in 1970 (the single was released on March 6th, the Album on May 8th). In 1964 they were top of the sales charts. In the week ending March 21st, 1964, they were Nos. 1, 2, 3, 4 and 5 in the US chart with *Twist and Shout*, *Can't Buy Me Love*, *She Loves You*, *I Want to Hold Your Hand* and *Please Please Me*; and Nos. 1 and 2 on the LP charts with *Meet the Beatles* and *Introducing the Beatles*. By May 1972, United Kingdom sales of *I Want to Hold Your Hand* had reached over 1½ million.

World sales of *With the Beatles* were at least 6,500,000 million to mid-1967 – a record for any 'pop' group. *Sergeant Pepper's Lonely Hearts Club Band* released in June 1967, had sold more than 7,000,000 copies by January 1970. By May 1972 UK sales were just over 1 million.

The best-selling LP is the 20th Century-Fox Album *Sing We Now Of Christmas*, issued in 1958. In 1963 this title was changed to *The Little Drummer Boy* and by January 1970 estimated sales were 13,000,000.

The all-time bestseller among LPs of musical film shows is the soundtrack album of *The Sound of Music*. Released in 1965 sales had reached 13,000,000 by January 1970.

Johnny Mathis has had the longest stay in the LP charts in the USA – a stay of 490 weeks with his Album *Johnny's Greatest Hits*.

Irving Berlin's record *White Christmas*, first recorded in 1941, has sold more copies than any other gramophone record. Thirty years later, sales had reached an estimated total of 100,000,000.

The songs most frequently sung in English are: *Happy Birthday to You* (sung in space by the American astronauts on their 1969 Apollo mission), *For He's a Jolly Good Fellow*, and *Auld Lang Syne*.

On January 11th, 1972, a BBC disc jockey played a record in the 'Late

Night Extra' programme. Its title: *Amazing Grace*, a 200-year-old Scottish hymn played by the Band of the Royal Scots Dragoon Guards. Within three weeks of its release it was No. 1 in the charts and has since sold well over half a million copies in Britain and is released in 17 different countries around the world.

The song with the longest title? Hoagy Carmichael's *I'm a Cranky Old Yank in a Clanky Old Tank on the Streets of Yokohama with my Honolulu Mama Doin' Those Beat-o, Beat-o, Flat-On-My-Seat-o, Hirohito Blues.*

# Great Composers

Henry Purcell (1659–95) English
George Friederich Handel (1685–1759) German
Johann Sebastian Bach (1685–1750) German
Franz Joseph Haydn (1732–1809) Austrian
Wolfgang Amadeus Mozart (1756–1791) Austrian
Ludwig Van Beethoven (1770–1827) German
Gioacchino Rossini (1792–1868) Italian
Franz Peter Schubert (1797–1828) Austrian
Gaetano Donizetti (1797–1848) Italian
Vincenzo Bellini (1801–1835) Italian
Hector Berlioz (1803–1869) French
Mikhail Ivanovitch Glinka (1804–1857) Russian
Frédéric Chopin (1810–1849) Polish
Robert Schumann (1810–1856) German
Franz Liszt (1811–1886) Hungarian
Richard Wagner (1813–1883) German
Giuseppe Verdi (1813–1901) Italian
Charles Gounod (1818–1893) French
Jacques Offenbach (1819–1880) German
César Franck (1822–1890) Belgian
Anton Bruckner (1824–1896) Austrian
Johannes Brahms (1833–1897) German
Alexander Borodin (1833–1887) Russian
Georges Bizet (1838–1875) French
Modest Petrovitch Mussorgsky (1839–1881) Russian
Peter Ilyich Tchaikovsky (1840–1893) Russian
Antonin Dvořák (1841–1904) Czechoslovakian
Arthur Sullivan (1842–1900) English
Nicolai Andreyevitch Rimsky-Korsakov (1844–1908) Russian

**Edward Elgar** (1857–1934) English
**Giacomo Puccini** (1858–1924) Italian
**Gustav Mahler** (1860–1911) Austrian
**Claude Debussy** (1862–1918) French
**Frederick Delius** (1862–1934) British
**Richard Strauss** (1864–1949) German
**Ralph Vaughan Williams** (1872–1958) English
**Serge Rachmaninov** (1873–1943) Russian
**Gustav Holst** (1874–1934) English
**Arnold Schoenberg** (1874–1951) Austrian
**Maurice Ravel** (1875–1937) French
**Béla Bartók** (1881–1945) Hungarian
**Igor Fedorovitch Stravinsky** (1882–1971) Russian
**Serge Prokofiev** (1891–1953) Russian
**Paul Hindemith** (1895–1963) German
**Jean Sibelius** (1865–1957) Finnish
**Kurt Weill** (1900–1950) German
**Aaron Copland** (1900–    ) American
**William Walton** (1902–    ) English
**Michael Tippett** (1905–    ) English
**Benjamin Britten** (1913–    ) English

# Principal Instruments of the Symphony Orchestra

| *Strings* | *Woodwind* |
|---|---|
| Violin | Flute |
| Viola | Piccolo |
| Cello | Oboe |
| Double Bass | Cor Anglais |
| Harp | Clarinet |
| | Bass Clarinet |
| | Bassoon |
| | Contra Bassoon |

| *Brass* | *Percussion* |
|---|---|
| Horn | Timpani (or Kettle Drums) |
| Trumpet | Side Drum |
| Trombone | Bass Drum |

Tuba

Cymbals
Triangle
Xylophone
Glockenspiel

# Some Musical Terms and their Meanings

ADAGIO – very slow
AGITATO – excited
ALLEGRO – cheerful, lively
ANDANTE – quiet, peaceful tempo
BARITONE – male voice between tenor and bass
BASS – deep-sounding; the lowest part in music
CONTRALTO – lowest register of the female voice
CRESCENDO – increasing the loudness gradually
DIMINUENDO – decreasing the loudness gradually
DOLCE – sweet
FALSETTO – highest register of the voice as used by male altos
FORTE – loud, strong
FORTISSIMO – very loud
HEAD-VOICE – the highest register of the human voice
LACRIMOSO – tearfully
LARGO – in slow, dignified style
MEZZO SOPRANO – female voice, between soprano and contralto
MODERATO – at a moderate pace
PIANISSIMO – very soft
PRESTO – fast
RECITATIVE – declamatory singing, free in tempo and rhythm
REPRISE – repeat
RHYTHM – measured time
SOLO – alone
SOPRANO – the highest female voice
SOTTO – below, beneath
SPIRITUOSO – spirited
TENOR – the highest natural male voice
TIMBRE – quality of tone
VIRTUOSO – performer of exceptional skill

*Flemish ~ Hubert Jan van EYCK*

# B. Painting

## I. RENAISSANCE AND MANNERIST PAINTING

(14th–16th centuries)
    **Giotto di Bondone** (1266–1337), Italian
    **Sandro Botticelli** (1441–1510), Florentine
    **Leonardo da Vinci** (1452–1519), Italian
    **Michaelangelo** (1475–1564), Italian
    **Raphael** (1483–1520), Italian
    **Albrecht Dürer** (1471–1528), German
    **Hans Holbein** (1497–1543), German
    **Giorgione** (c1478–1510), Venetian
    **Titian** (1487–1576), Venetian
    **El Greco** (1541–1614), Spanish

## II. BAROQUE THROUGH IMPRESSIONIST PAINTING

(17th–19th centuries)
    FLANDERS
      **Peter Paul Rubens** (1577–1640)
      **Anthony van Dyke** (1599–1641)

    THE NETHERLANDS
      **Jan Vermeer** (1632–1675)
      **Frans Hals** (?1580–1666)
      **Rembrandt** (1606–1669)

    SPAIN
      **Velasquez** (1599–1660)
      **Murillo** (1617–1682)
      **Goya** (1746–1828)

    FRANCE (17th and 18th centuries)
      **Antoine Watteau** (1684–1721)
      **Jean Honoré Fragonard** (1732–1806)
      **Jacques Louis David** (1748–1825)

    ENGLAND
      **William Hogarth** (1697–1764)
      **Sir Joshua Reynolds** (1723–1792)
      **Thomas Gainsborough** (1727–1788)

William Blake (1757–1827)
John Constable (1776–1837)
Joseph Turner (1775–1851)
George Romney (1734–1802)

PRE-RAPHAELITES
Ford Madox Brown (1821–1893)
Dante Gabriel Rossetti (1828–1882)
William Holman Hunt (1827–1910)
Sir John Millais (1829–1896)
Sir Edward Burne-Jones (1833–1898)

FRANCE (19th century)
Jean Auguste Dominique Ingres (1780–1867)
Eugene Delacroix (1798–1863)
Jean Corot (1796–1875)
Honoré Daumier (1808–1879)
Édouard Manet (1832–1883)

THE IMPRESSIONISTS
Claude Monet (1840–1926)
Pierre Auguste Renoir (1841–1919)
Degas (1834–1917)

## III. MODERN PAINTING (late 19th and 20th centuries)

POST IMPRESSIONISM
Toulouse-Lautrec (1864–1901), French
Vincent van Gogh (1853–1890), Dutch
Paul Gaugin (1848–1903), French
Paul Cézanne (1839–1906), French

FAUVISM
Henri Matisse (1869–1954), French
Raoul Dufy (1877–1953), French

CUBISM
Georges Braque (1882–1963), French
Juan Gris (1887–1927), Spanish
Pablo Picasso (1881–    ), Spanish

SURREALISM
Salvador Dali (1905–    ), Spanish

## SOME WELL-KNOWN BRITISH PAINTERS OF TODAY

| | | |
|---|---|---|
| Victor Pasmore | Bridget Riley | L. S. Lowry |
| David Hockney | Ben Nicholson | Mark Tobey |
| Graham Sutherland | Alan Davie | John Bratby |
| William Scott | Sidney Nolan | Ceri Richards |
| Francis Bacon | Peter Blake | Bernard Cohen |
| Lucian Freud | | |

## POP ART

Pop art appeared in England in the late 1950s and in America ten years later.

The highest price paid for an item of Pop Art was for 'Soup Can' by Andy Warhol. The 72″ × 54″ work was sold in May 1970 for £25,000.

# C. Literature

# Some Famous British Authors

| | | Best-known work |
|---|---|---|
| Daniel Defoe | 1661 ?–1731 | Robinson Crusoe |
| Sir Walter Scott | 1771–1832 | The Waverley novels |
| Jane Austen | 1775–1817 | Pride and Prejudice |
| Elizabeth Cleghorn Gaskell | 1810–1865 | Cranford |
| Frederick Marryat | 1792–1848 | The Children of the New Forest |
| William Makepeace Thackeray | 1811–1863 | Vanity Fair |
| Charles Dickens | 1812–1870 | David Copperfield |
| Charles Reade | 1814–1884 | The Cloister and the Hearth |
| Anthony Trollope | 1815–1882 | The Warden |
| Charlotte Brontë | 1816–1855 | Jane Eyre |
| Emily Brontë | 1818–1848 | Wuthering Heights |
| George Eliot (Mary Ann Evans) | 1819–1880 | The Mill on the Floss |
| Charles Kingsley | 1819–1875 | The Water Babies |
| Wilkie Collins | 1824–1889 | The Moonstone |
| Lord Lytton | 1831–1891 | The Last Days of Pompeii |
| Samuel Butler | 1835–1902 | The Way of All Flesh |
| Thomas Hardy | 1840–1928 | Tess of the D'Urbervilles |

|  |  | *Best-known work* |
|---|---|---|
| Henry James | 1843–1916 | *The Turn of the Screw* |
| Joseph Conrad | 1857–1924 | *Lord Jim* |
| Sir A. Conan Doyle | 1859–1930 | *The Hound of the Baskervilles* |
| W. W. Jacobs | 1863–1943 | *The Monkey's Paw* (and other short stories) |
| Rudyard Kipling | 1865–1936 | *The Jungle Book* |
| H. G. Wells | 1866–1946 | *Kipps* |
| Arnold Bennett | 1867–1931 | *The Old Wives' Tale* |
| John Galsworthy | 1869–1933 | *The Forsyte Saga* |
| Hilaire Belloc | 1870–1953 | *Cautionary Tales* |
| G. K. Chesterton | 1874–1936 | The *Father Brown* stories |
| John Buchan | 1875–1940 | *The Thirty-Nine Steps* |
| D. H. Lawrence | 1885–1930 | *Sons and Lovers* |
| George Orwell | 1903–1950 | *Animal Farm* |

## Some Famous English Essayists

| | | | |
|---|---|---|---|
| Francis Bacon | 1561–1626 | Robert Lynd | 1879–1949 |
| Joseph Addison | 1672–1719 | A. A. Milne | 1882–1956 |
| Oliver Goldsmith | 1728–1774 | Harold Nicolson | 1886– |
| Charles Lamb | 1775–1834 | Neville Cardus | 1889– |
| William Hazlitt | 1778–1830 | J. B. Priestley | 1894– |
| Leigh Hunt | 1784–1859 | Aldous Huxley | 1894–1963 |
| Robert Louis Stevenson | 1850–1894 | Ian Mackay | 1898–1952 |
| E. V. Lucas | 1868–1938 | V. S. Pritchett | 1900– |

## Some Famous British Poets

|  |  | *Best-known work* |
|---|---|---|
| William Langland | 1330?–1400? | Piers Plowman |
| Geoffrey Chaucer | 1340?–1400 | The Canterbury Tales |
| Edmund Spenser | 1552?–1599 | Faerie Queene |
| Michael Drayton | 1563–1631 | The Ballad of Agincourt |
| John Milton | 1608–1674 | Paradise Lost |
| Samuel Butler | 1612–1680 | Hudibras |
| Alexander Pope | 1688–1744 | Rape of the Lock |
| Thomas Gray | 1716–1771 | Elegy in a Country Churchyard |

| | | *Best-known work* |
|---|---|---|
| **William Cowper** | 1731–1800 | The Task |
| **William Blake** | 1757–1828 | Songs of Innocence and Songs of Experience |
| **Robert Burns** | 1759–1796 | Tam o'Shanter |
| **William Wordsworth** | 1770–1850 | Lyrical Ballads |
| **Samuel Taylor Coleridge** | 1772–1834 | Rime of the Ancient Mariner |
| **Lord Byron** | 1788–1824 | Don Juan |
| **Percy Bysshe Shelley** | 1792–1822 | Ode to the West Wind |
| **John Keats** | 1795–1821 | Endymion |
| **Thomas Hood** | 1799–1845 | Song of a Shirt |
| **Elizabeth Barrett Browning** | 1806–1861 | Sonnets from the Portuguese |
| **Edward Fitzgerald** | 1809–1893 | Rubaiyat of Omar Khayyam |
| **Alfred Lord Tennyson** | 1809–1892 | Idylls of the King |
| **Robert Browning** | 1812–1889 | The Pied Piper of Hamelin |
| **Edward Lear** | 1812–1888 | The Owl and the Pussycat |
| **Christina Rossetti** | 1830–1894 | Goblin Market |
| **Robert Bridges** | 1844–1930 | Testament of Beauty |
| **A. E. Housman** | 1859–1936 | A Shropshire Lad |
| **Walter de la Mare** | 1873–1956 | The Traveller |
| **John Masefield** | 1876–1967 | Sea Fever |
| **T. S. Eliot** | 1888–1965 | The Waste Land |
| **Dylan Thomas** | 1914–1953 | Under Milk Wood |

# The Poets Laureate

The origins of the office of Poet Laureate go back even before the time of Chaucer. Henry III ordered the payment of ten pounds to Henri d'Avranches, his 'official' poet, and the first holder of the title of *Versificator Regis* (the King's Versifier). From this stemmed the title and post of Poet Laureate as we know it today.

The first traditional poet laureate was Ben Jonson, who was granted a pension in recognition of his services as a poet, by James I in 1616. When he died the laurel crown passed to:

| | |
|---|---|
| **Sir William D'Avenant** | 1637 |
| **John Dryden** | 1670 |
| **Thomas Shadwell** | 1688 |

| | |
|---|---|
| Nahum Tate | 1692 |
| Nicholas Rowe | 1715 |
| Rev. Laurence Eusden | 1718 |
| Colley Cibber | 1730 |
| William Whitehead | 1757 |
| Rev. Thomas Warton | 1785 |
| Henry James Pye | 1790 |
| Robert Southey | 1813 |
| William Wordsworth | 1843 |
| Lord Tennyson | 1850 |
| Alfred Austin | 1896 |
| Robert Bridges | 1913 |
| John Masefield | 1930 |
| Cecil Day-Lewis | 1967 |
| Sir John Betjeman | 1972 |

# The Works of William Shakespeare

| | Date Written |
|---|---|
| *Henry VI*, Part I | 1591 |
| *Henry VI*, Part II | 1591 |
| *Henry VI*, Part III | 1591 |
| *The Comedy of Errors* | 1592 |
| *Richard III* | 1593 |
| *Titus Andronicus* | 1593 |
| *The Taming of the Shrew* | 1594 |
| *The Two Gentlemen of Verona* | 1594 |
| *Love's Labour's Lost* | 1594 |
| *Romeo and Juliet* | 1595 |
| *Richard II* | 1595 |
| *A Midsummer Night's Dream* | 1596 |
| *King John* | 1596 |
| *The Merchant of Venice* | 1596 |
| *Henry IV*, Part I | 1597 |
| *Henry IV*, Part II | 1598 |
| *The Merry Wives of Windsor* | 1598 |
| *Much Ado About Nothing* | 1598 |
| *Henry V* | 1599 |

|  | Date Written |
|---|---|
| Julius Caesar | 1599 |
| As You Like It | 1600 |
| Twelfth Night | 1601 |
| Hamlet | 1601 |
| Troilus and Cressida | 1602 |
| All's Well That Ends Well | 1603 |
| Measure for Measure | 1604 |
| Othello | 1604 |
| King Lear | 1605 |
| Macbeth | 1606 |
| Antony and Cleopatra | 1607 |
| Pericles | 1608 |
| Coriolanus | 1609 |
| Timon of Athens | 1609 |
| Cymbeline | 1610 |
| The Winter's Tale | 1611 |
| The Tempest | 1611 |
| Henry VIII | 1613 |
| Venus and Adonis | 1592 |
| The Rape of Lucrece | 1593 |
| The Sonnets | |

# British Newspapers

| NATIONAL MORNINGS | | Average net sales January–June 1972 (Audit Bureau of Circulation) |
|---|---|---|
| Daily Express | Est. 1900 | 3,348,752 |
| Daily Mail | Est. 1896 | 1,710,141 |
| Daily Mirror | Est. 1903 | 4,289,233 |
| Daily Telegraph | Est. 1855 | 1,436,354 |
| Financial Times | Est. 1888 | 187,781 |
| The Guardian | Est. 1821 | 341,075 |
| The Sporting Life | Est. 1859 | 87,775 |
| Sun | Est. 1964 | 2,625,532 |
| The Times | Est. 1785 | 345,016 |

|  |  | Average net sales January–June 1972 (Audit Bureau of Circulation) |
|---|---|---|
| **LONDON EVENINGS** | | |
| *Evening News* | Est. 1881 | |
| (Mon.–Fri. edition) | | 900,749 |
| (Sat. edition) | | 739,866 |
| *Evening Standard* | Est. 1827 | |
| (Mon.–Fri. edition) | | 519,154 |
| (Sat. edition) | | 436,928 |
| | | |
| **NATIONAL SUNDAYS** | | |
| *News of the World* | Est. 1843 | 6,014,010 |
| *The Observer* | Est. 1791 | 797,907 |
| *The Sunday People* | Est. 1881 | 4,615,424 |
| *Sunday Express* | Est. 1918 | 4,027,716 |
| *Sunday Mirror* | Est. 1915 | 4,473,200 |
| *Sunday Telegraph* | Est. 1961 | 753,654 |
| *Sunday Times* | Est. 1822 | 1,450,291 |

# Ten 'Bestselling' Magazines in Britain

|  |  | Average net sales January–June 1972 (Audit Bureau of Circulation) |
|---|---|---|
| 1. | *Woman* | 1,970,766 |
| 2. | *Woman's Weekly* | 1,830,311 |
| 3. | *Woman's Own* | 1,627,765 |
| 4. | *Weekend* | 1,171,933 |
| 5. | *Family Circle* | 1,161,250 |
| 6. | *Woman's Realm* | 1,001,147 |
| 7. | *Reveille* | 855,798 |
| 8. | *Woman and Home* | 736,437 |
| 9. | *Saturday Tit-Bits* | 633,216 |
| 10. | *Living* | 577,727 |
| | (*Radio Times* | 3,571,327 |
| | *TV Times*) | 3,329,364) |

## Some Alphabets

**HEBREW.**

מנסעפצקרשתשרקצפעסנמ
אבגדהוזחטיכל

**CYRILLIC.**

АБВГДЕЖЗИЙКЛМНОПР
СТУФХЦЧШЩЪЫЬЭЮЯ

**ARABIC.**

ظظغعغعغف ق ققف ق اكگگگك گك ك الل م ممم ن

على گى كى فى مى ں مىم ا ٢٢١ ٣٤ ٥٦٧٨٩ !؟ ٠ ( )؛ ؞ ــ ا س ـ ة

**GREEK.**

ΑΒΓΔΕΖΗΘΙΚΛΜΝΞΟΠΡΣΤΥΦΧΨΩ;˄˅

---

## Roman Numerals

| | | | |
|---|---|---|---|
| 1 ... I | 12 ... XII | 50 ... L | 700 ... DCC |
| 2 ... II | 13 ... XIII | 60 ... LX | 800 ... DCCC |
| 3 ... III | 14 ... XIV | 70 ... LXX | 900 ... CM |
| 4 ... IV | 15 ... XV | 80 ... LXXX | 1000 ... M |
| 5 ... V | 16 ... XVI | 90 ... XC | 1500 ... MD |
| 6 ... VI | 17 ... XVII | 100 ... C | 1700 ... MDCC |
| 7 ... VII | 18 ... XVIII | 200 ... CC | 1800 ... MDCCC |
| 8 ... VIII | 19 ... XIX | 300 ... CCC | 1895 ... MDCCCXCV |
| 9 ... IX | 20 ... XX | 400 ... CD | 1900 ... MCM |
| 10 ... X | 30 ... XXX | 500 ... D | 1944 ... MCMXLIV |
| 11 ... XI | 40 ... XL | 600 ... DC | 2000 ... MM |

A line placed over a numeral multiplies the number by 1,000 e.g.:
6,000 ... $\overline{\text{VI}}$; 16,000 ... $\overline{\text{XVI}}$; 160,000 ... $\overline{\text{CLX}}$; 666,000 ... $\overline{\text{DCLXVI}}$